PRAYER

PRAYER

Finding the Heart's True Home

Richard J. Foster

Hodder & Stoughton

LONDON SYDNEY AUCKLAND

Scriptural quotations are taken from the New Revised Standard Version
of the Bible, unless otherwise indicated.

British Library Cataloguing in Publication Data

A catalogue record for this book is available from the British Library

ISBN 0-340-58417-3

Copyright © Richard J. Foster 1992

First published in Great Britain 1992
Second impression 1993

Published by Hodder and Stoughton,
a division of Hodder and Stoughton Ltd,
Mill Road, Dunton Green, Sevenoaks, Kent TN13 2YA
Editorial Office: 47 Bedford Square, London WC1B 3DP

Typeset by Hewer Text Composition Services, Edinburgh
Printed in England by Clays Ltd, St Ives plc.

To Eugene and Jean Coffin
My Pastors

As a child I heard Eugene and Jean quip about
being a pair of jeans. They spoke more than they
knew. For over fifty years now they have had a
compassionate ministry that is inseparable and
wears well.

Contents

Acknowledgments

It is never possible for any of us to cover the list of those who have shaped us. When writing a book, the problem only intensifies. I cannot thank everyone, but I will thank some in hopes that they will symbolize the many who remain anonymous.

I am grateful to those who read all or part of the manuscript and provided valuable suggestions: Carolynn Foster, Nathan Foster, Lynda Graybeal, Dotsy Hill, Janet Janzen and Carol Mullikin. In addition, I read various chapters at the weekly meetings of The Milton Center, and its members gave me valuable critique and encouragement. I thank them: Harold Fickett, Janine Hathaway, Frank Kastor, David Owens, Virginia Stem Owens, Charles Parker, Bruce Parmenter and Jim Smith.

I want to thank my former parishioners and students, who helped me test these ideas over many years in both theory and practice. They have been my teachers. I am also indebted to a special group of individuals who prayed for me throughout this writing and held up my often sagging arms: Wendell Barnett, Ken and Doris Boyce, Karen Christensen, Taddie Gunn, Dotsy Hill, Ed and Alice Kerr, Claudia Mitchell, Bonnie Parker, Betse Rockwood, Sarah Smith, Dallas and Jane Willard, Jean Winslow, and Dick and Gayle Withnell. In addition, I express gratitude to Carolyn Armitage of Hodder & Stoughton for her editorial skill and warm encouragement.

I thank Lynda Graybeal for overseeing the office and fulfilling duties too numerous to mention so I could be free to write. And finally, I thank God for Carolynn who prayed with me and for me from the conception to the birth of this book.

Preface

For a long time I have wanted to write on the subject of prayer. To do so, however, would have been to commit the sin of presumption. I was not ready. I had more – much more – to learn, to experience. With many subjects it is perfectly acceptable to share one's wonderings and wanderings, but this is not true with prayer. Prayer ushers us into the Holy of Holies where we bow before the deepest mysteries of the faith, and one fears to touch the Ark. The years have come and gone, and while I am still a novice in the ways of prayer (who can ever master something in which the main object is to be mastered?) I somehow sense the divine nod of approval. Now is the time. And so I am writing, and in my writing I am speaking for all the prayerless persons I have been and all the prayerful persons I hope to become.

Throughout I will be seeking to name our experiences of prayer, a little like Adam in the Garden naming the animals. I hope in this way to define something of the character of our dialogue with God. Countless people, you see, pray far more than they know. Often they have such a "stained-glass" image of prayer that they fail to recognize what they are experiencing as prayer and so condemn themselves for not praying. And so I trust that many passages in this book will be instantly recognizable to you – making you think, "Of course! I've experienced that!" By naming our experiences, I hope to increase our understanding of what God is doing among us so we can be more intentional in our practice.

I should, at the outset, comment on the special linguistic

problem in addressing God. The personal pronoun is one expression of this, and attempts to solve this problem with dashes and slashes are semantically awkward and aesthetically abhorrent. I have, therefore, chosen to follow the standard usage of the masculine pronoun although I am keenly aware of the inadequacies of this approach. I am the first to admit that our language is simply limited here. Clearly, God incorporates and transcends our categories of sexuality – that is, God is not a male deity as opposed to a female deity.

Actually Jesus' use of "Abba praying" was an inclusive action. By the use of the diminutive for "father" Jesus reveals that our relationship with God involves not only the strength and empowerment commonly identified with masculinity, but also the nurture and caring intimacy often associated with femininity.

A brief note about the structure of this book might be useful. Without pressing the analogy too far, it is helpful to see that the three movements into prayer are trinitarian in character. The movement inward (Part I) is prayer to God the Son, Jesus Christ, which corresponds to his role as Saviour and Teacher among us. The movement upward (Part II) is prayer to God the Father, which corresponds to his role as sovereign King and eternal Lover among us. The movement outward (Part III) is prayer to God the Holy Spirit, which corresponds to his role as Empowerer and Evangelist among us. The movement inward comes first simply because God has revealed himself to us most fully and most clearly in Jesus Christ.

One small word of counsel before we strike out on to this disciplined journey into the holy place: healthy prayer necessitates frequent experiences of the common, earthy, run-of-the-mill variety. Like walks, and talks, and good wholesome laughter. Like work in the yard, and chitchat with the neighbours, and washing windows. Like loving our spouse, and playing with our kids, and working with our colleagues. To be spiritually fit to scale the Himalayas of the spirit we need regular exercise in the hills and valleys of ordinary life.

Richard J. Foster
January 1, 1992

Coming Home: An Invitation to Prayer

True, whole prayer is nothing but love.
— St Augustine

God has graciously allowed me to catch a glimpse into his heart, and I want to share with you what I have seen. Today the heart of God is an open wound of love. He aches over our distance and preoccupation. He mourns that we do not draw near to him. He grieves that we have forgotten him. He weeps over our obsession with muchness and manyness. He longs for our presence.

And he is inviting you — and me — to come home, to come home to where we belong, to come home to that for which we were created. His arms are stretched out wide to receive us. His heart is enlarged to take us in.

For too long we have been in a far country: a country of noise and hurry and crowds, a country of climb and push and shove, a country of frustration and fear and intimidation. And he welcomes us home: home to serenity and peace and joy, home to friendship and fellowship and openness, home to intimacy and acceptance and affirmation.

We do not need to be shy. He invites us into the living-room of his heart where we can put on old slippers and share freely. He invites us into the kitchen of his friendship where chatter and batter mix in good fun. He invites us into the dining-room of his strength, where we can feast to our heart's delight. He invites us into the study of his wisdom where we can learn and grow and stretch . . . and ask all the questions we want. He invites us into the workshop of his creativity, where we can be co-labourers with him, working together to determine the outcomes of events. He invites us into the bedroom of his rest where new peace is found, and where we can be naked and vulnerable and free. It is also the place of deepest intimacy, where we know and are known to the fullest.

The Key and the Door

The key to this home, this heart of God, is prayer. Perhaps you have never prayed before except in anguish or terror. It may be that the only time the Divine Name has been on your lips has been in angry expletives. Never mind. I am here to tell you that the Father's heart is open wide – you are welcome to come in.

Perhaps you do not believe in prayer. You may have tried to pray and been profoundly disappointed ... and disillusioned. You seem to have little faith, or none. It does not matter. The Father's heart is open wide – you are welcome to come in.

Perhaps you are bruised and broken by the pressures of life. Others have wronged you and you feel scarred for life. You have old, painful memories that have never been healed. You avoid prayer because you feel too distant, too unworthy, too defiled. Do not despair. The Father's heart is open wide – you are welcome to come in.

Perhaps you have prayed for many years but the words have grown brittle and cold. Little ever happens any more. God seems remote and inaccessible. Listen to me. The Father's heart is open wide – you are welcome to come in.

Perhaps prayer is the delight of your life. You have lived in the divine milieu for a long time and can attest to its goodness. But you long for more: more power, more love, more of God in your life. Believe me. The Father's heart is open wide – you too are welcome to come higher up and deeper in.

If the key is prayer, the door is Jesus Christ. How good of God to provide us a way into his heart. He knows that we are stiff-necked and hard-hearted, so he has provided a means of entrance. Jesus, the Christ, lived a perfect life, died in our place, and rose victorious over all the dark powers so that we might live through him. This is wonderfully good news. No longer do we have to stand outside, barred from nearness to God by our rebellion. We may now enter through the door of God's grace and mercy in Jesus Christ.

The Syntax of Prayer

This book is written to help you explore this "many splendoured" heart of God. It is not about definitions *of* prayer or terminology *for* prayer or arguments *about* prayer, though all of these have their place. Nor is it about methods and techniques of prayer, though I am sure we will discuss both. No, this book is about a love relationship: an enduring, continuing, growing love relationship with the great God of the universe. And overwhelming love invites a response. Loving is the syntax of prayer. To be effective pray-ers, we need to be effective lovers. In *The Rime of the Ancient Mariner* Samuel Coleridge declares, "He prayeth well, who loveth well."[1] Coleridge, of course, got this idea from the Bible, for its pages breathe the language of divine love. Real prayer comes not from gritting our teeth but from falling in love. This is why the great literature on prayer is frankly and wonderfully erotic. "The Trinity," writes Juliana of Norwich, "is our everlasting lover."[2] "O my love!" exclaims Richard Rolle. "O my Honey! O my Harp! O my psalter and canticle all the day! When will you heal my grief? O root of my heart, when will you come to me?"[3] "Jesus, Lover of my soul," pleads Charles Wesley. "Let me to thy bosom fly."[4]

One day a friend of mine was walking through a shopping mall with his two-year-old son. The child was in a particularly cantankerous mood, fussing and fuming. The frustrated father tried everything to quiet his son but nothing seemed to help. The child simply would not obey. Then, under some special inspiration, the father scooped up his son and, holding him close to his chest, began singing an impromptu love song. None of the words rhymed. He sang off key. And yet, as best he could, this father began sharing his heart. "I love you," he sang. "I'm so glad you're my boy. You make me happy. I like the way you laugh." On they went from one store to the next. Quietly the father continued singing off key and making up words that did not rhyme. The child relaxed and became still, listening to this strange and wonderful song. Finally, they finished shopping and went to the car. As the father opened the door and prepared to buckle his son into the car seat, the child lifted his head and said simply, "Sing it to me again, Daddy! Sing it to me again!"[5]

Prayer is a little like that. With simplicity of heart we allow ourselves to be gathered up into the arms of the Father and let him sing his love song over us.

------------◆------------

Dear God, I am so grateful for your invitation to enter your heart of love. As best I can I come in. Thank you for receiving me.

— Amen.

PART I

Moving Inward
Seeking the Transformation We Need

To pray is to change. This is a great grace. How good of God to provide a path whereby our lives can be taken over by love and joy and peace and patience and kindness and goodness and faithfulness and gentleness and self-control.

The movement inward comes first because without interior transformation the movement up into God's glory would overwhelm us and the movement out into ministry would destroy us.

A disciple once came to Abba Joseph saying, "Father, according as I am able, I keep my little rule, my little fast, and my little prayer. And according as I am able I strive to cleanse my mind of all evil thoughts and my heart of all evil intents. Now, what more should I do?" Abba Joseph rose up and stretched out his hands to heaven, and his fingers became like ten lamps of fire. He answered, "Why not be totally changed into fire?"

I

Simple Prayer

Pray as you can, not as you can't.

— Dom Chapman

We today yearn for prayer and hide from prayer. We are attracted to it and repelled by it. We believe prayer is something we should do, even something we want to do; but it seems as if a chasm stands between us and actually praying. We experience the agony of prayerlessness.

We are not quite sure what holds us back. Of course we are busy with work and family obligations, but that is only a smoke screen. Our busyness seldom keeps us from eating or sleeping or making love. No, there is something deeper, more profound keeping us in check. In reality, there are any number of "somethings" preventing us, all of which we will explore in due time. But for now there is one "something" that needs immediate attention. It is the notion — almost universal among us modern high achievers — that we have to have everything "just right" in order to pray. That is, before we can really pray, our lives need some fine tuning, or we need to know more about how to pray, or we need to study the philosophical questions surrounding prayer, or we need to have a better grasp of the great traditions of prayer. And on it goes.

It isn't that these are wrong concerns or that there is never a time to deal with them. But we are starting from the wrong end of things — putting the cart before the horse. Our problem is that we assume prayer is something to master the way we master algebra or motor mechanics. That puts us in the "on top" position, where we are competent and in control. But when praying we come "underneath", where we calmly and deliberately surrender control and become incompetent. "To pray," writes Emilie Griffin, "means to be willing to be naïve."[1]

I used to think that I needed to get all my motives straightened out before I could pray, really pray. I would be in some prayer group, for example, and I would examine what I had just prayed and think to myself, "How utterly foolish and self-centred; I can't pray this way!" And so I would determine never to pray again until my motives were pure. You understand, I did not want to be a hypocrite. I knew that God is holy and righteous. I knew that prayer is no magic incantation. I knew that I must not use God for my own ends. But the practical effect of all this internal soul-searching was to completely paralyse my ability to pray.

The truth of the matter is, we all come to prayer with a tangled mass of motives – altruistic *and* selfish, merciful *and* hateful, loving *and* bitter. Frankly, this side of eternity we will *never* unravel the good from the bad, the pure from the impure. But what I have come to see is that God is big enough to receive us with all our mixture. We do not have to be bright, or pure, or filled with faith, or anything. That is what grace means, and not only are we saved by grace, we live by it as well. And we pray by it.

Jesus reminds us that prayer is a little like children coming to their parents. Our children come to us with the craziest requests at times. Often we are grieved by the meanness and selfishness of their requests, but we would be all the more grieved if they never came to us even with their meanness and selfishness. We are simply glad that they do come – mixed motives and all.

This is precisely how it is with prayer. We will never have pure enough motives, or be good enough, or know enough in order to pray rightly. We simply must set all these things aside and begin praying. In fact, it is in the very act of prayer itself – the intimate, ongoing interaction with God – that these matters are cared for in due time.

Just as We Are

What I am trying to say is that God receives us just as we are and accepts our prayers just as they are. In the same way that a small child cannot draw a bad picture so a child of God cannot offer a bad prayer. So we are brought to the most basic, the most primary form of prayer: Simple Prayer. Let me describe it for you. In Simple Prayer we bring ourselves before God just as we are, warts and all. Like children before a loving father, we open our hearts and make our requests. We do not try to sort things out, the good from the bad. We simply and unpretentiously share our concerns and make our petitions. We tell God, for example, how frustrated we are with the co-worker at the office or the neighbour down the road. We ask for food, favourable weather, and good health.

In a very real sense we *are* the focus of Simple Prayer. Our needs, our wants, our concerns dominate our prayer experience. Our prayers are shot through with plenty of pride, conceit, vanity, pretentiousness, haughtiness and general all-around egocentricity. No doubt there are also magnanimity, generosity, unselfishness and universal goodwill.

We make mistakes – lots of them; we sin; we fall down, often, but each time we get up and begin again. We pray again. We seek to follow God again. And again our insolence and self-indulgence defeat us. Never mind. We confess and begin again ... and again ... and again. In fact, sometimes Simple Prayer is called the "Prayer of Beginning Again".

Simple Prayer is the most common form of prayer in the Bible. There is little that is lofty or magnanimous about the faith heroes who journey across the pages of Scripture. Think of Moses complaining to God about his stiff-necked and erstwhile followers: "Why have I not found favour in your sight, that you lay the burden of all this people on me? Did I conceive all this people? Did I give birth to them, that you should say to me, 'Carry them in your bosom, as a nurse carries a sucking child,' to the land that you promised

on oath to their ancestors?" (Num. 11:11b-12). Or consider
Elisha retaliating against the children who had jeered at
him, calling him a "baldhead": "He cursed them in the
name of the LORD. Then two she-bears came out of the
woods and mauled forty-two of the boys" (2 Kings 2:24).
And then there is the Psalmist delighting in the violent
death of the babies of his enemies: "Happy shall they be
who take your little ones and dash them against the rock!"
(Ps. 137:9).

Yet right in the midst of all this self-serving prayer are
some of the most noble and sublime utterances of the
human spirit. Think of Moses interceding before God on
behalf of a stubborn and disobedient Israel: "But now, if
you will only forgive their sin – but if not, blot me out of
the book that you have written" (Exod. 32:32). Or consider
this same Elisha who had cursed the children, on another
day showing mercy to a barren woman of Shunem and
prophesying over her: "At this season, in due time, you
shall embrace a son" (2 Kings 4:16). Or look into the heart
of the Psalmist crying out to Yahweh, "Oh, how I love
your law! It is my meditation all day long" (Ps. 119:97).
In Simple Prayer the good, the bad, and the ugly are all
mixed together.

Simple Prayer is found throughout Scripture. Abraham
prayed this way, as did Joseph, Joshua, Hannah, David,
Gideon, Ruth, Peter, James, John, and a host of other
biblical luminaries.

Simple Prayer involves ordinary people bringing ordinary
concerns to a loving and compassionate Father. There is no
pretence in Simple Prayer. We do not pretend to be more
holy, more pure, or more saintly than we actually are. We
do not try to conceal our conflicting and contradictory
motives from God – or ourselves. And in this posture we
pour out our heart to the God who is greater than our heart
and who knows all things (1 John 3:20).

Simple Prayer is beginning prayer. It is the prayer of children and yet we will return to it again and again. St Teresa
of Avila notes, "There is no stage of prayer so sublime that

it isn't necessary to return often to the beginning."[2] Jesus, for example, calls us to Simple Prayer when he urges us to ask for daily bread. As John Dalrymple rightly observes, "We never outgrow this kind of prayer, because we never outgrow the needs which give rise to it."[3]

There is a temptation, especially by the "sophisticated", to despise this most elementary way of praying. They seek to skip over Simple Prayer in the hopes of advancing to more "mature" expressions of prayer. They smile at the egotistical asking, asking, asking of so many. Grandly they speak of avoiding "self-centred prayer" in favour of "other-centred prayer". What these people fail to see, however, is that Simple Prayer is necessary, even essential, to the spiritual life. The only way we move beyond "self-centred prayer" (if indeed we do) is by going through it, not by making a detour round it.

Those who think they can leap over Simple Prayer deceive themselves. Most likely they themselves have not prayed. They may have discussed prayer, analysed prayer, even written books about prayer, but it is highly unlikely that they have actually prayed. But when we pray, genuinely pray, the real condition of our heart is revealed. This is as it should be. This is when God truly begins to work with us. The adventure is just beginning.

Beginning Where We Are

Up to this point we have been describing Simple Prayer. That is theory. But we must move beyond theory to ask the question for which all that has gone before is a prelude. How do we practise Simple Prayer? What do we do? Where do we begin?

Very simply, we begin right where we are: in our families, at our jobs, with our neighbours and friends. Now, I wish this did not sound so trivial because on the practical level of knowing God it is the most profound truth we will ever hear. To believe that God can reach us and bless us in the ordinary junctures of daily life is the stuff of prayer. But we

want to throw this away, so hard is it for us to believe that
God would enter our space. "God can't bless me here," we
moan. "When I graduate . . ." "When I'm the chairman of
the board . . ." "When I'm the president of the company
. . ." "When I'm the senior pastor . . . then God can bless
me." But you see, the only place God can bless us is where
we are, because that is the only place we are!

Do you remember Moses at the burning bush? God had to
tell him to take off his shoes – he did not know he was on holy
ground. And if we can just come to see that where we are is
holy ground – in our jobs and homes, with our co-workers
and friends and families – this is where we learn to pray.

In the most natural and simple way possible we learn to
pray our experiences by taking up the ordinary events of
every-day life and giving them to God. Perhaps we have
a crushing failure that gives us more than one sleepless
night. Well, we pace the floor *with* God, telling him of
our hurt and our pain and our disappointment. "Why
me?" we cry out, "why me?" for frustration and tears
and anger are also the language of Simple Prayer. We
invite God to walk with us as we grieve the loss of our
dream. Maybe the offhand remark of a neighbour triggers
a whole explosion of emotions within us: anger, jealousy,
fear. Very well, we speak frankly and honestly with God
about what is happening and ask him to help us see the
hurt behind the emotion.

We should feel perfectly free to complain to God, or
argue with God, or yell at God. The prophet Jeremiah once
shouted out, "You have seduced me, Yahweh, and I have
let myself be seduced; you have overpowered me: you were
the stronger. I am a daily laughing-stock, everybody's butt"
(Jer. 20:7, JB). And I can well imagine that Jeremiah shook
his fist to heaven as he spoke! God is perfectly capable of
handling our anger and frustration and disappointment. C.
S. Lewis counsels us to "lay before him what is in us, not
what ought to be in us".4

We must never believe the lie which says that the details
of our lives are not the proper content of prayer. For

example, we may have been taught that prayer is a sublime and otherworldly activity; that in prayer we are to talk to God *about* God. As a result we are inclined to view our experiences as distractions and intrusions into proper prayer. This is an ethereal, decarnate spirituality. We, on the other hand, worship a God who was born in a smelly stable, who walked this earth in blood, sweat, and tears, but who nevertheless lived in perpetual responsiveness to the heavenly Monitor.

And so I urge you: carry on an ongoing conversation with God about the daily stuff of life, a little like Tevye in *Fiddler on the Roof*.* For now, do not worry about "proper" praying, just talk to God. Share your hurts; share your sorrows; share your joys — freely and openly. God listens in compassion and love, just as we do when our children come to us. He delights in our presence. When we do this we will discover something of inestimable value. We will discover that by praying we learn to pray.

Counsels Along the Way

I would like to give a few beginning words of counsel as we start on this studied adventure into prayer. My first counsel is simply a reminder that prayer is nothing more than an ongoing and growing love relationship with God the Father, Son and Holy Spirit. This is especially true with Simple Prayer. Here no one has any advantage. The bruised and broken enter Simple Prayer as freely as the healthy and wealthy. Madame Guyon writes:

This way of prayer, this simple relationship to your

---

* Tevye's prayers, by the by, appeal to us precisely because they are Simple Prayer. There is no better example of this than his song, "If I Were a Rich Man", in which he prays the question many of us wish we could ask the Almighty, "Lord, Who made the lion and the lamb/ You decreed I should be what I am./ Would it spoil some vast, eternal plan/ If I were a wealthy man?"

Lord, is so suited for everyone; it is just as suited for the dull and the ignorant as it is for the well-educated. This prayer, this experience which begins so simply, has as its end a totally abandoned love to the Lord. Only one thing is required – Love.5

Second, as we begin, we must never be discouraged by our lack of prayer. Even in our prayerlessness we can hunger for God. If so, the hunger is itself prayer. "The desire for prayer" writes Mary Clare Vincent, "is prayer, the prayer of desire."6 In time the desire will lead to practice, and practice will increase the desire. When we cannot pray, we let God be our prayer. Nor should we be frightened by the hardness of our heart: prayer will soften it. We give even our lack of prayer to God.

An opposite but equally important counsel is to let go of trying too hard to pray. Some people work at the business of praying with such intensity that they get spiritual indigestion. There is a principle of progression in the spiritual life. We do not take occasional joggers and put them in a marathon race, and we must not do that with prayer either. The desert mothers and fathers spoke of the sin of "spiritual greed", that is, wanting more of God than can be digested. If prayer is not a fixed habit with you, instead of starting with twelve hours of prayer-filled dialogue, single out a few moments and put all your energy into them. When you have had enough, tell God simply, "I must have a rest; I have no strength to be with you all the time." This, by the way, is perfectly true, and God knows that you are still not capable of bearing his company continuously. Besides, even the most spiritually advanced – perhaps *especially* the most spiritually advanced – need frequent times of laughter and play and good fun.

I now want to give a counsel that may sound strange. It is that we should learn to pray even while we are dwelling on evil. Perhaps we are waging an interior battle over anger, or lust, or pride, or greed, or ambition. We need not isolate these things from prayer. Instead we talk to God about what is going on inside, that we know displeases him. We lift even our disobedience into the arms of the Father; he is strong enough to carry the weight. Sin, to be sure, separates us from God, but trying to hide our sin separates us all the more. "The Lord," writes Emilie Griffin, "loves us – perhaps most of all – when we fail and try again."7

Finally, I would suggest that in the beginning it is wise to strive for uneventful prayer experiences.8 Divine revelations and ecstasies can overwhelm us and distract us from the real work of prayer. Our approach needs to be more like that of the Psalmist, who sought to avoid "marvels beyond my scope. Enough for me to keep my soul tranquil and quiet like a child in its mother's arms" (Ps. 131:1–2, JB). Besides, if we are unaccustomed to it, just slipping quietly into the presence of God can be so exotic and fresh that it delights us enormously.

The Conversion of the Heart

Simple Prayer is often ignored in many of the books written about prayer. I have often wondered why this is so. Perhaps it is because devout writers fear the self-centred aspects of Simple Prayer. To focus so much on the "self" can easily lead to selfishness and narcissism. Further, we are always in danger of rationalizing and manipulating our experiences so that we hear only what we want to hear. We may in the end become so consumed with ourselves that we lose sight of God altogether and end up worshipping "the creature rather than the Creator", as Paul put it (Rom. 1:25).

It is a legitimate concern. The dangers are all too real. But as Joseph Schmidt notes, "They are dangers on the right road. We must move with some caution but not turn back."9 Nor shall we turn back. Seeking divine protection, we venture forward with honesty and openness.

In the beginning we are indeed the subject and the centre of our prayers. But in God's time and in God's way a Copernican revolution takes place in our heart. Slowly, almost imperceptibly, there is a shift in our centre of gravity. We pass from thinking of God as part of our life to the realization that we are part of his life. Wondrously and mysteriously God moves from the periphery of our prayer experience to the centre. A conversion of the heart takes place, a transformation of the spirit. This wonderful work of Divine Grace is the major burden of this book, and it is to this that we must now turn our attention.

———————◆———————

Dear Jesus, how desperately I need to learn to pray. And yet, when I am honest I know that I often do not even want to pray.
    I am distracted!
      I am stubborn!
        I am self-centred!
In your mercy, Jesus, bring my "want-er" more in line with my "need-er" so that I can come to want what I need.
    In your name and for your sake, I pray.
                    — Amen.

2

Prayer of the Forsaken

*To come to the pleasure you have not you must
go by a way in which you enjoy not.*
— St John of the Cross

There is no more plaintive or heartfelt prayer than the cry
of Jesus: "My God, my God, why hast thou forsaken me?"
(Matt. 27:46b, KJV). Jesus' experience on the cross was, of
course, utterly unique and unrepeatable for he was taking
into himself the sin of the world. But in our own way you
and I *will* pray this Prayer of the Forsaken if we seek the
intimacy of perpetual communion with the Father. Times
of seeming desertion and absence and abandonment appear
to be universal among those who have walked this path of
faith before us. We might just as well get used to the idea
that, sooner or later, we too will know what it means to
feel forsaken by God.

The old writers spoke of this reality as *Deus Absconditus*
– the God who is hidden. Almost instinctively you understand the experience they were describing, do you not?
Have you ever tried to pray and felt nothing, saw nothing,
sensed nothing? Has it ever seemed as if your prayers did
no more than bounce off the ceiling and ricochet around an
empty room? Have there been times when you desperately
needed some word of assurance, some demonstration of
divine presence, and you got nothing?

Sometimes God seems to be hidden from us. We do
everything we know. We pray. We serve. We worship. We
live as faithfully as we can. And still there is nothing . . .
nothing! It feels as if we are "beating on heaven's door with
bruised knuckles in the dark", to use the words of George
Buttrick.[1]

I am sure you understand that when I speak of the absence of God, I am talking not about a true absence but rather a *sense* of absence. God is always present with us – we know that theologically – but there are times when he withdraws our consciousness of his presence.

But these theological niceties are of little help to us when we enter the Sahara of the heart. Here we experience real spiritual desolation. We feel abandoned by friends, spouse and God. Every hope evaporates the moment we reach for it. Every dream dies the moment we try to realize it. We question, we doubt, we struggle. Nothing helps. We pray and the words seem empty. We turn to the Bible and find it meaningless. We turn to music and it fails to move us. We seek the fellowship of other Christians and discover only backbiting, selfishness and egoism.

The biblical metaphor for these experiences of forsakenness is the desert. It is an apt image for we do indeed feel dry, barren, parched. With the Psalmist we cry out, "I call all day, my God, but you never answer" (Ps. 22:2). In fact, we begin to wonder if there is a God to answer.

These experiences of abandonment and desertion have come and will come to us all. Therefore it is good to see if anything helpful can be said as we face the barren wasteland of God's absence.

A Major Highway

The first word that should be spoken is one of encouragement. We are not on a rabbit trail, but a major highway. Many have travelled this way before us. Think of Moses exiled from Egypt's splendour, waiting year after silent year for God to deliver his people. Think of the Psalmist's plaintive cry to God, "Why have you forgotten me?" (Ps. 42:9). Think of Elijah in a desolate cave keeping a lonely vigil over wind and earthquake and fire. Think of Jeremiah lowered down into a dungeon well until he "sank in the mire". Think of Mary's solitary vigil at Golgotha. Think of those solitary

words atop Golgotha, "My God, my God, why . . . why
. . . why?"

Christians down through the centuries have witnessed
the same experience. St John of the Cross named it "the
dark night of the soul". An anonymous English writer
identified it as "the cloud of unknowing". Jean-Pierre de
Caussade called it "the dark night of faith". George Fox
said simply, "When it was day I wished for night, and when
it was night I wished for day."[2] Be encouraged – you and I
are in good company.

In addition I want you to know that to be faced with the
"withering winds of God's hiddenness"[3] does not mean
that God is displeased with you, or that you are insensitive
to the work of God's Spirit, or that you have committed
some horrendous offence against heaven, or that there is
something wrong with you, or anything. Darkness is a
definite experience of prayer. It is to be expected, even
embraced.

Tailor-Made Journey

The second thing that can be said about our experience
of abandonment is that every faith journey is tailor-made.
Our sense of God's absence does not come to us in any
preset timetable. We cannot simply draw some universal
road map that everyone will be able to follow.

It is true that those in the first flush of faith are often
given unusual graces of the Spirit, just as a new baby is
cuddled and pampered. It is also true that some of the
deepest experiences of alienation and separation from
God have come to those who have travelled far into
the interior realms of faith. But we can enter the bleak
deserts of barrenness and the dark canyons of anguish at
any number of points in our sojourn.

Since there is no special sequence in the life of prayer, we
simply do not move from one stage to the next knowing, for
example, that at stages five and twelve we will experience
abandonment by God. Of course, it would be much easier

if that were the case, but then we would be describing a mechanical arrangement rather than a living relationship.

A Living Relationship

That is the next thing that should be said about our sense of the absence of God, namely that we are entering into a living relationship that begins and develops in mutual freedom. God grants us perfect freedom because he desires creatures who freely choose to be in relationship with him. Through the Prayer of the Forsaken we are learning to give to God the same freedom. Relationships of this kind can never be manipulated or forced.

If we could make the Creator of heaven and earth instantly appear at our beck and call, we would not be in communion with the God of Abraham, Isaac and Jacob. We do that with objects, with things, with idols. But God, the great iconoclast, is constantly smashing our false images of who he is and what he is like.

Can you see how our very sense of the absence of God is, therefore, an unsuspected grace? In the very act of hiddenness God is slowly weaning us from fashioning him in our own image. Like Aslan, the Christ figure in *The Chronicles of Narnia*, God is wild and free and comes at will. By refusing to be a puppet on our string or a genie in our bottle, God frees us from our false, idolatrous images.

Besides, we should probably be thankful that God does not always present himself whenever we wish, because we might not be able to endure such a meeting. Often in the Bible people were scared out of their wits when they encountered the living God. "Do not let God speak to us, or we will die," pleaded the children of Israel (Exod. 20:19). At times this should be our plea as well.

Anatomy of an Absence

Allow me to share with you a time when I entered the Prayer of the Forsaken. By every outward standard things were going well. Publishers wanted me to write for them. Speaking invitations were too numerous and too gracious. Yet through a series of events it seemed clear to me that God wanted me to retreat from public activity. In essence God said, "Keep quiet!" And so I did. I stopped all public speaking, I stopped all writing and I waited. At the time this began I did not know if I would ever speak or write again – I rather thought I would not. As it turned out, this fast from public life lasted about eighteen months.

I waited in silence. And God was silent too. I joined in the Psalmist's query: "How long will you hide your face from me?" (Ps. 13:1). The answer I got: nothing. Absolutely nothing! There were no sudden revelations. No penetrating insights. Not even gentle assurances. Nothing.

Have you ever been there? Perhaps for you it was the tragic death of a child or spouse that plunged you into the desolate desert of God's absence. Maybe it was a crisis in marriage or vocation, or a failure in business. It may have been none of these. There may have been no dramatic event at all – you simply slipped from the warm glow of intimate communion to the icy cold of . . . nothing. At least "nothing" is how it feels . . . well, actually there is no feeling at all. It is as if all feelings have gone into hibernation. (You see how I am struggling for the language to describe this experience of abandonment, for words are fragmentary approximations at best, but if you have been there, you understand what I mean.)

As I mentioned earlier this discipline of silence lasted some eighteen months. It ended finally and simply with gentle assurances that it was time to re-enter the public square.

The Purifying Silence

As best I can discern, the silence of God month after weary month was a purifying silence. I say "as best I can discern" because the purifying was not dramatic or even recognizable at the time. It was a little bit like when you do not realize that a child has grown until you measure her against the mark on the hall door from last year.

St John of the Cross says that two purifications occur in the dark night of the soul, and in some measure I experienced both. The first involves stripping us of dependence upon *exterior results*. We find ourselves less and less impressed with the religion of the "big deal" – big buildings, big budgets, big productions, big miracles. Not that there is anything wrong with big things, but *they* are no longer what impress us. Nor are we drawn towards praise and adulation. Not that there is anything wrong with kind and gracious remarks, but *they* are no longer what move us.

Then, too, we become deadened to that impressive corpus of religious response to God. Liturgical practices, sacramental symbols, aids to prayer, books on personal fulfilment, private devotional exercises – all of these become as mere ashes in our hands. Not that there is anything wrong with acts of devotion, but *they* are no longer what fascinate us.

The final stripping of dependence upon exterior results comes as we become less in control of our destiny, and more at the mercy of others. St John calls this the "Passive Dark Night". It is the condition of Peter who once girded himself and went where he wanted but in time found that others girded him and took him where he did not want to go (John 21:18–19).

For me the greatest value in my lack of control was the intimate and ultimate awareness that I could not manage God. God refused to jump when I said "Jump!" Neither by theological acumen nor by religious technique could I conquer God. God was, in fact, to conquer me.

The second purifying of St John involves stripping us of dependence upon *interior results*. This is more disturbing and painful than the first purification because it threatens us at the root of all we believe in and have given ourselves to. In the beginning we become less and less sure of the inner workings of the Spirit. It is not that we disbelieve in

God, but more profoundly we wonder what kind of God we believe in. Is God good and intent upon our goodness, or is God cruel, sadistic and a tyrant?

We discover that the workings of faith, hope and love become themselves subject to doubt. Our personal motivations become suspect. We worry whether this act or that thought is inspired by fear, vanity and arrogance rather than faith, hope and love.

Like a frightened child we walk cautiously through the dark mists that now surround the Holy of Holies. We become tentative and unsure of ourselves. Nagging questions assail us with a force they never had before. "Is prayer only a psychological trick?" "Does evil ultimately win out?" "Is there any real meaning in the universe?" "Does God really love me?"

Through all of this, paradoxically, God is purifying our faith by threatening to destroy it. We are led to a profound and holy distrust of all superficial drives and human strivings. We know more deeply than ever before our capacity for infinite self-deception. Slowly we are being taken off vain securities and false allegiances. Our trust in all exterior and interior results is being shattered so that we can learn faith in God alone. Through our barrenness of soul God is producing detachment, humility, patience, perseverance.

Most surprising of all, our very dryness produces the habit of prayer in us. All distractions are gone. Even all warm fellowship has disappeared. We have become focused. The soul is parched. And thirsty. And this thirst can lead us to prayer. I say "can" because it can also lead us to despair or simply to abandon the search.

The Prayer of Complaint

This brings us to the issue of what we do during these times of abandonment. Is there any kind of prayer in which we can engage when we feel forsaken? Yes – we can begin by praying the Prayer of Complaint. This is a form of prayer that has been largely lost in our modern, sanitized religion, but the Bible abounds with it.

The best way I know to relearn this time-honoured approach to God is by praying that part of the Psalter traditionally known as the "Lament Psalms".4 The ancient singers really knew how to complain, and their words of anguish and frustration can guide our lips into the prayer we dare not pray alone. They expressed reverence *and* disappointment: "God whom I praise, break your silence" (Ps. 109:1, JB). They experienced dogged hope *and* mounting despair: "I am here, calling for your help, praying to you every morning: why do you reject me? Why do you hide your face from me?" (Ps. 88:13–14, JB). They had confidence in the character of God *and* exasperation at the inaction of God: "I say to God, my rock, 'Why have you forgotten me?'" (Ps. 42:9).

The Lament Psalms teach us to pray our inner conflicts and contradictions. They allow us to shout out our for-sakenness in the dark caverns of abandonment and then hear the echo return to us over and over until we bitterly recant them, only to shout them out again. They give us permission to shake our fist at God one moment and break into doxology the next.

Short Darts of Longing Love

A second thing we can do when we are buffeted by the silence of God is to beat upon the cloud of unknowing "with a short dart of longing love".5 We may not see the end from the beginning but we keep on doing what we know to do. We pray, we listen, we worship, we carry out the duty of the present moment. What we learned to do in the light of God's love, we also do in the dark of God's absence. We ask and continue to ask even though there is no answer. We seek and continue to seek even though we do not find. We knock and continue to knock even though the door remains shut.

It is this constant, longing love that produces a firmness

of life orientation in us. We love God more than the gifts God brings. Like Job, we serve God even if he slays us. Like Mary, we say freely, "Here am I, the servant of the Lord; let it be with me according to your word" (Luke 1:38). This is a wonderful grace.

Trust Precedes Faith

I would like to offer one more counsel to those who find themselves devoid of the presence of God. It is this: wait on God. Wait, silent and still. Wait, attentive and responsive. Learn that trust precedes faith. Faith is a little like putting your car into gear, and right now you cannot exercise faith, you cannot move forward. Do not berate yourself for this. But when you are unable to put your spiritual life into drive, do not put it into reverse; put it into neutral. Trust is how you put your spiritual life in neutral. Trust is confidence in the character of God. Firmly and deliberately you say, "I do not understand what God is doing or even where God is, but I know that he is out to do me good." This is trust. This is how to wait.

I do not fully understand the reasons for the wildernesses of God's absence. This I do know; while the wilderness is necessary, it is never meant to be permanent. In God's time and in God's way the desert will give way to a land flowing with milk and honey. And as we wait for that promised land of the soul, we can echo the prayer of Bernard of Clairvaux, "O my God, deep calls unto deep (Ps. 42:7). The deep of my profound misery calls to the deep of your infinite mercy."[6]

———————◆———————

GOD, WHERE ARE YOU!? What have I done to make you hide from me? Are you playing cat and mouse with me or are your purposes larger than my perceptions? I feel alone, lost, forsaken.

You are the God who specializes in revealing yourself. You showed yourself to Abraham, Isaac and Jacob. When Moses wanted to know what you looked like, you obliged him. Why them and not me?

I am tired of praying. I am tired of asking. I am tired of waiting. But I will keep on praying and asking and waiting because I have nowhere else to go.

Jesus, you too knew the loneliness of the desert and the isolation of the cross. And it is through your forsaken prayer that I speak these words.

— Amen.

3

The Prayer of Examen

Prayer is the inner bath of love into which the soul plunges itself.

— St John Vianney

How very strange that the Prayer of Examen* has been lost to us in an age of obsessive introspection. It is actually possible today for people to go to church services week in and week out for years without having a single experience of spiritual examen. What a tragedy! What a loss! No wonder people today are weak. No wonder they are barely hanging on.

How much richer and fuller is the biblical witness. The Psalmist declares, "Yahweh, you examine me and know me" (Ps. 139:1, JB). King David — who ought to know — witnesses, "The LORD searches every mind, and understands every plan and thought" (1 Chron. 28:9). And the Apostle Paul reminds us that "the Spirit searches everything, even the depths of God" (1 Cor. 2:10). And on it goes. These folk of faith knew the examen of God, and they experienced it not as a dreadful thing but as something of immeasurable strength and empowerment.

So what is this Prayer of Examen? It has two basic aspects, like the two sides of a door. The first is an *examen*

---

* Some small explanation should be given for the use of the rather unfamiliar word "examen". It is, of course, immediately identifiable with the commonly used word "examination", and it carries much the same meaning, minus the academic context. Examen comes from the Latin and refers to the tongue, or weight indicator, on a balance scale, hence conveying the idea of an accurate assessment of the true situation.

of consciousness through which we discover how God has
been present to us throughout the day and how we have
responded to his loving presence. The second aspect is an
examen of conscience in which we uncover those areas that
need cleansing, purifying and healing. It may be helpful to
look at these two aspects separately.

The Remembrance of Love

In the examen of consciousness we prayerfully reflect on the
thoughts, feelings and actions of our days to see how God
has been at work among us and how we responded. We
consider, for example, whether the boisterous neighbour
of last night was more than just a rude interruption of a
quiet evening. Maybe, just maybe, he was the voice of God
urging us to be attentive to the pain and loneliness of those
around us. Perhaps in the glorious sunrise of this morning
God was shouting out to us his love of beauty and inviting
us to share in it, but we were too sleepy or distracted to
participate. Maybe we responded to the Divine Whisper
to write a letter or call a friend on the telephone, and
the results of our simple obedience were nothing short of
startling.

The examen of consciousness is the means God uses to
make us more aware of our surroundings. Recently I sat
next to a student from Tehran, sensing that God wanted
me to be present and attentive to him. Reza is his name, and
in our few moments together he taught me about dignity
and courage and faith. His words to me were few, but they
were, each one, life giving. I had seen Reza before, but I
had not been present to him before. I am the better for our
meeting.

You see, I am not talking about something complicated
or unusual in the least. God wants us to be present where
we are. He invites us to see and to hear what is around us
and, through it all, to discern the footprints of the Holy.

Actually, the examen of consciousness is one way we
heed the call to rehearse the mighty deeds of God. Have you

ever noticed how frequently the Bible urges us to remember? Remember the covenant God made with Abraham. Remember how Yahweh delivered his people from the land of Egypt, from the house of bondage. Remember the holy Decalogue, the Ten Commandments. Remember the kingdom promise to David. Remember the heir of David whose body was broken and whose blood was poured out. In the bread and the wine remember ... remember Calvary.

After Israel defeated the Philistines, Samuel set up a stone memorial between Mizpah and Jeshanah and named it Ebenezer for "hitherto the Lord has helped us" (1 Sam. 7:12, RSV). He was giving the people a specific way of remembering. That is what we are doing in the examen of consciousness. We are raising our own personal Ebenezer and declaring, "Here is where God met me and helped me." We are remembering.

The Scrutiny of Love

In the examen of conscience we are inviting the Lord to search our hearts to the depths. Far from being dreadful this is a scrutiny of love. We boldly speak the words of the Psalmist, "Search me, O God, and know my heart; test me and know my thoughts. See if there is any wicked way in me, and lead me in the way everlasting" (Ps. 139:23–24).

Without apology and without defence we ask to see what is truly in us. It is for our own sake that we ask these things. It is for our good, for our healing, for our happiness.

I want you to know that God goes with us in the examen of conscience. It is a joint search, if I may put it that way. This fact is helpful for us to know for two equally important but opposite reasons.

To begin with, if we are the lone examiners of our heart, a thousand justifications will arise to declare our innocence. We will "call evil good, and good evil", as Isaiah says (Isa. 5:20). But since God is with us in the search, we are listening more than we are defending. Our petty rationalizations and evasions of responsibility simply will not tolerate the light of his presence. He will show us what we need to see when we need to see it.

At the other end of the spectrum is our tendency for self-flagellation. If left to our own devices, it is so easy for us to take one good look at who we truly are and declare ourselves unredeemable. Our damaged self-image votes against us, and we begin beating ourselves mercilessly. But with God alongside us, we are protected and comforted. He will never allow us to see more than we are able to handle. He knows that too much introspection can harm more than help.

Madame Guyon warns us of "depending on the diligence of our own scrutiny rather than on God for the discovery and knowledge of our sin".[1] If the examination is solely a *self*-examination, we will always end up with excessive praise or blame. But under the searchlight of the great Physician we can expect only good always.

Not that there is no pain. Guyon notes, "When you are accustomed to this type of surrender, you will find that as soon as a fault is committed, God will rebuke it through an inward burning. He allows no evil to be concealed in the lives of His children."[2] And so there is a painful "inward burning", but we know that it is a purifying fire and can welcome its cleansing.

The Priceless Grace

By now a question may have arisen in your mind. What is the purpose of all this examination business anyway? Just what are we expecting it to accomplish? It is an honest question, and it deserves an honest answer. Actually the answer is easy to state: it is the value of the answer that is difficult to articulate.

The Prayer of Examen produces within us the priceless grace of self-knowledge. I wish I could adequately explain to you how great a grace this truly is. Unfortunately, contemporary men and women simply do not value self-knowledge in the same way that all preceding generations have. For us technocratic knowledge reigns supreme. Even when we pursue self-knowledge, we all too often reduce it to a hedonistic search for personal peace and prosperity. How poor we are! Even the pagan philosophers were wiser than this generation. They knew that an unexamined life was not worth living. "Know thyself" is the famous dictum of Socrates.

St Teresa of Avila understood the value of self-knowledge. In her autobiography she writes, "This path of self knowledge must never be abandoned, nor is there on this journey a soul so much a giant that it has no need to return often to the stage of an infant and a suckling."[3] Self-knowledge is not only foundational but also a foundation that can never be forgotten. We are to come back to this most basic way of prayer over and over again.

In attempting to explain to us the value of self-knowledge, Teresa adds something that sounds quite strange to us. She writes, "Along this path of prayer, self knowledge and the thought of one's sins is the bread with which all palates must be fed no matter how delicate they may be; they cannot be sustained without this bread."[4] How startling to think that our own sinfulness can be the bread by which we are fed. How can this be?

Paul, you may remember, urges us to offer our bodies – our very selves – as a living sacrifice to God (Rom. 12:1). This offering cannot be made in some abstract way with pious words or religious acts. No, it must be rooted in the acceptance of the concrete details of who we are and the way we live. We must come to accept and even honour our creatureliness. The offering of ourselves can only be the offering of our lived experience because this alone is who we are. And who we are – not who we want to be – is the only offering we have to give. We give God therefore not just our strengths but also our weaknesses, not just our gift-edness, but also our brokenness. Our duplicity, our lust, our narcissism, our sloth – all are laid on the altar of sacrifice.

We must not deny or ignore the depth of our evil, for, paradoxically, our sinfulness becomes our bread. When in honesty we accept the evil that is in us as part of the truth about ourselves and offer that truth up to God, we are in a mysterious way nourished. Even the truth about our shadow side sets us free (John 8:32).

There is, therefore, no need to repress, suppress or sublimate any of God's truth about ourselves. Full, total, unvarnished self-knowledge is the bread by which we are sustained. A yes to life means an honest recognition of our own evil, but it is also a yes to God who in the midst of our evil sustains us and draws us into his righteousness.

Through faith, self-knowledge leads us to a self-acceptance and a self-love that draw their life from God's acceptance and love. So St Teresa is right after all; this is "the bread with which all palates must be fed." Her words are wise counsel indeed: "This path of self knowledge must never be abandoned."

Turning Inward

Earlier I said that the Prayer of Examen had two aspects. That is accurate enough in analysis, but when we come to practice, it can be misleading. In reality, the experience is more like an animated computer graphic of two concentric circles that are constantly overlapping, interfacing, and weaving into and out of one another. We watch, for example, for God's activity in our lives, and when we find it we discover that he has exposed our blind side. The examen of consciousness and the examen of conscience are a little like the waves of the ocean: distinct from one another and yet constantly on top of and never totally separate from each other. Understanding this, we now turn to *the* question: how do we practise the Prayer of Examen?

We practise it by turning inward. Not outward, not upward, but inward. Anthony Bloom writes, "Your prayer must be turned inwards, not towards a God of Heaven nor towards a God far off, but towards God who is closer to you than you are aware."5

With examen more than any other form of prayer, we bore down deeper and deeper, the way a drill would bore down into the bowels of the earth. We are constantly turning inward – but inward in a very special way. I do not mean to turn inward by becoming ever more introspective, nor do I mean to turn inward in hopes of finding within ourselves some special inner strength or an inner saviour who will deliver us. Vain search! No, it is not a journey *into* ourselves that we are undertaking but a journey *through* ourselves so that we can emerge from the deepest level of the self into God. As St John Chrysostom notes, "Find the door of your heart, you will discover it is the door of the kingdom of God."6

Madame Guyon calls this special kind of inward turning "the law of central tendency". "As you continue holding your soul deep in your inward parts, you will discover that God has a *magnetic* attracting quality! Your God is like a magnet! The Lord naturally draws you more and more towards himself."7 We are drawn into the Divine Centre, says Guyon, through God's grace rather than by our own efforts. She concludes, "Your soul, once it begins to turn inward, is brought under this . . . law of central tendency. It . . . gradually falls towards its proper centre, which is God. The soul needs no other force to draw it than the weight of love."8

Personal Ebenezers

"But how," you may ask, "is this turning inward accomplished? Are there activities of body, mind and spirit that help us?" Oh yes, many – more than I can number. Let me give you a few of the more common.

One time-tested way to enter the examen of consciousness is by means of a spiritual journal. From the *Confessions* of St Augustine to the *Markings* of Dag Hammarskjöld, Christians throughout the centuries have found value in recording their spiritual trek. "Like a lathe," writes Virginia Stem Owens, "a journal forces us inward to the heart of the wood."9

Journal-keeping is a highly intentional reflection on the events of our days. It differs from a diary by its focus on why and wherefore, rather than who and what. The external events are springboards for understanding the deeper workings of God in the heart. One special value of a journal is the record that it keeps – a personal Ebenezer, if you will. We can turn back to the pages of our personal history with God as often as we like and see the issues we have struggled with and the progress we have made.

The many diaries and journals of Frank Laubach are a disciplined adventure into the examen of consciousness. I think especially of his *Game with Minutes* in which he sought to see how many minutes in a day he could become conscious of God's presence. On New Year's Day 1937 he wrote, "God, I want to give you every minute of this year. I shall try to keep you in mind every moment of my waking hours."10 On another occasion he notes, "God, after a sleepless night, I open my eyes, laughing, for we are together! Sleep is not necessary. Disturbances like that man coughing below me all night are good for character if I do not let them keep me from you."11

I think also of Laubach's *Learning the Vocabulary of God*, in which he dedicates one entire year to learning how God speaks through the course of ordinary events. Early into that experiment he writes, "God, this going in search of your vocabulary promises to open a whole *world* of new vision. I have a little book in my pocket to record your words as they come to me all day long, just as I might learn any language."12 Interestingly, the experience of that year led him into his life's work, known worldwide as the Laubach Literacy Method. On a Tuesday in Baroda Bazaar, India, he writes, "Over three hundred and thirty millions who cannot read are calling for help. Need is your language, is a word from you. How to approach this problem is baffling. Unsolved problems are your language, for in them you are our schoolmaster training us."[13]

While I encourage the discipline of journal-keeping as a means of spiritual growth, I do not want to elevate it out of proper perspective. As far as we know, Jesus never engaged in this practice, nor did Francis of Assisi or any number of other well-known Christians. They seem to have fared quite well in their own spiritual formation without it. This needs to be said today because there are some groups that have found journal-keeping so valuable that they mistakenly assume that everyone must "journal". This is simply not the case. Journal-keeping is valuable for certain people – usually those who are especially verbal – and not valuable for others. We can never dictate the means of God's grace.

Many other things can be done. One summer I went outside each evening at about 10 p.m. to the little basketball court we had set up in our driveway. Alone, I would shoot baskets, all the time inviting God to do a spiritual inventory on the day. Many things would surface to memory. Sin was there to be sure: an angry word, a missed courtesy, a failed opportunity to encourage someone. But there was also the good: a small obedience, a quiet prayer that seemed to do so much, a word fitly spoken. It was for one summer only, and I have never tried to repeat the experience, but it was one way of experiencing the examen of consciousness.

There are also many ways to enter the examen of conscience. Martin Luther encouraged regular and prayerful meditation on the Ten Commandments and the Lord's Prayer as means of holding our lives before a moral standard. Many use personal retreat times to review their lives.

Perhaps you will want to try the unique way a friend of mine has of experiencing the examen of conscience. All week she tries to live as an heir of God's power, doing his works and thinking his thoughts. Then on Friday or Saturday evening she leaves the heights and comes down into the depths of her being, asking the Spirit of God to guide her memory back over the week to any sin or failing that needs his forgiveness. Then she enters a definite time of repentance which is concluded by receiving the Eucharist in the Sunday morning worship service.

This leads us directly into the subject of our next chapter – the Prayer of Tears. It is to this wonderful way of prayer that we now turn.

Precious Saviour, why do I fear your scrutiny? Yours is an examen of love. Still, I am afraid . . . afraid of what may surface. Even so, I invite you to search me to the depths so that I may know myself – and you – in fuller measure.

– Amen.

4

The Prayer of Tears

Tears are like blood in the wounds of the soul.
— Gregory of Nyssa

Penthos is the Greek word for it. There is simply no good English equivalent. It is a frequent experience for those who walked across the pages of the Bible, and a recurring theme in the works of the great devotional writers. *Penthos* means a broken and contrite heart. *Penthos* means inward godly sorrow. *Penthos* means blessed, holy mourning. *Penthos* means deep, heartfelt compunction. Above all, *Penthos* means the Prayer of Tears.

Gregory of Nyssa said of St Ephrem, "When I start to remember his floods of tears I myself begin to weep, for it is almost impossible to pass dry-eyed through the ocean of his tears. There was never a day or night . . . when his vigilant eyes did not appear bathed in tears."[1] Abba Anthony declared boldly, "Whoever wishes to advance in building up virtue will do so through weeping and tears."[2]

The Soft Rain of Tears

What is it, this Prayer of Tears? It is being "cut to the heart" over our distance and offence to the goodness of God (Acts 2:37). It is weeping over our sins and the sins of the world. It is entering into the liberating shocks of repentance. It is the intimate and ultimate awareness that sin cuts us off from the fullness of God's presence. On the morning of October 18, 1740, David Brainard, that stalwart pioneer missionary to Native Americans, wrote in his journal:

My soul was exceedingly melted, and bitterly mourned

over my exceeding sinfulness and vileness. I never before had felt so pungent and deep a sense of the odious nature of sin as at this time. My soul was then unusually carried forth in love to God and had a lively sense of God's love to me.[3]

Recently I experienced a special grace of the soft rain of tears. I had been considering my sin and the sin of God's people. I had also been meditating on the Gospel teaching (and the ancient teaching of the Church) on "compunction" – heart sorrow. As I did this, God graciously helped me enter into a holy mourning in my heart on behalf of the Church, and a deep tear-filled thanksgiving at God's patience, love, and mercy towards us. As Micah declares, "Who is a God like you, pardoning iniquity?" (Mic. 7:18).

For me this heart-weeping lasted only a few days. I wished for more. These experiences seem to be the exception today; there was a time when they were the rule. It was reported of the French actress Eve LaVallière that after her conversion her eyes were constantly irritated from perpetual weeping.[4]

A Litany of Tears

Certainly the men and women who march across the pages of Scripture were well acquainted with the grace of tears. In his anguish Job declares, "My eye pours out tears to God" (Job 16:20). Crushed over the sin and desolation of Moab, Isaiah cries out, "I weep with the weeping of Jazer; I drench you with my tears, O Heshbon and Elealeh" (Isa. 16:9).

Jeremiah is known as the "weeping prophet" and the reputation is well deserved. "O that my head were a spring of water," he moans, "and my eyes a fountain of tears, so that I might weep day and night for the slain of my poor people!" (Jer. 9:1). If Jeremiah did not pen the book of Lamentations, he should have! "Cry aloud to the Lord!

O wall of daughter Zion! Let tears stream down like a torrent day and night! Give yourself no rest, your eyes no respite!" (Lam. 2:18).

Almost every page of the Psalter is wet with the tears of the singers. "I am weary with my moaning," laments David, "every night I flood my bed with tears; I drench my couch with my weeping" (Ps. 6:6). Weeping, in fact, was such a habitual practice for David that he could appeal to his tears as a witness before God: "You have kept count of my tossings; put my tears in your bottle. Are they not in your record?" (Ps. 56:8). The singer who so beautifully describes our soul's thirst for God as a hart longing for flowing streams goes on to confess, "My tears have been my food day and night" (Ps. 42:3). Psalm 119, that extended paean of praise to Torah, contains this haunting lament: "My eyes shed streams of tears because your law is not kept" (Ps. 119:136).

Consider Jesus, who "offered up prayers and supplications, with loud cries and tears" (Heb. 5:7). See him weeping over his beloved Jerusalem: "How often have I desired to gather your children together as a hen gathers her brood under her wings, and you were not willing!" (Matt. 23:37). Listen to his beatitude upon the broken, the bruised, the disposed, "Blessed are those who mourn" (Matt. 5:4). "Blessed are you who weep" (Luke 6:21). Watch his tenderness towards the Mary who bathed his feet with her tears: "She has shown great love." Hear his word of absolution: "Your sins are forgiven," and his benedictus: "Go in peace" (Luke 7:36–50).

Or think of Paul, who came to Asia "serving the Lord with all humility and with tears" (Acts 20:19). To the Ephesians he said, "For three years I did not cease night or day to warn everyone with tears" (Acts 20:31). To his flock at Corinth he declared, "I wrote you out of much distress and anguish of heart and with many tears," and later he could rejoice that their "mourning" and "godly grief" had led them to repentance (2 Cor. 2:4; 7:7–11).

Deep Joy

What is it about all this sorrow and weeping and mourning?
It sounds a bit depressing, at least to those of us who
have been brought up on a religion of good feelings and
prosperity. The old writers, however, had a very different
view. They saw it as a gift to be sought after, the "charism
of tears". For them the people most to be pitied are those
who go through life with dry eyes and cold hearts. They
actually called this inner heart turmoil "deep joy".

In fact, joy is the most obvious result of a heart perpetually
bowed in contrition. Basilea Schlink writes, "The first
characteristic of the kingdom of heaven is the overflowing
joy that comes from contrition and repentance. . . . Tears
of contrition soften even the hardest hearts."5 The Psalmist
sings, "May those who sow in tears reap with shouts of joy"
(Ps. 126:5).

And so it is. A good friend of mine was recently given
an unusual expression of this deep joy. He is the pastor of
a small congregation that is a microcosm of all the sin and
hurt of the modern world. Often he is brought into times
of brokenness and weeping for the sins and sorrows of his
people, and at times when he is praying for individuals, the
spirit of sobbing comes.

But on this occasion he was attending a conference and
staying in a motel by himself. He awoke early one morning
with the words of Psalm 91:14–16 on his lips: "Those who
love me, I will deliver. . . . When they call to me, I will
answer them." Immediately he opened his Bible and began
praying Scripture to God. In the midst of praying the Scripture, he started chuckling and then laughing out loud – deep
down belly laughter; high, holy, uproarious laughter. He
rolled over and over on his bed laughing, laughing, laughing. Laughing until his sides ached. Laughing until he had to
put a pillow over his face to muffle the noise. This wonderful release of his spirit into holy laughter lasted for perhaps
thirty minutes. After it subsided, he exclaimed to no one in
particular, "What a wonderful way to start the day!"

Now, my friend is not prone to levity. In fact he takes his spiritual walk so seriously that on occasion I have encouraged him to lighten up a bit. So what happened? I rather imagine God was bringing him into the deep joy reserved for those who are well acquainted with heart sorrow and tear-filled repentance. St Ammonas, a disciple of Abba Anthony, writes, "Fear produces tears, and tears joy. Joy brings strength, through which the soul will be fruitful in everything."[6] And Father Hausherr observes, "Compunction ends in beatitude."[7]

Labyrinthine Questions

But perhaps I have gone too quickly for you. You do not yet understand why there is so much emphasis upon the more emotional side of prayer – weeping and mourning and all. I am not sure that I understand it either. I do know that unless the emotive centre of our lives is touched, it is as if a fuse remains unlit. Tears are a sign – not an infallible sign to be sure, but a sign nevertheless – that God has touched this centre. Through the Prayer of Tears we give God permission to show us our sinfulness and the sinfulness of the world at the emotional level. As best I can discern, tears are God's way of helping us descend with the mind into the heart and there bow in perpetual adoration and worship.

Numerous other questions press upon the mind. Is not all this talk of sin and contrition and repentance a bit archaic – a throwback to the days of false guilt and unhealthy repressions? What theological realities give rise to this form of prayer? To pray in this way, do we literally have to cry? And . . . and . . . and . . .

I understand your concerns and your questions. I have more of both than I can ever address in one short chapter, even if I had all the answers. There is probably no kind of prayer that elicits more wonderings than this one. Perhaps this is why Madame Lot-Borodine calls it the "Mystery of Tears".[8] But rather than fret about what

we do not know, let's try to be clear about what we
do know.

The Rock-Bottom Reality

The most rock-bottom reality for the Prayer of Tears is
that we are sinners. I do not mean that we commit sins
– though I am quite sure that is true too. I am giving not
a moralistic judgment on our activities but a theological
judgment on our separation from God. We are not sinners
because we commit sinful acts; rather we commit sinful acts
because we are sinners. The theologians call this essential
corruption *peccatum originis*, or original sin, and the sin
that is at the heart of all sin is a refusal to believe, a
lack of faith, a *defectus fidei*. From this fundamental lack
and estrangement from God flow all of the warped and
distorted actions we call sins.

The New Testament opens with the frequent, almost
monotonous call of John the Baptist to "repent for the
kingdom of God is at hand." The refrain is taken up
by Peter at Pentecost, and finally our Bible closes with
Jesus' call to the seven churches to repent and turn into
God's way.

It is, of course, the cross of Jesus Christ that makes
such repentance possible. In some mysterious way, through
shedding his blood Jesus took into himself all the evil
and all the hostility of all the ages and redeemed it. He
reconciled us to God, restoring the infinitely valuable
personal relationship that had been shattered by sin. By
means of the cross Christ opened the "spigot of grace",
as Adrienne von Speyr put it.[9]

That is not all. Christian theology tells us that Christ
died and passed through hell, "making captivity captive"
(Eph. 4:8). Then, on the third day, Jesus burst forth from
death's grip, and the first act of the resurrected one was to
institute the ministry of confession and forgiveness (John
20:23). The resurrection is God's abrupt absolution!

One more thing is needed, namely our response of

repentance – not just once but again and again. Martin
Luther declares that the life of the Christian should be one
of daily repentance. Daily we confess, daily we repent, daily
we "turn, turn, 'til we turn 'round right." The Prayer of
Tears is the primary aid to our turning. How this is done,
however, is not well understood in our day. It is to this
concern that we now turn.

Acts of Contrition

God never despises "a broken and contrite heart", says
the Psalmist (Ps. 51:17). But the real question for us in the
modern world is how do we experience a contrite heart, a
grieving, broken, sorrowing, repentant heart?

We begin by asking. I wish that did not sound so trite, for
it is the deepest truth we can ever know about our turning
towards God. *We* simply cannot make heart repentance
happen. It is not something that we cause to come about
by creating a certain kind of mood with a certain kind of
atmosphere and a certain kind of music. It is a gift from
God, pure and simple. But it is a gift that God loves to
bestow upon all who ask.

And so with boldness and persistence we ask for contrite
hearts. We ask for weeping, lamenting hearts. "Lord," we
may pray, "let me receive the gift of tears." If at first heart
sorrow does not come we keep asking, we keep seeking, we
keep knocking.

Like the tax collector in Jesus' parable we plead, "God,
be merciful to me, a sinner!" (Luke 18:13). Not just once,
or now and again, but with every breath. The ancient
liturgical refrain *Kyrie, Eleison* (Lord, have mercy), comes
from this parable. So does the famous Jesus Prayer, "Lord
Jesus Christ, Son of God, have mercy on me, a sinner." We
join with the multitude of voices from all the ages, asking
for the gift of repentance, the Prayer of Tears. At times our
prayer may be reduced to a single word: "Mercy!"

Second, we confess. We acknowledge our lack of faith,
our distance, our hardheartedness. Before a loving and

gracious Father we declare our sins without excuse or abridgement; unbelief and disunity, arrogance and self-sufficiency, and offences too personal to name and too many to mention. C. S. Lewis notes, "The true Christian's nostril is to be continually attentive to the inner cesspool."[10] Paul's shocking declaration "Wretched man that I am!" is the cry of the mature Christian longing for the spirit of repentance (Rom. 7:24).

We leave no space for excuses or extenuating circumstances; we say, "By my own fault, my own most grievous fault," as the old confessional rite reads. And like the old rite, we "confess these sins, and all those I cannot remember." The seventeenth-century poet Phineas Fletcher writes:

> Drop, drop, slow tears,
>   And bathe those beauteous feet,
> Which brought from heaven
>   The news and Prince of peace.
>
> Cease not, wet eyes,
>   His mercies to entreat;
> To cry for vengeance
>   Sin doth never cease.
>
> In your deep floods
>   Drown all my faults and fears;
> Nor let his eye
>   See sin, but through my tears.[11]

Third, we receive. Our God who is faithful and just — and also full of mercy — *will* forgive and *will* cleanse (1 John 1:9). Like the father of the prodigal, he rushes to us at the first sign of our turning towards home. He lavishes us with good gifts that we do not deserve and cannot earn.

In my book *Celebration of Discipline* I provide detailed counsel for those times when we are unable to experience forgiveness and cleansing by ourselves and need the help of our brothers and sisters in faith.[12] Suffice it to say here that we who follow Jesus Christ have been given the gracious ministry of bringing God's forgiveness to one another (John 20:23). You are probably aware of the priestly confessional in the Roman Catholic Communion. It might help you to know, also, that the early monastic movement was entirely noncleric, and that these laypeople began by giving reciprocal confession to one another, receiving the assurance of Christ's forgiveness from one another. We are privileged to do the same.

Even more, through the power of Christ we release within people the spirit of forgiveness and compassion. The entire eighteenth chapter of the Gospel of Matthew is devoted to Jesus' teaching on the giving and receiving of forgiveness, and right in the middle of that penetrating discussion Jesus promises us, "Whatever you bind on earth will be bound in heaven, and whatever you loose on earth will be loosed in heaven" (Matt. 18:18). And so we do. We bind bitterness and hardheartedness. We loose forgiveness and tenderheartedness. It is a ministry we can indulge in lavishly.

Fourth, we obey. It is not enough to ask God for a heart soft and broken where there is space for repentance. It is not enough to confess freely and openly our many offences. Embedded in the word of forgiveness is the call to obedience.

Perhaps there surfaces to the conscious mind an attitude of self-righteousness. We confess it instantly. Maybe we remember an unkindness spoken. We go to the person without hesitation and ask forgiveness. Perhaps a past act of injustice comes to mind. Immediately we make restitution.

On the affirmative side of the ledger we engage in the practice of virtue with boundless zeal. Perhaps at work we have a chance to strike a blow against injustice. We speak up right away. Maybe we see an opportunity to influence our children for good. We do it posthaste. Perhaps a neighbour needs a hand in repairing the fence. We rush to help. Through it all we experience the joy of obedience.

When We Cannot Weep

I want to conclude this discussion of the Prayer of Tears with a few words to those who cannot weep. There are those who, as St Symeon tells us, "even puncturing would not cause compunction".[13] I know because I am one of them, and only by special graces has it been otherwise.

Few things in our culture move us in this direction. Besides, certain temperaments are slow to furnish tears. If this is the case with you, do not be discouraged. I have been where you are. Allow me to share a few counsels that have been helpful to me.

Be both firm and friendly with yourself. Do not let yourself get away with the "I'm just not the emotional type" excuse. Also remember that you did not take on the modern macho "I am a rock, I am an island" attitude overnight, and it will take more than a day to change such ingrained habits. Be encouraged by the observation of Thomas à Kempis that "habit overcomes habit".[14] You are building new habits of prayer, and patient, kind, firm persistence is what you need with yourself.

Next, if you will immerse yourself in the Gospels, they will cure you of the "stiff-upper-lip" religion that is so foreign to the one who was "a man of sorrows and acquainted with grief". Jesus knew the Prayer of Tears, and he will show you how to follow "in his steps" (1 Pet. 2:21). Follow the counsel of St Theodore the Studite: "Let us go in the Spirit to the Jordan . . . and let us receive baptism with him, I mean the baptism of tears."[15]

Also, when you cannot weep outwardly, shed tears before God in your intention. Have a weeping heart. Keep your soul in tears. Even if the eyes are dry, the mind and the spirit can be broken before God.

Finally, as you wait patiently for the baptism of tears to come, rest in the words of John Chrysostom: "The fire of sin is intense, but it is put out by a small amount of tears, for the tear puts out a furnace of faults, and cleans our wounds of sin."[16]

Gracious Jesus, it is easier for me to approach you with my mind than with my tears. I do not know how to pray from the emotive centre of my life or even how to get in touch with that part of me. Still, I come to you just as I am.

I am sorry for my many rejections of your overtures of love. Please forgive all my offences against your law. I repent of my callous and insensitive ways. Break my stony heart with the things that break your heart.

Jesus, you went through your greatest trial in unashamed agony and wept tears of deep, deep sorrow. In remembrance of your sorrow help me to weep over my sin . . . and my sins.

For your sake and in your name, I pray.

— Amen.

5

The Prayer of Relinquishment

The Spirit teaches me to yield my will entirely to the will of the Father. He opens my ear to wait in great gentleness and teachableness of soul for what the Father has day by day to speak and to teach. He discovers to me how union with God's will is union with God himself; how entire surrender to God's will is the Father's claim, the Son's example, and the true blessedness of the soul.

— Andrew Murray

As we are learning to pray we discover an interesting progression. In the beginning our will is in struggle with God's will. We beg. We pout. We demand. We expect God to perform like a magician or shower us with blessings like Father Christmas. We major in instant solutions and manipulative prayers.

As difficult as this time of struggle is, we must never despise it or try to avoid it. It is an essential part of our growing and deepening in things spiritual. To be sure, it is an inferior stage, but only in the sense that a child is at an inferior stage to that of an adult. The adult can reason better and carry heavier loads because both brain and brawn are more fully developed, but the child is doing exactly what we would expect at that age. So it is in the life of the spirit.

In time, however, we begin to enter into a grace-filled releasing of our will and a flowing into the will of the Father. It is the Prayer of Relinquishment that moves us from the struggling to the releasing.

Instructed by a Commercial

I want to plant a visual icon in your mind for the Prayer of Relinquishment. To do so I need to tell you a little story — you will see how it fits presently.

A social worker friend of mine who lived some distance away would often ask me to come to her town to teach on the prayer of inner healing for her and her colleagues. I would always decline, knowing that there were many good resource people in her town. She persisted. Finally I said to her, "Let's make the idea of my coming a matter of prayer itself. Here is what I want you to do. Go back home and speak to no one except God about the idea of my coming, and if at least six people share with you a desire for this kind of teaching in the next week or so, then we will know God is in it and I'll come." She agreed.

Please understand, I was not trying to hear from God; I was trying to get out of doing the teaching session! Four days later she called and said, "Twelve people have approached me about this since I have been home!" I was trapped. I consented to come.

It was a small gathering of about fifteen social workers. We met in my friend's home. The first night one gentleman shared frankly, "Be easy on me because I am not one of you." This was his way of saying that he was not a Christian, and the group received his comment graciously.

Throughout the weekend the Spirit of God rested tenderly upon the entire group, so much so that on Sunday afternoon this same gentleman asked quietly, "Would you pray for me that I might know Jesus the way you know Jesus?"

What were we to do? None of the normal responses seemed appropriate. We waited in silence. Finally one young man stood up and gently placed his hands on the man's shoulders. I have never forgotten his prayer. I felt like taking off my shoes — we were on holy ground.

Strange as it may seem, he prayed a commercial. He described a popular advertisement of the day for NesTea in which different people, sweltering from the summer sun, would fall into a swimming pool with a thirst-quenching sense of "ahhh!" on their faces. He then invited this man to fall into the arms of Jesus in the same way. The gentleman suddenly began to weep, heaving deep sighs of sorrow and grief. We watched in reverent wonder as he received the gift of saving faith. It was a tender, grace-filled moment. Later he shared with us how the prayer touched a deep centre in his past relating to his baptism as a child.

This picture of a person falling into the arms of Jesus with a thirst-quenching sense of "ahhh!" is, for me, a perfect image of the Prayer of Relinquishment. It is the mental icon I want you to hold on to.

The end result of the Prayer of Relinquishment brings us into this soul-satisfying rest. As you read on in this chapter, I hope you will engrave in your mind's eye the picture of yourself falling into the arms of Jesus, fully satisfied, fully at rest. As I am sure you are aware, this picture describes the end result of the Prayer of Relinquishment rather than the process, and we need to have the end result clearly before us to give us courage to face the process.

The School of Gethsemane

We learn the Prayer of Relinquishment in the school of Gethsemane. Gaze in adoring wonder at the scene. The solitary figure etched against gnarled olive trees. The bloodlike sweat falling to the ground. The human longing: "Let this cup pass." The final relinquishment: "Not my will but yours be done" (Luke 22:39–46). We do well to meditate often on this unparalleled expression of relinquishment.

Here we have the incarnate Son praying through his tears and not receiving what he asks. Jesus, you see, knew the burden of unanswered prayer. He really did want the cup to pass, and he asked that it would pass. "If you are willing" was his questioning, his wondering. The Father's will was not yet absolutely clear to him. "Is there any other way?"

"Can people be redeemed by some different means?" The answer – No! Andrew Murray writes, "For our sins, he suffered beneath the burden of that unanswered prayer."[1]

Here we have the complete laying down of human will. The battle cry for us is, "My will be done!" rather than, "Thy will be done." We have excellent reasons for the banner of self-will: "Better for me than them to be in control." "Besides, I would use the power to such good ends." But in the school of Gethsemane we learn to distrust whatever is of our own mind, thought and will, even though it is not directly sinful. Jesus shows us a more excellent way. The way of helplessness. The way of abandonment. The way of relinquishment. "My will be done" is conquered by "not my will".

Here we have the perfect flowing into the will of the Father. "Your will be done" was Jesus' consuming concern. To applaud the will of God, to do the will of God, even to fight for the will of God is not difficult . . . until it comes at cross-purposes with our will. Then the lines are drawn, the debate begins, and the self-deception takes over. But in the school of Gethsemane we learn that "my will, my way, my good" must yield to higher authority.

The Necessity of Struggle

We must not, however, get the notion that all of this comes to us effortlessly. That would not even be desirable. Struggle is an essential feature of the Prayer of Relinquishment. Did you notice that Jesus asked repeatedly for the cup to pass? Make no mistake about it: he could have avoided the cross if he had so chosen. He had a free will and a genuine choice, and he freely chose to submit his will to the will of the Father.

It was no simple choice or quick fix. Jesus' prayer struggle – replete with bloody sweat – lasted long into the night. Relinquishment is no easy task.

All of the luminaries in Scripture struggled as well: Abraham as he relinquished his son, Isaac; Moses as he relinquished his understanding of how the deliverer of Israel should function; David as he relinquished the son given to him by Bathsheba; Mary as she relinquished control over her future; Paul as he relinquished his desire to be free of a debilitating "thorn in the flesh".

Struggle is important because the Prayer of Relinquishment is Christian prayer and not fatalism. We do not resign ourselves to fate. Catherine Marshall writes, "Resignation is barren of faith in the love of God . . . Resignation lies down quietly in the dust of a universe from which God seems to have fled, and the door of Hope swings shut."[2]

We are not locked into a preset, determinist future. Ours is an open, not a closed universe. We are "co-labourers with God", as the Apostle Paul put it – working with God to determine the outcome of events. Therefore our prayer efforts are a genuine give and take, a true dialogue with God – and a true struggle.

Severing Precious Roots

As I write these words, Carolynn and I are personally experiencing the Prayer of Relinquishment. A little over a year ago prophetic utterance was spoken over me, the first half of which relates to our family and has been occurring in the most encouraging and faith-building ways. The second half of this message had to do with some deep trials we would go through that would result in our being catapulted into a new realm of effective ministry.

I did not know what to think of the last part of this message until a few months ago when I received an unusual revelation from God, the gist of which indicated that I would be severing some very precious roots in my life. At first I misunderstood these words, assuming that they referred to my relationship with a small group of writers I was with at the time. (The fact that God speaks to us is no guarantee that we hear or understand correctly!) In time I came to see that God was speaking about our deep roots in the city where we live and the university where I teach.

This has been confirmed by numerous circumstances and the wise counsel of many from around the country.

But it has been only the beginning of our experience of the Prayer of Relinquishment. We are releasing far more than the warm friendships of more than a dozen years, far more than the base from which to operate our new renewal effort, *RENOVARÉ*.

I am the executive director of a small fellowship of writers called The Milton Center. I founded this centre five years ago, and I continue to have very high hopes for its future. I am having to relinquish it. For years Carolynn and I dreamed of building a toxin-free home in hope of gaining an upper hand over her rather severe allergies. Carolynn spent one entire year designing and overseeing the building of the house. We moved in only recently. We are having to relinquish it. And so much more.

These decisions do not come easily. We pray. We struggle. We weep. We go back and forth, back and forth, weighing option after option. We pray again, struggle again, weep again. Believe me, we have tangled with God plenty over this decision. At the time of this writing we do not know what all this will mean, but our relinquishment is a full and wholehearted agreement with God that his way is altogether right and good.

Release with Hope

The Prayer of Relinquishment is a bona fide letting go, but it is a release with hope. We have no fatalist resignation. We are buoyed up by a confident trust in the character of God. Even when all we see are the tangled threads on the back of life's tapestry, we know that God is good and is out to do us good always. That gives us hope to believe that we are the winners regardless of what we are being called upon to relinquish. God is inviting us deeper in and higher up. There is training in righteousness, transforming power, new joys, deeper intimacy.

Sometimes the very thing we relinquish is given back to

us. Before writing my first book, *Celebration of Discipline*, I did nothing but talk about it for a solid year. Carolynn grew tired of hearing me rattle on. It was my grand obsession.

Then I attended a large conference where a well-known author – one of the featured speakers – shared rather offhandedly how destructive his writing career had been to his marriage. It was a casual comment, not pertinent to the topic of the conference, but I heard nothing else the entire week. Echoing in my ears was the query: "Are you willing to relinquish this book in favour of Carolynn and the boys?"

God was speaking to me, of course, but I was simply frustrated and angry: "Why would God put a book idea in my heart and then tell me not to write it? And besides, here I've come all this way and spent all this money and I can't concentrate on a single thing the speakers are saying. What a waste!" But the question kept hounding me.

My flight got home late Sunday evening. The ride from the airport was filled with chitchat about the children and the leaky tap, and the bills that were due. Carolynn knew nothing about my internal struggle. Once in the house I held her in my arms and said firmly, "Honey, I want you to know that you are more important to me than this book project. I won't write it if it will ever damage our relationship." That was that. I went to bed sure I would never write the book.

That was Sunday night. On Tuesday morning I met the person who was to become my publishing editor. The rest is history. And, you know, to this day I cannot remember a single thing the speakers at that conference said!

A Priceless Treasure

This does not always happen, of course. There are times when the release is permanent. At such times we are to trust in the wisdom of God and ask for the grace to rest in his peace. A settled peace, in fact, is the most frequent experience of those who have trod the path of relinquishment.

But, as I said earlier, the very thing we release is sometimes returned to us. Why would God take us through such a roller-coaster process? Why, for example, did Jesus say, "Unless a grain of wheat falls into the earth and dies, it remains just a single grain; but if it dies, it bears much fruit" (John 12:24)? Why does God seemingly require relinquishment before bringing something into being?

Part of the answer lies in the fact that, frequently, we hold on so tightly to the good we know that we cannot receive the greater good that we do not know. God has to help us let go of our tiny vision in order to release the greater good he has in store for us.

But this is only a partial answer. The fuller answer lies in the purposes of God in transforming the human personality. Relinquishment brings to us a priceless treasure: *the crucifixion of the will*. Paul knew what a great gift this is. "I have been crucified with Christ," he joyfully announces. There is relinquishment. There is crucifixion. There is death to the self-life. But there is also a releasing with hope: "It is no longer I who live, but it is Christ who lives in me. And the life I now live in the flesh I live by faith in the Son of God, who loved me and gave himself for me" (Gal. 2:19–20).

John Woolman, the Quaker tailor who did so much to remove slavery from the American continent, once had a dramatic vision in which he "heard a soft, melodious voice, more pure and harmonious than any I had heard with my ears before; I believed it was the voice of an angel who spake to other angels. The words were, '*John Woolman is dead*.'" Woolman was very puzzled over these words and sought to "get so deep that I might understand this mystery". Finally he "felt divine power prepare my mouth" and he declared, "I am crucified with Christ." "Then the mystery was opened, and I perceived . . . that the language John Woolman is dead meant no more than the death of my own will."[3]

"The death of my own will" – strong language. But all

of the great devotional masters have found it so. Søren Kierkegaard echoes Woolman's experience when he notes, "God creates everything out of nothing — and everything which God is to use he first reduces to nothing."[4]

Do you know what a great freedom this crucifixion of the will is? It means freedom from what A. W. Tozer called "the fine threads of the self-life, the hyphenated sins of the human spirit".[5] It means freedom from the self-sins: self-sufficiency, self-pity, self-absorption, self-abuse, self-aggrandizement, self-castigation, self-deception, self-exaltation, self-depreciation, self-indulgence, self-hatred and a host of others just like them. It means freedom from the everlasting burden of always having to get our own way. It means freedom to care for others, to genuinely put their needs first, to give joyfully and freely.

Little by little we are changed by this daily crucifixion of the will. Changed, not like a tornado changes things, but like a grain of sand in an oyster changes things. New graces emerge: new ability to cast all our care upon God, new joy at the success of others, new hope in a God who is good.

Please remember, we are dealing with the crucifixion of the will, not the obliteration of the will. Crucifixion always has resurrection tied to it. God is not destroying the will, but transforming it so that over a process of time and experience we can freely will what God wills. In the crucifixion of the will we are enabled to let go of our tightfisted hold on life and follow our best prayers.

The Practice of Prayer

Only through the specifics of daily life can you be led into the Prayer of Relinquishment. The will is surrendered moment by moment as you face the ordinary decisions of home, family and job. I cannot prescribe for you how this is done. In fact, you will not know the shape of relinquishment until specific issues arise. So the practice will come through lived experience. I am able, however, to give you some practised prayers that you can interpret into your individual situation.

First, learn the prayer of self-emptying. Meditatively pray through Philippians, chapter 2 which describes the *kenosis*, the self-emptying of Christ, who was in the form of God but who voluntarily took on the form of a servant and became obedient to the point of death. Bid the brooding Spirit of God to apply your prayer to the specifics of your day. Wait quietly. Listen carefully. Obey immediately.

Second, learn the prayer of surrender. Using any of the synoptic Gospels, go with Jesus into the Garden. Stay awake and watch. See his sorrowing soul. Let your heart be saddened too. Struggle with him in seeking other options, hoping to avoid the cup. Now, speak his words as your own: "Not my will, but yours be done." Invite the resurrected one to interpret the words into your life, your family, your vocation.

Third, learn the prayer of abandonment. De Caussade's book *Self-Abandonment to Divine Providence* may be helpful. You might want to use the words of Charles de Foucauld, "Father, I abandon myself into your hands; do with me what you will. Whatever you may do, I thank you: I am ready for all, I accept all. Let only your will be done in me, and in all your creatures — I wish no more than this, O Lord."[6] Allow the Sovereign of your heart to specify what needs to be laid at his feet.

Fourth, learn the prayer of release. First, lift up into his arms your children, your spouse, your friends. Next, place into his loving care your future, your hopes, your dreams. Finally, hold up to him your enemies, your angers, your desire for retaliation. Give it all into his hands and then turn around and walk away. He will care for everything as he sees fit.

Fifth, learn the prayer of resurrection. "Lord," you may pray, "bring back to life what will please you and advance your kingdom. Let it come in whatever form you desire. Let it be in your time and your way. Thank you, Lord, for resurrection." Some things will remain dead — it is better for you that they do. Others will burst forth into new life in such a way that you will hardly recognize them. In either case, rest in the confidence that God is better than you are at resurrection.

Our sojourn into the Prayer of Relinquishment has only begun. We have so much to learn, so far to go. Relinquishment takes us into rugged terrain. The climb is steep, the rocks are sharp, and the trail passes by precarious ridges. From every human viewpoint, at times it looks as if we have fallen over the precipice to our death. But we know better. We know that we are only falling into the arms of Jesus fully satisfied, fully at rest.

---◆---

O Lord, how do I let go when I'm so unsure of things? I'm unsure of your will, and I'm unsure of myself. . . . That really isn't the problem at all, is it? The truth of the matter is I hate the very idea of letting go. I really want to be in control. No, I need to be in control. That's it, isn't it? I'm afraid to give up control, afraid of what might happen. Heal my fear, Lord.

How good of you to reveal my blind spots even in the midst of my stumbling attempts to pray. Thank you!

But now what do I do? How do I give up control? Jesus, please, teach me your way of relinquishment.

— Amen.

6

Formation Prayer

Prayer — secret, fervent, believing prayer — lies at the root of all personal godliness.
— William Cary

"Prayer changes things," people say. It also changes us. The latter goal is the more imperative. The primary purpose of prayer is to bring us into such a life of communion with the Father that, by the power of the Spirit, we are increasingly conformed to the image of the Son. This process of transformation is the sole focus of Formation Prayer.

None of us will keep up a life of prayer unless we are prepared to change. We will either give it up or turn it into a little system that maintains the form of godliness but denies the power of it — which is the same thing as giving it up.

When we begin to walk with God, he is gracious and marvellously answers our feeble, egocentric prayers. We think, "This is wonderful. God is real after all!" In time, however, when we try to push this button again, God says to us, "I would like to be more than your Provider. I also want to be your Teacher and your Friend. Let me lead you into a more excellent way. I want to free you of the greed and avarice, the fear and hostility that make your life one great sorrow." Now, we may chafe under this and struggle against it, but in time we learn the goodness of rightness and begin to move into holy obedience. Each day in a new and living way the brooding Spirit of God teaches us. As we begin to follow these nudgings of the Spirit, we are changed from the inside out.

The old writers had a term for this dynamic of change

— *conversatio morum*.[1] It is a hard phrase to translate. Negatively, it means death to the status quo, death to things as they have always been. Positively, it means constant change, constant conversion, constant openness to the movings of the Spirit. Jean-Pierre de Caussade writes, "The soul, light as a feather, fluid as water, innocent as a child, responds to every movement of grace like a floating balloon."[2]

In earlier chapters I have made passing reference to the way prayer changes the ingrained habit structures of our lives. In Formation Prayer this issue becomes the centre of our concern. Crucial questions must be addressed. How does prayer of this sort enable us to throttle egoism and shed the burden of self-importance? In what way does it stimulate spiritual growth? What role does it play in producing in us the fruit of love, joy, peace, patience, kindness, generosity, faithfulness, gentleness and self-control (Gal. 5:22)?

The Limitation of Prayer

Before proceeding, I must offer a caution. We should not overstate the place of prayer in the formation of "holy habits". Prayer by itself is severely limited in the good it can accomplish. It is only a part — albeit an important part — of a much larger whole.

Dallas Willard speaks of the three major areas God uses in our continuing transformation — a "golden triangle" of formation, if you will. The first area is the classical disciplines of the spiritual life: solitude, fasting, worship, celebration and the like. The second area is our continual interaction with the movings of the Spirit of God: resistance, disobedience, repentance, submission, faith, obedience, and more. The third major area is the patient endurance God develops in us by means of the various frustrations, trials and temptations we face daily.[3]

Therefore, we must never isolate prayer from the rest of Christian devotion and claim more for it than God

intended. No, instead we want to see the dynamic interaction of prayer in concert with an overall spiritual life.

Another caution. When I speak of Formation Prayer, I
am talking not about perfectionism but about progress
in the spiritual life. Such issues as "sinless perfection"
and "entire sanctification" are much debated among the
theologians, and while I believe the issues are important,
and I even have opinions on them, I am not trying to solve
these matters here.

What I do want to insist on is the importance of progress,
of growth, of change, of formation. God desires to mould
us more and more into Christ's way: "Those whom he
foreknew he also predestined to be conformed to the image
of his Son" (Rom. 8:29). We want to see the part Formation
Prayer plays in this ongoing conformity.

Pursuing and Being Pursued

There are both active and passive sides to Formation
Prayer. On the active side we are pursuing God. We are
sojourners seeking a city whose builder and maker is God.
We are a pilgrim people on a journey of faith. We are
working out our own salvation with fear and trembling.
We are exercising ourselves unto godliness. We are pressing
on towards the goal of the upward call of God in Christ
Jesus (Phil. 2:12; 1 Tim. 4:7; Phil. 3:12–14).

On the passive side we are being pursued by God. We are
attentive and responsive. We are warm clay in the hands of
the Master Potter (Jer. 18).

Both the active and the passive sides are necessary, and
both stand in a dynamic tension with one another – a little
like Michelangelo's fresco in the Sistine Chapel of God and
Adam stretching out to one another.

Stretching Out to God

Look with me at three classical ways of proactive prayer
whose principal aim is our transformation. The first is

derived from the *Spiritual Exercises* of Ignatius of Loyola.[4] Although Ignatius designed this approach to prayer primarily as a retreat experience for those who came under his leadership, it is also a school of prayer for all of us.

The regimen of the *Exercises* has four basic sections, or weeks. The first focuses upon our sins in the light of God's love. The second centres on the life of Christ, the third on the passion of Christ, and the fourth on the resurrection of Christ.

Each of the four weeks is accompanied by a generous supply of meditation exercises, often taken from the Gospels. Here Ignatius is at his best by insisting upon the use of all the senses in each meditation. If, for example, we are considering Christ on trial for his life, we are to "see" the crowd, "hear" the accusations, "feel" the sting of the whip. The point of all this emphasis upon the senses is to move us from reading about to entering in. We are seeing, hearing, smelling, tasting, and touching the story.

Since the purpose is to bring about conformity to Christlikeness, there is throughout the *Exercises* an uninterrupted asking for special *charisms* or graces of the Spirit. In the first week we are habitually seeking the grace of being loved by God and being bathed in his love. Throughout the second week our unbroken request is for the grace of being formed into the image of Christ. When we contemplate the passion of Christ, we are continually asking for the grace to die to the attachments of this world. In the final week, which focuses on the resurrection of Christ, the grace we seek is the power of the Spirit always to choose God and God's way.

Many who read these words would be uncomfortable with various details of the Ignatian retreat, but I want to commend this four-part rhythm to you. We all need a deeper musing upon our perennial knack of disobedience and God's unbounded habit of forgiving. We all need a richer contemplation upon that *life*, which shows us the way so we may follow "in his steps". We all need a fuller meditation upon that *death*, which sets us free. We all need a more profound experience of that *resurrection*, which empowers us to obey Christ in all things.

The Twelve Steps of Saint Benedict

A second classical approach to Formation Prayer is the active pursuit of humility described in *The Rule of St Benedict*.5 Using the metaphor of Jacob's ladder, Benedict discusses twelve steps into humility.

Humility has received such a bad press in our day that we really must correct at least a few of the distortions before we are able to assess whether we want to take even one step into it, not to mention twelve.

Put in simple terms, humility means to live as close to the truth as possible: the truth about ourselves, the truth about others, the truth about the world in which we live. It has nothing whatever to do with a Casper Milquetoast kind of personality. It does not mean grovelling or finding the worst possible things to say about ourselves.

Humility is in fact filled with power to bring forth life. The word itself comes from the Latin *humus*, which means fertile ground. "Humility," writes Anthony Bloom, "is the situation of the earth." In one sense humility is nothing more than staying close to the earth. The earth, Bloom reminds us, is always with us, always taken for granted, always walked on by everyone. It is the place where we dump our refuse:

> It's there, silent and accepting everything and in a miraculous way making out of all the refuse new richness . . . transforming corruption itself into a power of life and a new possibility of creativeness, open to the sunshine, open to the rain, ready to receive any seed we sow and capable of bringing thirtyfold, sixtyfold, a hundredfold out of every seed.6

Such is the power of humility. As Teresa of Avila reminds us, "Humility is the principal aid to prayer."7

But how do we get it? Humility is one of those virtues that we never attain by focusing on it. The idea is ludicrous. As a result, however, many have concluded that there is therefore nothing we can do to deal with the arrogant, ego-centred drives that plague us – so we simply wait for God to pour humility on our heads. Vain wait!

Benedict has done a great service by showing us that there is spiritual work we can undertake in this realm. There are activities of mind, body and spirit that will conquer pride and bring the joy of a meek and humble life. While not all of us would agree with each of his steps, we can all be grateful to Benedict for helping us see that there *are* things we can do that will move us forward in the life of humility.

Several of Benedict's steps focus on our relationship with God: "Have a constant reverence for God before our eyes; reject our own will and desires and, instead, do God's will; confess all of our evil thoughts and all of our evil actions to the Lord." Three of the steps deal with our use of the tongue, underscoring the importance of this single aspect of our lives. We are to cultivate silence, avoid frivolous talk, and use plain, simple speech. One of the steps of humility is "enduring with patience the injuries and afflictions we face". Another is "to be content in all things".

In each case the point of the teaching is its triviality. Simple ordinary things are undertaken for the love of God. As we experience the many little deaths of going beyond ourselves, we increasingly enter into the grace of humility.

The Little Way

This leads directly into a third classical approach to Formation Prayer: the Little Way of Thérèse of Lisieux.[8] This simple woman, known only as "the Little Flower", devised a prayer-filled approach to life that has helped many. This Little Way, as she called it, is deceptively simple. It is, in short, to seek out the menial job, to welcome unjust criticisms, to befriend those who annoy us, to help those who are ungrateful. For her part, Thérsè was convinced that these "trifles" pleased Jesus more than the great deeds of recognized holiness. The beauty of the Little Way is how utterly available it is to everyone. From the child to the adult, from the sophisticated to the simple, from the most powerful to the least influential, all can undertake this ministry of small things. The opportunities to live in this way come to us constantly, while the great fidelities happen only now and again. Almost daily we can give smiling service to nagging co-workers, listen attentively to silly bores, express little kindnesses without making a fuss.

We may think these tiny, trivial activities are hardly worth mentioning. That, of course, is precisely their value. They are unrecognized conquests over selfishness. We will never receive a medal or even a "thank you" for these invisible victories in ordinary life – which is exactly what we want.

An incident from Thérèse's autobiography, *The Story of a Soul*, underscores the hiddenness of the Little Way. One uneducated and rather conceited sister had managed to irritate Thérèse in everything she did. Rather than avoid this person, however, she took the Little Way straight into the conflict: "I set myself to treat her as if I loved her best of all." Thérèse succeeded so well in her Little Way that following her death, this same sister declared, "During her life, I made her really happy." Thérèse, I am sure, would be pleased.9

The Communion of Solitude

We must now turn our attention to that aspect of Formation Prayer that focuses upon receiving more than striving, yielding more than initiating. The quintessential image here is of clay in the hands of a potter – soft, pliable, malleable. Look with me, then, at three classical approaches to this more passive side of Formation Prayer.

Solitude is the first and the most foundational of these approaches. "Without solitude it is virtually impossible to live a spiritual life," writes Henri Nouwen.[10] The reason for this is simple to see: by means of solitude God frees us from our bondage to people and our own inner compulsions.

To enter solitude, we must disregard what others think of us. Who will understand this call to aloneness? Even our closest friends will see it as a waste of precious time and rather self-centred. But, oh, the liberty that is released in our hearts when we let go of the opinions of others! The less we are mesmerized by human voices, the more we are able to hear the Divine Voice. The less we are manipulated by the expectations of others, the more we are open to the expectations of God.

In solitude, however, we die not only to others but also to ourselves. To be sure, at first we thought solitude was a way to recharge our batteries in order to enter life's many competitions with new vigour and strength. In time, however, we find that solitude gives us power not to win the rat race but to ignore the rat race altogether. Slowly we find ourselves letting go of our inner compulsions to acquire more wealth than we need, look more youthful than we are, attain more status than is wise. In the stillness, our false, busy selves are unmasked and seen for the impostors they truly are.

St Jerome reminds us that we are "never less alone than when alone".[11] I invite you into this communion of solitude.

Peering Into the Abyss

Strange as it may sound to modern ears, the contemplation of one's own death is among the most time-honoured approaches to personal transformation. In our day of runaway narcissism it is a practice we would do well to revive. What would happen if you were to die today? If I were to die today? One of the most sobering insights from such a meditation is the realization that life would continue right on without us – and quite well for that matter. The sun would come up the next day. People would go about their normal duties. Nothing of substance would be changed.

This is a hard reality for us who carry the illusion that the world revolves around our decisions. How could anything of importance happen without us there? How *dare* anything of importance happen without us there! You see, we are a little like the fly on the chariot wheel in *Aesop's Fables* who looked back and declared, "My, what a dust storm I'm causing!"

A Lutheran pastor friend – the Reverend Bill Vaswig – and I once were discussing Galatians 2:19 and wondering what it means to be crucified with Christ. I mean, what are we actually talking about? Bill said, "Let's pray the passage into each other." I had wanted to keep the discussion at arm's length, but I gulped and said, "All right, how do we do it?" "I don't know exactly," was Bill's response, "but you go first!" So I went over to him, placed my hands on his head, and began to pray. I have no idea what I said beyond the hope that he would experience what it means to be crucified with Christ.

When I finished and sat down, Bill looked at me wide-eyed and whispered, "It happened!" "What happened?" I responded blankly. He proceeded to explain that as I began praying, he saw a vivid mental picture of his church with a funeral service going on inside. He could see everything clearly: the coffin with the lid open, the chancel, the high arching beams. But he was seeing it all from inside the coffin. It was his funeral! As the people, filled with sorrow, filed past the coffin, he tried to tell them that everything was okay, that he was fine, and that what was happening was good. They could not hear him; all they could see was a corpse and yet he was more alive than he had ever been.

His prayer for me had equally powerful results for we were bathed in the milieu of the Holy Spirit that day. Most important of all, we both entered into a deeper understanding of death to the self.

The Prayer of Docility

A third form of passive Formation Prayer is what Evelyn Underhill calls "the prayer of docility".[12] It is the experience of being "completely supple, completely transparent, completely abandoned in the hands of God".[13]

Let me try to explain it by analogy. Picture a child with a pencil in hand making indecipherable scribbles on a piece of paper. Now watch his mother place her hand over her child's and guide it on the page, making big beautiful letters. This is the prayer of docility.

Again, watch a sail pick up the wind on first one side of a boat and then the other as the person at the helm tacks with skilful ease. The very pliability of the sail is what makes it able to take advantage of the wind. Put a board in its place, and the boat will go nowhere. It is this frailty, this unguarded accessibility that is at the heart of the prayer of docility.

So, as you read these words, yield yourself into the loving hands of the Master Potter. Do not be afraid. He will not "break a bruised reed or quench a smouldering wick", as Scripture says (Matt. 12:20). He never steps on the weak, never snuffs out the smallest hope. Allow his hand to rest upon yours and guide you. Become weak, frail, vulnerable. Now listen to the voice of the true Shepherd and learn from him.

The Blessedness of Winter

As winter approaches each year, I like to watch our large maple in the back yard begin to lose its covering of summer green and take on a funereal brown. As the leaves drop, one by one all of the irregularities and defects of the tree are exposed. The imperfections are always there, of course, but they have been hidden from my view by an emerald blanket. Now, however, it is denuded and desolate, and I can see its real condition.

Winter preserves and strengthens a tree. Rather than

expending its strength on the exterior surface, its sap is forced deeper and deeper into its interior depth. In winter a tougher, more resilient life is firmly established. Winter is necessary for the tree to survive and flourish.

Instantly you see the application. So often we hide our true condition with the surface virtues of pious activity, but, once the leaves of our frantic pace drop away, the transforming power of a wintry spirituality can have effect.

To the outward eye everything looks barren and unsightly. Our many defects, flaws, weaknesses and imperfections stand out in bold relief. But only the outward virtues have collapsed; the principle of virtue is actually being strengthened. The soul is venturing forth into the interior. Real, solid, enduring virtues begin to develop deep within. Pure love is being birthed.

———◆———

Dear Lord Jesus, in my better moments I want nothing more than to be like you. But there are other moments. . . . Help me to see how good conformity to your way really is. In my seeking for you may I be found by you. I love you, Lord.

— Amen.

7

Covenant Prayer

What we need is a desire to know the whole will of God, with a fixed resolution to do it.
— John Wesley

Covenant Prayer is a profound interior heart call to a God-intoxicated life. It leads us to the crossroad of personal decision. It guides us through the valley of sacred commitment. It beckons us up the alpine pathway of holy obedience.

The essence of Covenant Prayer is captured in the confession of the Psalmist: "My heart is fixed, O God, my heart is fixed" (Ps. 57:7, KJV). At the altar of Covenant Prayer we vow unswerving allegiance; we make high resolves; we promise holy obedience.

Understandable Fear

I can well imagine that you almost instinctively draw back from all this language of commitment. I draw back from it too. Why is this?

Well, first of all, many people today are simply not good at commitments of any kind. In one sense it is hardly our fault. It is in the air. It is the mood of the times. Commitment means responsibility and responsibility sounds confining.

For example, it is common in our day to define freedom as the complete absence of restraint. Once we think about it — even for a moment — we realize how utterly ludicrous this idea really is. Absolute freedom is absolute nonsense! We gain freedom in anything through commitment, discipline and fixed habit. Demosthenes was free to be a great orator only because he had gone through the discipline of speaking above the roar of the ocean with pebbles in his mouth. George Frederick Handel was able to compose his magnificent *Messiah* only because he had schooled himself in musical composition. By means of intense personal discipline Flannery O'Connor was able to rise above a debilitating disease to become one of the finest fiction writers of the twentieth century. Freedom is the product of discipline and commitment.

Then, too, we fear that commitment will take all the spontaneity and joy out of our lives. Solemn vows sound so grim, so much like going through life with clenched teeth. When it comes to prayer, we do not want to feel duty bound. We want to pray as we feel drawn to it. We fear that commitments will make prayer seem like compulsory exercises rather than free-will offerings.

As Dietrich Bonhoeffer reminds us, however, the truth of the matter is that "prayer is not a free-will offering to God; it is an obligatory service, something which he requires."[1] But duty does not need to be grim. Do we think just because many of the Psalms we love were born out of the context of ritual ceremonies that they had no joy to them? Do we think just because Peter and John went up to the temple at the regularly appointed hour of prayer that there was no spontaneity in their words to the lame man: "I have no silver or gold, but what I have I give you; in the name of Jesus Christ of Nazareth, stand up and walk"? Or that this man went about the temple "walking and leaping and praising God" with clenched teeth (Acts 3:1–10)? No, when undertaken in the power of the Spirit, acts of duty can be filled with great joy and blessing. In fact, duty is, as de Caussade teaches us, "the sacrament of the present moment".

I want to mention one other reason why we shy away from commitment. It is, very simply, the fear that we will not be able to fulfil our covenant. We may have made commitments in the past that we were not able to fulfil – perhaps a marriage vow or a promise to our children. Or it

could have been something far more simple – a pledge to be
diligent in devotional reading, for example. We may even
have come across the Bible verse that warns, "It is better
that you should not vow than that you should vow and
not fulfil it" (Eccles. 5:5). As a result, we feel condemned
in our hearts over these broken covenants.

To this fear I want to speak words of grace and mercy.
Remember, even the great Apostle Peter made promises
that were too much for him (John 13:36–38). Remember
also that God knows the intentions of your heart. He
knows your weaknesses and your frailties. Oftentimes
your heart will condemn you for things for which God
does not condemn you. Even more, he is pleased with your
attempts to please him. The promises and commitments of
your heart are not made in vain. God is working at the
desire level of your formation. He has a way of bringing
to pass the longings deep within – after all, he placed those
longings there!

Life-Giving Covenants

Covenant is a Bible word. You may be aware of the covenant God made with Noah, with Abraham, with Moses,
with David. Jesus, you will remember, established the New
Covenant in his blood for the forgiveness of sins.

The point of a covenant is commitment – the very thing
to which we have such an aversion. But where would we
be if God had not committed himself to blessing the world
through the offspring of Abraham? Where would we be if
Jesus had refused to commit himself to washing away the
sins of the world? Where would we be?

When God made his covenant with Moses, he promised
to deliver his people from the land of Egypt, from the
house of bondage. He promised to be their God, to
protect them, to guide them, to bless them. There were
also stipulations to the covenant – what we today call
the Ten Commandments. These were to be the response
of the people to the overwhelming grace and goodness of

God, their promise to live faithful, obedient lives, not as a way of earning God's pleasure but as a way of expressing gratitude for God's mercy.

The New Covenant that Jesus established in his blood demands no less. He has written his law not on tablets of stone, but on the fleshy tablets of our hearts. We have seen the glory of God in the face of Jesus Christ. Calvary's sacrifice is God's binding commitment. He has made covenant with us. Commitment demands commitment. What is our response? Are we willing to offer up lives of obedience in return?

The Covenant of Holy Obedience

We respond to the heavenly overtures of God's love first through the Covenant of Holy Obedience. Without reservation we vow to follow the Father's faintest whisper. In utter devotion and total simplicity we promise to obey the voice of the true Shepherd. Thomas Kelly writes, "There is a degree of holy and complete obedience and of joyful self-renunciation and of sensitive listening that is breath-taking."[2]

I know that all this sounds so frighteningly absolute and final. How can we possibly fulfil such promises? Well, *we* cannot. The matter of obedience is God's business and not ours. We cannot do a single good act unless God first gives us the desire for it and then empowers us to do it. But that is just the point. God *is* giving you the desire — you would not be reading these words if the desire was not already bubbling up inside you. And he will never give the desire to do something that he will not also give the power to obey.

Besides, obedience is really not as burdensome as it seems at first blush. We are doing nothing more than falling head over heels in love with the everlasting Lover of our souls. "O love that will not let me go," confesses the hymn writer George Matheson.[3] We are responding in the only way we can to the invading, urging, inviting, persuading call of Eternal Love.

God, you see, rushes to us at the first hint of our openness. He is the hound of heaven baying relentlessly upon our track. And he places within us such an insatiable God hunger that absolutely nothing satisfies us except the genuine whole-wheat Bread of Life.

Sometimes we are invaded to the depths by an overwhelming experience of the love of God. Walking down the streets of New York, D. L. Moody was so overcome by God's loving presence that he rushed to the home of a friend in order to have a room alone where, for two hours, wave after wave of God's ravishing love swept over him. At other times we experience such a flaming vision of light that we are for ever blinded to all competing loyalties. In the centre of his greatest spiritual moment Blaise Pascal wrote the single word, "Fire!" Still others have a visitation of such indescribable peace that they stand and walk and sit and lie in wordless adoration and submission and wonder and glory.

We emerge from such soul-shaking, love-invaded times for ever changed. We have swung like a needle to the polestar of the Spirit. Never again will any ordinary goodness do. No half measures will suffice. We are consumed by a relentless, inexorable divine standard of holy obedience.

I have discovered that such God-intoxicating experiences are far more common than we might at first assume. However, it is possible that we have never had such a soul-shaking encounter. That is all right. Nothing is wrong with us. We can share in the joyous wonder of such flaming visions through the biographies and journals of the saints and the wonderful stories of countless unnamed, unheralded ordinary people. After all, these experiences are given for the encouragement of all the people of God, not just a few individuals.

Also, we can cultivate the habit of a Godward directed mind and heart. As we carry on the business of the day, inwardly we keep pressing in towards the Divine Centre. At every opportunity we place our mind before God with inward confessions and petitions: "Mercy, Lord"; "I love you, Jesus"; "Show me your way today." Even more, we descend with the mind into the heart and live in quiet wonder and adoration and praise.

We obey him *now* in everything we can and in everything we know. We take up the prayer of Elizabeth Fry: "O Lord! enable me to be more and more, singly, simply and purely obedient to Thy service."[4]

If we fall down – and we *will* fall down – we get up and seek to obey again. We are forming the habit of obedience, and all habits begin with plenty of slips and falls and false starts. We did not learn to walk overnight. Or to play the piano. And we do not condemn ourselves unduly when we stub our toe or play a wrong note, now, do we? We must not condemn ourselves unduly in the spiritual life either. At first it will feel as if we are doing the work, that *we* are the initiators. But in time we will see that it is God who inflames our heart with a burning craving for absolute purity. A. W. Tozer writes, "We pursue God because, and only because, he has first put an urge within us that spurs us to the pursuit."[5]

And here is the beautiful thing: finding God only deepens and heightens the pursuit. One taste of obedience and we want more. "O taste and see that the Lord is good," invites the Psalmist (Ps. 34:8). The paradoxical experience of the children of the burning heart is that by feasting on God we hunger for him all the more. Bernard of Clairvaux put this holy addiction into verse:

> We taste Thee, O Thou living Bread,
>   And long to feast upon Thee still:
> We drink of thee, the Fountainhead
>   And thirst our souls from Thee to fill.[6]

Here is what I am trying to say: obedience has a way of strengthening rather than depleting our resources. If we obey in one small corner, we will have power to obey elsewhere. Obedience begets obedience.

I hope you know that I am talking about holy obedience

within the dishevelled friction of home and office and
school and shopping mall. We are learning the obedience
of unwearied patience in the midst of pestering children.
We are learning the obedience of absolute gentleness with
the frustrations and fears and pains of our spouse. We are
learning the obedience of settled peace in the expectation
of events beyond our control. This is the Covenant of Holy
Obedience.

The Covenant of Time

Covenant Prayer does not leave us in the broad commitment of holy obedience. It also calls us to detailed resolves.
In *The Saints' Everlasting Rest* Richard Baxter counsels us
to seek out the "fittest time for prayer, the fittest place for
prayer, and the fittest preparation of heart" for prayer.7
These constitute the specific fidelities of Covenant Prayer.

The Covenant of Time means a commitment to a *regular*
experience of prayer. In his *Rule* St Benedict insisted on
regularity in prayer because he did not ever want his
followers to forget who was in charge. It is an occu-
pational hazard of devout people to confuse their work
with God's work. How easy it is to replace "this work
is really significant" with "I am really significant." With
a profound understanding of this, Benedict would call for
prayer at regular intervals throughout the day – right in the
middle of apparently urgent and important work. We too
will find that a commitment to regular prayer will defeat
self-importance and the wiles of the devil.

But what is "regular"? That will depend on you; your
personality, your needs. The ancient Hebrew pattern was
three times a day – morning, afternoon and evening. Peter
and John encountered the lame man because they were
going up to the temple at the three o'clock hour of prayer,
as was their custom (Acts 3:1). (I know of one group in
India that has chimes that ring at ten in the morning and
three in the afternoon as a signal for everyone to stop what
they are doing and gather up the needs of the community

in silent prayer.) Many have found a daily — especially early morning — regimen especially useful. "O LORD, in the morning you hear my voice," declares the Psalmist (Ps. 5:3).

We must be careful here not to lay impossible burdens upon people. Rural life tends to function around a daily cycle, whereas urban life tends to function around a weekly cycle. In the country there are chores to be done morning and evening — such as milking the cows and feeding the chickens. A daily prayer discipline makes good sense in this context. In urban life, in contrast, everything presses hard towards Friday — TGIF, Thank God it's Friday, as we say — and the weekends are much more discretionary. In this context it might make more sense to order a prayer life around a weekly pattern. Instead of feeling guilty that we cannot set aside time for prayer on a daily basis, perhaps it would be better to devote Saturday mornings, for example, to more extended experiences of prayer and devotional reading.

Over this matter I want to give some counsel for parents of infants. The demands that your baby makes are immense — more than you realize at first — especially if you are a single parent. The interruptions never end. Also, your sleep is seldom deep because you always have one ear open for your baby. It is important to recognize this fact and be easy with yourself. This time will pass — sooner than you think. Rather than trying to pray in some fanciful isolation that you will never find, discover God in your times with your baby. God will become real to you through your baby. The times of play with your baby are your prayer. You may be able to pray during feeding time — this is especially true for nursing mothers — so sing your prayers to the Lord. In a few short months you will be able to return to a more regular pattern of prayer.

Once we have made generous latitude for individual differences and schedules, we must firmly discipline ourselves to a regular pattern of prayer. We cannot assume that time will somehow magically appear. We will never *have* time for prayer — we must *make* time. On this score we have to be ruthless with our rationalizations. We must never, for instance, excuse our prayerlessness under the guise of "always living prayerfully". John Dalrymple rightly observes, "The truth is that we only learn to pray all the time everywhere after we have resolutely set about praying some of the time somewhere."[8]

Accountability to others helps immensely. I meet weekly with a small group, and at every gathering each of us answers several questions, the first one being, "What experiences of prayer and meditation have you had this week, and what is your determination for next week?"

Simple, practical decisions can aid us in maintaining our covenant. I like to date each time of prayer in a simple spiral notebook that is always with me. When I travel, I usually plan to use the first leg of the plane flight for worship, prayer and meditation. One winter I scheduled a three o'clock appointment into my datebook for each working day. I would then leave the office for one hour, drive five minutes to the local zoo, and, with Bible and personal journal in hand, spend fifty minutes on a bench in a lovely indoor rain forest. Most people do not have such discretionary time on the job, but we all have time available to us if we once get the idea.

I hope you know that there is no need to answer the telephone, or the door, for that matter. Archbishop Anthony Bloom tells of his father who would put a note on his door saying, "Don't go to the trouble of knocking. I am at home but I will not open the door."[9] I have never quite been able to do that, but I have, on occasion, put a sign on my office door that everyone understands — "In Conference with the Boss!"

Be assured of this: everything will try to pull you away from this sacred time. Your phone will ring. Your pen will run dry. Someone will knock at your door. You will suddenly have an urgent need to do something you have left undone for years. And in that split second you alone will decide whether you will hold steady in the inner sanctuary of the heart or rush out of the holy place, tyrannized by the urgent.

The Covenant of Place

If the Covenant of Time calls us to constancy, then the Covenant of Place calls us to stability. In his day St Benedict saw so many roving prophets without any kind of accountability that he made the vow of stability a central feature of his *Rule*. We too need to be anchored somewhere.

The Covenant of Place gives us the gift of focus. When I was a new Christian I used to go out behind the garage each morning and sit on a cinder-block wall with my feet on the dustbins, Bible in hand. This was holy ground. On those days when it was too cold to be outside, I went literally into a closet in our tiny duplex in New Mexico. There I found darkness and silence, both of which taught me focus. I urge you, too, to find a place of focus – a loft, a garden, a spare room, an attic, even a designated chair – somewhere away from the routine of life, out of the path of distractions. Allow this spot to become a sacred "tent of meeting". Thomas Merton writes:

> My chief joy is to escape to the attic of the garden house and the little broken window that looks out over the valley. There in the silence I love the green grass. The tortured gestures of the apple trees have become part of my prayer. . . . So much do I love this solitude that when I walk out along the road to the old barns that stand alone, far from the new buildings, delight begins to overpower me from head to foot and peace smiles even in the marrow of my bones.[10]

The Covenant of Place includes a commitment to community. We are part of a people; we identify with them and commit ourselves to them. Some have a spiritual director, a person who listens with them on their walk with God.

Others gather in small bands – the church within the Church – for mutual nurture and accountability.

But remember, this community is a gift. We cannot just make it happen by logistical arrangements. Sometimes and in some places we live without this special grace. Our covenant, however, is always to seek it out, always to welcome its appearing, always to nurture its development.

The Covenant of Heart Preparation

We are to have the "fittest preparation of heart", says Richard Baxter. Long before anyone knew that body language reveals our innermost feelings, Baxter was urging people to meet God in such an uninhibited way that their deepest feelings could burst forth. We can run, jump, walk, stand, kneel, or lie prostrate on the floor. We can close our eyes bowed in awe and reverence, or we can raise our eyes upward in praise and devotion. We can lift our hands, clap our hands, fold our hands. We can weep, laugh, sing, shout. We can use trumpet, lute, harp, tambourine, strings, pipe, and loud clashing cymbals. We can kneel in silent wonder and adoration.

We can also prepare the heart by cultivating "holy expectancy". With our mind's eye we pass through the outer court and into the inner court. The veil is lifted from our hearts and we enter the Holy of Holies. The air becomes charged with expectancy. We listen in utter silence for the *Kol Yahweh*, the voice of the Lord.

Another way we make the heart ready to enter the awesome Presence is by disciplining the tongue. How much more fitting to come in absolute silence before the Holy One of eternity than to rush into his presence with hearts and minds askew and tongues full of words. The scriptural admonition is, "The LORD is in his holy temple; let all the earth keep silence before him!" (Hab. 2:20).

Specific preparations can be extremely helpful. The Psalter is the prayer book of the Church, and I will often precede personal prayer with the prayerful reading of a Psalm. My own church tradition is decidedly non-liturgical which is precisely why at times I use one of the great books of liturgy designed to aid private prayer. Sometimes I choose John Baillie to cultivate my heart by means of his famous *Diary of Private Prayer*, or I may turn to the lesser-known *Doctor Johnson's Prayers*. At other times I write out my own prayers and pray them as a daily private ritual of heart preparation.

The preparation of your own little sanctuary can draw the heart into worship. I have a friend who lights a candle in her small study whenever she goes to prayer. Fresh flowers can delight both sight and smell. I like to have a cup of coffee in hand whenever I pray in the morning.

I know you have preparations of your own. The idea is to use all the means at our disposal to urge all that is within us into doxology; "Bless the LORD, O my soul, and all that is within me, bless his holy name" (Ps. 103:1). As Richard Baxter reminds us, the rewards are well worth the effort: "There is none on earth that live such a life of joy and blessedness as those that are acquainted with this heavenly conversation."[11]

The Trysting Prayer

We usually think of a tryst as a prearranged meeting of lovers. How appropriate! The trysting prayer is our special date with God. We can be free and at ease because we are entering into the heart's true home. Our Eternal Lover lures us back regularly into his presence with anticipation and delight. It is not hard to honour this regular time of meeting for the language of lovers is the language of waste. We are glad to waste time with God, for we are pleased with the company.

Blessed Saviour, I pace back and forth at the altar of commitment. I really do want a fixed habit of prayer. At least, that is what I want at the moment. I'm not sure if that is what I will want two weeks from now. I do know that without some kind of consistent communion with you I will not know holy obedience.

So, as best I can, I promise to set aside time regularly for prayer, meditation and spiritual reading. Strengthen me in this covenant. Help me so to delight in your presence that I will want to come home to you often.

In your name and for your sake I make this covenant.

— Amen.

PART II

Moving Upward
Seeking the Intimacy We Need

We are exiles and aliens until we can come into God, the heart's true home. Pride and fear have kept us at a safe distance. But as the resistance within us is overcome by the operations of faith, hope and love, we begin moving upward into the divine intimacy. This in turn empowers us for ministry to others.

Leo Tolstoy tells the story of three hermits who lived on an island. Their prayer of intimacy and love was as simple as they were simple: "We are three; you are three; have mercy on us. Amen." Miracles sometimes happened when they prayed in this way.

The bishop, however, hearing about the hermits decided that they needed guidance in proper prayer, and so he went to their small island. After instructing the monks, the bishop set sail for the mainland, pleased to have enlightened the souls of such simple men.

Suddenly, off the stern of the ship he saw a huge ball of light skimming across the ocean. It got closer and closer until he could see that it was the three hermits running on top of the water. Once on board the ship they said to the bishop, "We are so sorry, but we have forgotten some of your teaching. Would you please instruct us again?" The bishop shook his head and replied meekly, "Forget everything I have taught you and continue to pray in your old way."

The Prayer of Adoration

In the school of adoration the soul learns why the approach to every other goal had left it restless.

– Douglas Steere

Prayer is the human *response* to the perpetual outpouring of love by which God lays siege to every soul. When our reply to God is most direct of all, it is called adoration. Adoration is the spontaneous yearning of the heart to worship, honour, magnify and bless God.

In one sense adoration is not a special form of prayer, for all true prayer is saturated with it. It is the air in which prayer breathes, the sea in which prayer swims. In another sense, though, it *is* distinct from other kinds of prayer, for in adoration we enter the rarefied air of selfless devotion. We ask for nothing but to cherish him. We seek nothing but his exaltation. We focus on nothing but his goodness. "In the prayer of *adoration* we love God for himself, for his very being, for his radiant joy."[1]

Adventure in Adoration

I went to the annual meeting of a small group of writers in high spirits. The *esprit de corps* and tête-à-tête are always exhilarating. This particular year we were meeting at a lovely resort near the Canadian border. Quickly, however, I found myself withdrawing from the intellectual bantering. I did not fully understand the reasons for my inner seclusion. "I am weary from a hectic travel schedule," I reasoned, "and my spirit has grown sad, weighted down by the pains and sorrows of many. Perhaps a little solitude would solve the problem." Deep within, however, I sensed the need for something more than mere solitude . . . but what?

The next day the early afternoon was free, and optional readings were scheduled for the late afternoon – a perfect time to be alone. Following lunch, I went on a solo hike near a lovely lake, thrilling at the infinite variety of blues and greens. Then, I drove to a nearby town and strolled about the shops, my anonymity allowing for solitude in the midst of many people.

It was time to return for the readings, yet somehow I sensed that what needed to happen within me was not complete. On the drive back I spied an obscure sign pointing to a nearby waterfall. I turned up the winding road that cut its way through lush woods and ended at the falls. The sun darted in and out of the trees in a playful game of tag as I explored the area.

Following the river downstream for perhaps an hour or so, I eventually found myself off all existing paths and far beyond tourists and day hikers. I picked my way around boulders and over fallen trees until I came upon a huge outcropping of rock that jutted into the river, causing it to form a twisted U-turn. With much ado I made my way up this elongated granite thumb, and for some time I simply revelled in the glory of the canyon above me and the surging waters below.

What happened next is difficult to put into words. With the roar of the river quickly swallowing up any cry my voice could make, I felt free to shout out my thanksgiving and praise to God. A spirit of adoration and celebration sprang up within me, and I started dancing to the tune of a heavenly drummer and singing words unknown to my conscious mind. I sang with my mind too – hymns and psalms springing up from distant memory as well as spiritual songs that cascaded down in impromptu splendour. Thanksgivings poured forth for all things great and small. Praises joined with the river in joyous exaltation. It felt as if I was being invited to join, in my feeble way, in the ceaseless paean of praise that ascends before the throne of God.

In the beginning the experience was wholly effervescent, but in time the exuberance began to give way to a whispered, "Holy! Holy! Holy!" Worship grew deeper, more fertile. I had begun by blessing the name of God and was finally reduced to breathing the name of God. Exaltation sank into adoration.

Quiet murmurings of reverence continued for some time. Then a listening stillness came over me that yielded needed instruction for the days ahead. By now the long shadows in the canyon signalled the end of the day. In utter silence I made my way back upstream, bowed in awe and adoration. The inner hush remained for several days. That afternoon I experienced no ecstasy in the classic sense of the term, but I did enter a loving adoration that heals our sorrows and draws us near to the heart of the Father.

The Two Sides of Adoration

There are two sides to the Prayer of Adoration: thanksgiving and praise. The usual distinction between these two experiences is this: in thanksgiving we give glory to God for *what he has done for us*; in praise, we give glory to God for *who he is in himself*.

The distinction is valid, but we must not make too much of it. In experience the two weave themselves in and out of one another and become part of an organic whole. The biblical authors frequently use the words interchangeably and even on top of one another: "I will thank you in the great congregation; in the mighty throng I will praise you" (Ps. 35:18). Simultaneously, thanksgiving and praise splash across the experience of all true adoration.

The Old Testament world is soaked with the language of thanksgiving. In the days of the monarchy King David chose certain priests to be ministers before the Ark of the Covenant with a singular commission. "To invoke, to thank, and to praise the LORD, the God of Israel." He appointed special singers to do nothing but "the singing of praises to the LORD" (1 Chron. 16:4–36). Then, too, there was the "thank offering" that was such a prominent feature in the worship of ancient Israel (Lev. 7:12, and so on).

It is hard to find a page of the Psalter that does not contain the rhetoric of thanksgiving: "O give thanks to the LORD, for he is good; for his steadfast love endures for ever" (Ps. 106:1); "I will give thanks to the LORD with my whole heart" (Ps. 9:1). "O LORD my God, I will give thanks to you for ever" (Ps. 30:12). On and on goes the litany, thanksgiving on top of thanksgiving.

Jesus was the ultimate grateful person. The signature written across his life was the prayer "I thank you, Father, Lord of heaven and earth" (Luke 10:21). Paul too knew the spirit of gratitude: "I thank my God through Jesus Christ for all of you" (Rom. 1:8). Certainly the biblical witnesses speak with one voice, urging us to give "thanks to God the Father at all times and for everything in the name of our Lord Jesus Christ" (Eph. 5:20).

To the extent we can draw a line of demarcation, praise lies on a higher plane than thanksgiving. In his classic work entitled simply *Prayer*, Ole Hallesby observes, "When I give thanks, my thoughts still circle about myself to some extent. But in praise my soul ascends to self-forgetting adoration, seeing and praising only the majesty and power of God, His grace and redemption."[2]

The Bible is certainly packed with praise. The ancient law code startles us with its trenchant words: "He is your praise; he is your God" (Deut. 10:21). The Psalms reverberate with the tumult of praise: "Praise the LORD! Praise the LORD, O my soul! I will praise the LORD as long as I live; I will sing praises to my God all my life long" (Ps. 146: 1–2); "I will bless the LORD at all times; his praise shall continually be in my mouth" (Ps. 34:1); "You who fear the LORD, praise him!" (Ps. 22:23); "He put a new song in my mouth, a song of praise to our God" (Ps. 40:3).

The writer to the Hebrews urges us to "continually offer a sacrifice of praise to God, that is, the fruit of lips that confess his name" (Heb. 13:15). And the writer of Revelation assures us that praise is the serious business of heaven:

I heard the voice of many angels surrounding the throne and the living creatures and the elders; they numbered myriads of myriads and thousands of thousands, singing with full voice "Worthy is the Lamb that was slaughtered to receive power and wealth and wisdom and might and honor and glory and blessing!" (Rev. 5:11–12).

Blessing is jubilant praise, praise raised to its highest point. "Bless the LORD, O my soul," enjoins the Psalmist, "and all that is within me, bless his holy name" (Ps. 103:1). Luke closes his Gospel with the enthralling words of blessing "and they were continually in the temple blessing God" (Luke 24:53). When we are brought into experiences of blessing God, the soul is enraptured in praise.

Who can question the significance of these twin activities of heart and mind? Together they help us exegete the meaning of adoration. May our hearts be stirred. May our minds be rejuvenated. May we ardently join with that ancient processional up the holy hill of Zion. "Enter his gates with thanksgiving, and his courts with praise. Give thanks to him, bless his name" (Ps. 100:4).

Tears in the Eyes of God

If we could only see the heart of the Father, we would be drawn into praise and thanksgiving more often. It is easy for us to think that God is so majestic and so highly exalted that our adoration makes no difference to him. To be sure, the self-sufficiency of God is a precious doctrine, but we should always remember the words of St Augustine: "God thirsts to be thirsted after."[3]

Our God is not made of stone. His heart is the most sensitive and tender of all. No act goes unnoticed, no matter how insignificant or small. A cup of cold water is enough to put tears in the eyes of God. Like the proud mother who is thrilled to receive a wilted bouquet of dandelions from her child, so God celebrates our feeble expressions of gratitude.

Think of Jesus healing the ten lepers. Only one returned to give thanks, and he a Samaritan. How moved Jesus was by the one, how saddened by the nine! Think of the woman who bathed her Master's feet with the tears of gratitude. How stirred he was by her simple devotion! Think of the woman who in outlandish waste anointed Jesus' head with costly perfume. How touched he was by this lavish act of adoration! And what about us? Dare we hold back? It brings joy to the heart of God when we grip that pierced hand and say simply and profoundly, "Thank you, bless you, praise you!"

Obstacles to Adoration

C. S. Lewis identifies several things that keep us from adoration.4 The first is inattention. How easy to be caught up into the whirl of life and miss the overtures of Divine Love. And it is not just that we are trapped in a rat race of acquiring things. It is the quite legitimate demands of home and family and school and work that conspire to make life a blur. Like Jack's beanstalk, our obligations seem to grow overnight. We cannot adore when we do not see.

A second obstacle is the wrong kind of attention. We see a sunset and are drawn into analysis rather than doxology. Frustrations occur and all we are aware of is frustrations – we "ignore the smell of Deity".5

Once I was leading a worship service in a home on a hot summer evening. The doors were left open in hope of a breeze. At one point in the meeting I encouraged everyone to "wait on the Lord" in listening silence. The stillness, however, was quickly interrupted by the homeowner's cat scratching at the screen door, seeking entrance. The more I tried to ignore the cat, the worse it got. I prayed that God would do something – send the cat away, magically open the door, and other more drastic prayers that I shall not mention, since you may have a fondness for cats.

(Strangely, it never occurred to me to get up and let the cat in!)

Later in the evening someone mentioned the cat. Everyone began sharing how distracting the cat had been to their ability to focus on God. Everyone, that is, except Bill — a former missionary filled with wisdom and the Holy Spirit. Bill sat pensive, uttering not a word. "Bill," I queried, "what are you thinking?" "Oh," he spoke deliberately. "I was just wondering what God wanted to say to us through the cat." Now, as far as I know, we never got any "message" from the cat scratching on the screen door . . . except this: I was looking upon the cat as a distraction; Bill was looking upon the cat as a possible messenger. And that may well be enough "message" for anyone for one evening.

A third obstacle to adoration is greed. "Instead of saying, 'this also is Thou,' one may say the fatal word *Encore*."[6] One reason our addiction for more, more, more destroys our ability to adore is because it keeps us from reflection. Lingering over a rose or a phrase of Scripture — smelling, tasting, chewing, drinking it all in — this is the stuff of adoration. When we ask for an encore, we are asking for more than God is pleased to give. Instead of simply enjoying pleasures, we demand more pleasures — whether we enjoy them or not. Allow me to misuse an ancient passage: sufficient unto the day are the pleasures thereof!

Lewis mentions one more obstruction: conceit. How easy for those who discover God in the ordinary to get very smug about it all. We are appalled that others can see only grey in the sky when we are "delightedly observing such delicacies of pearl and dove and silver".[7] We who teach are especially prone to this temptation. "Don't you get it?" we lament. "It's right in front of your nose." Of course, we have been studying and reflecting on this reality for fifteen years while our students have only now encountered it! When conceit takes over, the focus is once again on how wonderful we are — which is why it so effectively severs the cords of adoration.

Stepping-Stones

The Prayer of Adoration must be learned. It does not come
automatically. Notice our own children! They do not need
to be trained to ask for things. To get empirical verification
for this, all we need is one trip with our children to a
shopping mall or a supermarket! But to express thanks?
That is a wholly different matter. What endless effort it
takes to help our children cultivate a habit of gratitude.

The same thing is true for us. Thanksgiving, praise,
adoration – these are seldom the first words in our minds
. . . or on our lips. We need all the help we can get in
order to move into a deeper, fuller adoring. The following
"stepping stones" will, I hope, help to mark the way.

We begin right where we are in the nooks and crannies,
the frustrations and fears, of ordinary life. When we are
filled with sadness, for example, it seldom helps to count
our many blessings or rehearse the glorious attributes of
God. We do not learn adoration on the grand cosmic
scale by centring on the grand and the cosmic, at least not
at first. It wears us out and defeats us to start in this way.

No, we start more simply. We learn about the goodness
of God not by contemplating the goodness of God, but
by watching a butterfly. So here is my counsel: begin by
paying attention to the little creatures that creep upon the
earth. Do not try to study or analyse them. Just watch
the birds and the squirrels and the ducks. Watch, do not
evaluate, watch.

Go to a brook and splash some water on to your burning
face. In that instant do not seek to solve all the problems
of pollution and the ecosystem; just feel the water. Most of
all do not try to find God in the water or to make yourself
be thankful for the water. Simply allow the cool wetness
to refresh your skin. Now sit back and listen to the sound
of the brook. Watch the branches of the tree overhead
swaying back and forth. Notice the leaves fluttering in
the breeze – notice their shape, their colour, their texture.
Listen to the symphony of rustling leaves and scampering

chipmunks and twittering birds. Remember, I am asking you not to analyse, only to notice.

When we do these kinds of things with some degree of regularity, we, in time, begin to *experience* pleasures rather than merely scrutinize them. What this does within us is altogether wonderful. We are first drawn into these tiny pleasures and then beyond them to the Giver of pleasures. True pleasures are, after all, "shafts of the glory," to use the phrase of C. S. Lewis. As this happens, thanksgiving and praise and adoration will flow naturally in their proper time: "To experience the tiny theophany is itself to adore."[8]

This is where we begin, but it is not where we end. Another stone to place across the waters of our narcissism is what Sue Monk Kidd calls "the grateful center".[9] Each of us has such a centre in our lives – a time and a place where we were free of all the grasping and grabbing, all the pushing and shoving, all the disapproving and dissenting.

Let me describe my grateful centre to you. I was seven years old, and my parents were trying to move to the American West Coast. Our relative poverty, however, caught up with us, and we were forced to winter in the cabin of an uncle in the Rocky Mountains. The time was difficult for my parents, I am sure, but for me it was glory. For a city boy to be suddenly plopped down into a paradise of towering pines, rose quartz, and splashing streams – well, *paradise* is too mild a term. Even the primitive nature of the cabin – lighting by candle, heating by fireplace, plumbing by outhouse – only added to the adventure.

My brothers and I conquered many a granite fortress, finding arrowheads and secret hiding-places. When the winter snows came, we "joined" Admiral Byrd on many a frozen expedition. For Christmas I helped Mum paint pine cones silver.

But my most vivid memory is of the fireplace. (I had never been around a fireplace before, all our heat heretofore having come from the coal furnace in our Nebraska home.) Every night I would pull out the bed that hid in the couch

by day and climb under the heavy quilts, my head less than
ten feet away from the crackling warmth. Night after night
I would fall asleep, watching this strange yellow blaze that
warmed us all. I was in my grateful centre.

Even today as an adult I can go back to that centre via
the marvellous capacity of memory and there experience
thanksgiving and gratitude to the God who gives every
good gift. I am not trying to escape or retreat from
the struggles and hardships of modern life, rather I am
giving myself a point of reference from which to face those
struggles and hardships.

You too have such a centre, I am sure. Go to it in your
imagination as often as you can and from that place allow
whispered prayers of thanksgiving to flow forth.

Such experiences help us on to the next stepping-stone:
the practice of gratitude. We can now develop a habit
of giving thanks for the simple gifts that come our way
day by day. Carolynn and I have just returned from
feeding some geese that now and then visit a small pond
behind our house. That is something to be grateful for.
I am glad for the cooler air today that cuts the edge
off summer's heat. And for the marvellously symmetri-
cal white fir outside my study window, I give thanks.
You get the idea – food, home, clothes, life itself –
for all these and more we practise gratitude. Try to
live one entire day in utter thanksgiving. Balance every
complaint with ten gratitudes, every criticism with ten
compliments. When we *practise* gratitude, a time will
come when we find ourselves saying, "Not 'please' but
'thank you'", as Annie Dillard notes in *Pilgrim at Tinker
Creek*.[10]

We are now ready for a stepping-stone that we could
never have managed in the beginning; magnifying God. To
magnify something you make it look larger, increasing it
out of proportion. To talk about ourselves or our activities
out of true proportion is dangerous indeed, but when we
magnify God, we are on safe ground. We simply cannot
say too much about God's goodness or love. The most

exaggerated things we can think of will still be far below what is actually the case.

The easiest way to begin magnifying God is to use the Psalter. In nearly any Psalm we can find a passage that will aid us in praising God. "O magnify the LORD with me," says the Psalmist, "and let us exalt his name together" (Ps. 34:3). And so we do, allowing the words to become our own.

In time, the words will not only become our own, but will also lead us to our own words. We can begin by speaking forth the words of indebtedness which in turn will lead us to acknowledgment, appreciation, gratitude, thanksgiving, praise and adoration.[11]

Music is a marvellous aid in all this. Praise music abounds today that can ease even sad hearts into adoration. Joyfully we can join in with these songs even if we have little musical talent. At home or in the car no one hears but God, and he is pleased.

The final stepping-stone I want to mention is joyous, hilarious, foot-stomping celebration. We clap, laugh, shout, sing, dance. Celebration is best done in community, but even when we are alone we are never alone, for we are joining the jubilee chant of angels and archangels and living creatures about which we can only guess. Like Miriam we dance and sing to the Lord for he has triumphed gloriously, the horse and rider thrown into the sea (Exod. 15). Like Mary our soul magnifies the Lord and our spirit rejoices in God our Saviour (Luke 1).

Well, we have come a long way in our consideration of adoration. We began with baby steps, what C. S. Lewis calls "adoration in infinitesimals".[12] But in God's time and in God's way we are led irresistibly into the adoration of him who is eternal, immortal, invisible, the only wise God (1 Tim. 1:17). Richard Baxter urges us: "Be much in that angelic work of praise. As the most heavenly Spirits will have the most heavenly employment, so the more heavenly the employment the more it will make the spirit heavenly."[13]

O most high, glorious God, how great is my dilemma! In your awful presence silence seems best. And yet, if I keep my peace, the rocks themselves will cry out. But if I do speak, what will I say?

It is Love that calls forth my speech, though it still feels like stammering. I love you, Lord God. I adore you. I worship you. I bow down before you.

Thank you for your gifts of grace:
  — the consistency of sunrise and sunset,
    — the wonder of colours,
      — the solace of voices I know.

I magnify you, Lord. Let me see your greatness — to the extent that I can receive it. Help me bow in your presence in endless wonder and ceaseless praise.

In the name of him whose adoration never failed.

— Amen.

9

The Prayer of Rest

Rest. Rest. Rest in God's love. The only work you are required now to do is to give your most intense attention to his still, small voice within.

— Madame Jeanne Guyon

Through the Prayer of Rest God places his children in the eye of the storm. When all around us is chaos and confusion, deep within we know stability and serenity. In the midst of intense personal struggle we are still and relaxed. While a thousand frustrations seek to distract us, we remain focused and attentive. This is the fruit of the Prayer of Rest.

There is perhaps no more appealing invitation in all the Bible than Jesus' gracious words, "Come to me, all you that are weary and are carrying heavy burdens, and I will give you rest" (Matt. 11:28). Nothing is more needed today than this rest of body, mind and spirit. We live so much of our lives in "an intolerable scramble of panting feverishness", as Thomas Kelly calls it.[1] All of the grasping and grabbing, all of the controlling, all of the manipulative dynamics of life exhaust us.

If only we could slip over into that life free from strain and anxiety and hurry! If only we could know that steady peace of God where all strain is gone and Christ is already victor over the world! If only ... But listen, my friend, I am here to tell you that this way of living can be ours. We *can* know this reality of rest, and trust, and serenity, and firmness of life-orientation. We *can* know as lived experience the words of Jean Sophia Pigott:

Jesus, I am resting, resting
    In the joy of what Thou art;
I am finding out the greatness
    Of Thy loving heart.[2]

Today, this very moment, Jesus is inviting you, Jesus is inviting me, into his rest: "Take my yoke upon you, and learn from me; for I am gentle and humble in heart, and you will find rest for your souls" (Matt. 11:29).

Sabbath Prayer

We are promised by the writer to the Hebrews that "a Sabbath rest still remains for the people of God" (Heb. 4:9). Those words have been familiar to me from my earliest days as a Christian, but I learned only more recently about "Sabbath Prayer" while on a small island off the Pacific coast of Canada. I was with a small study group, and, during a morning break period, I found a canoe and paddled over to a tiny island. Beaching the canoe, I began exploring the fir-covered outcropping. When I reached the crown of the island, I discovered a small wooden platform someone had built and an old weathered chair that sat atop it like a lonely sentinel.

Easing myself into the chair, I waited to see if it would sustain my weight. It held firm. I sat back into the warm sun and drank in the stillness of land and sea and sky. The trees were absolutely motionless – tranquil testimonials to the majesty of God. The songs of chickadee and blue jay did not break the silence, but only continued it.

I paddled over to this lovely spot not to pray, only to explore. Sitting there, however, I recalled Carolynn's goodbye words to me at the airport; "I want you to come home refreshed!" Soon I found myself praying simply, "Refresh me, Lord. Refresh me." It was not hard to wait in silence – that entire outdoor sanctuary seemed hushed in reverence. What next surfaced to my conscious mind was this: "I want to teach you Sabbath Prayer." I leaned forward in anticipation – I was far from sure what Sabbath Prayer was, but I was eager to learn. "You will have to lead me, because I don't know what I am supposed to do," I responded. Then came the words, "Be still . . . Rest . . . Shalom." That was all. Those words and no more. For some moments I sought to enter into the experience of each word.

The encounter was wonderful, but I was also aware that time was slipping by. I became concerned and thought, "It's nearly noon. People will begin to miss me and wonder why I've stayed here so long. I'd better get back for lunch." The same words were spoken over me: "Be still . . . Rest . . . Shalom." They seemed to calm my spirit, and I returned to a quiet attentiveness.

After a while, however, my mind became agitated by a kind of hyper-responsibility – perhaps you know the feeling. "The next session will begin soon," I reasoned. "I need to be there. What kind of example will my truancy make? Besides, everyone will really begin to be concerned about my absence." In full gear now, my mind began envisioning self-centred surrealistic scenarios: "People may be thinking that I tipped over in the canoe, and right now they are probably discussing whether to mount a rescue effort!" The same words served to discipline my mind: "Be still . . . Rest . . . Shalom."

The final temptation, however, was the most alluring. I began thinking to myself, "This experience is absolutely wonderful. I must capture this moment for the future. But how? I cannot possibly remember everything that is happening to me here. Where is some paper? I must write it all down!" Again: "Be still . . . Rest . . . Shalom." All the more focused, I settled back into Sabbath Prayer. In a short time it seemed like "the Presence in the midst" ended, and so I made my way back to the group, which, as you probably guessed, had scarcely noticed my absence and were going right on with the day's schedule.

Resting in God

The Bible tells us that, after speaking all things into existence from ant to aardvark, and after breathing into the human species the breath of life, God rested. This "resting of God" on the seventh day became the theological framework for the Sabbath regulation that summons us to rest in God. Now, before we dismiss this Old Testament Sabbath rule out of hand, it is important to see that there is a lot more behind it than the desire for a periodic breather. For instance, it has a way of tempering our gnawing need always to get ahead. If we ever want to know the degree to which we are enslaved by the passion to possess, all we have to do is observe the difficulty we have maintaining a Sabbath rhythm.

No teaching flowing out of the Sabbath principle is more important than the centrality of our resting in God. Instead of striving to make this or that happen, we learn trust in a heavenly Father who loves to give. This does not promote inactivity, but it does promote dependent activity. No longer do we take things into our own hands. Rather, we place all things into divine hands and then act out of inner promptings.

You may recall that the children of Israel failed to enter God's rest even though he had brought them out of the land of Egypt, out of the house of bondage. Unable to trust in Yahweh, they rebelled and spent their remaining days wandering in the deserts of Sinai. With tragic finality God declared, "'They shall not enter my rest'" (Heb. 4:3).

Today we are invited into the Sabbath rest of God which the children of Israel failed to enter. "It remains open for some to enter it," declares the writer to the Hebrews. The literal translation for "pray always" is "come to rest." Through the Prayer of Rest we enter this intense stillness, this quiet alertness.

Prayer in the Middle Voice

But how? How do we enter the Prayer of Rest? It is here that we face a serious dilemma. Our tendency is, on the one hand, to take firm control, or, on the other hand, to do absolutely nothing.

We most often begin by tackling prayer in the same way we have been taught to tackle every other problem – by hard work. We grit our teeth, intensify our willpower, and try, try, try. In reality this is a pagan concept of prayer in which we rouse the gods to action by our many incantations and vain repetitions.

Anthony Bloom tells the story of an elderly woman who had been working at prayer with all her might but without ever sensing God's presence. Wisely, the archbishop encouraged the old woman to go to her room each day and "for fifteen minutes knit before the face of God, but I forbid you to say one word of prayer. You just knit and try to enjoy the peace of your room."

The woman received this counsel, and at first her only thought was, "Oh, how nice. I have fifteen minutes during which I can do nothing without being guilty!" In time, however, she began to enter the silence created by her knitting. Soon, she said, "I perceived that this silence was not simply an absence of noise, but that the silence had substance. It was not absence of something but presence of something." As she continued her daily knitting, she discovered that "at the heart of the silence there was he who is all stillness, all peace, all poise."[3] She had let go of her tight-fisted efforts to enter God's presence and, by doing so, discovered God's presence already there.

But we must not get the wrong idea. Total passivity is not the answer either. Resting in God does not mean resignation or idleness. It does not mean that we sit back and hope God will do something. That is a Hindu concept of prayer in which we sink passively into the impersonal and fated will of gods and goddesses.

I remember one night well, even though it was many

years ago. I was in charge of a gathering of several hundred teenagers, and the meetings had gone well. The speaker of the evening had just finished and was inviting these young men and women to commit their lives to Jesus Christ. A hush fell over everyone. It was a tender moment. But just then a belt on one of the air-conditioning blowers began to squeak, and a distracting, disconcerting screech echoed throughout the auditorium.

I began to pray: "Lord, this is a special moment in the lives of these kids. Please, stop that noise – oil the belt, blow up the motor – do something, anything!" Nothing happened, and a minor crisis of faith joined forces with my frustration. But soon I began to quiet down, and as I did, I heard this: "Why don't you go over and turn off the blower yourself?" I was less than five steps away from the switch! In my youthful enthusiasm I was expecting God to intervene by some divine fiat when what was needed was a simple action on my part.

No, neither manipulative control nor listless passivity is an appropriate model for the Prayer of Rest. So, what approach are we to take? How do we break the horns of this dilemma?

"Prayer takes place in the middle voice," writes Eugene Peterson.[4] In grammar the active voice is when we take action, and the passive voice is when we receive the action of another, but in the middle voice we both act and are acted upon. We participate in the formation of the action and reap the benefits of it. "We neither manipulate God (active voice) nor are manipulated by God (passive voice). We are involved in the action and participate in its results but do not control or define it (middle voice)."[5]

You see, we are not bound by the categories of activism and quietism. They are simply not sufficient to describe what is happening in the Prayer of Rest. To be sure, it is "Sabbath rest" which sounds passive. But we must also "enter in", which sounds active. We are praying in the middle voice, entering that way of receiving and responding "that radiates into a thousand subtleties of participation and intimacy, trust and forgiveness and grace."[6]

The devotional masters often spoke of *Otium Sanctum*, "holy leisure". It refers to a sense of balance in life: activity and rest, work and play, sunshine and rain. It means the ability to carry on the activities of the day filled with the cosmic patience of God. Holy leisure means living – and praying – in the middle voice.

Activity of the Everlasting Trinity

The wonderful news I am trying to explain is this: while we are full participants in the grace-filled work of prayer, the work of prayer does not depend upon us. We often pray in struggling, halting ways. Many times we have only fragmentary glimpses of the heavenly glory. We do not know what to pray. We do not know how to pray. Often our best prayers feel like inarticulate groans.

This is why the promise of Scripture comes as such good news: "The Spirit helps us in our weakness; for we do not know how to pray as we ought, but that very Spirit intercedes with sighs too deep for words. And God, who searches the heart, knows what is the mind of the Spirit, because the Spirit intercedes for the saints according to the will of God" (Rom. 8.26–27).

Do you realize what a relief this is? The Holy Spirit of God, the third member of the Trinity, himself accompanies us in our prayers. When we stumble over our words, the Spirit straightens out the syntax. When we pray with muddy motives, the Spirit purifies the stream. When we see through a glass darkly, the Spirit adjusts and focuses what we are asking until it corresponds to the will of God.

The point is that we do not have to have everything perfect when we pray. The Spirit reshapes, refines and reinterprets our feeble, ego-driven prayers. We can rest in this work of the Spirit on our behalf.

But it gets even better. The writer to the Hebrews reminds us that Jesus Christ is our great High Priest, and, as you

know, the function of the High Priest in ancient Israel
was to intercede before God on behalf of the people (Heb.
7–9). Do we realize what this means? Today, as we carry
on the activities of our lives, Jesus Christ is praying for us.
Tonight, as we sleep through the long darkness, Jesus Christ
is praying for us. Continual prayer is being offered at the
throne of God on our behalf by none other than the eternal
Son. You are being prayed for now. I am being prayed for
now. We can rest in this work of the Son on our behalf.

But the best is yet to come. Hard as it may be for us
to imagine, God is in everlasting communion with himself
through our stumbling, bumbling prayers. P. T. Forsyth
writes, "When we speak to God it is really the God
who lives in us speaking through us to himself ... The
dialogue of grace is really the monologue of the divine
nature in self-communing love."7 How incredible! How
beyond belief! "We pray, and yet it is not we who pray, but
a Greater who prays in us."8 One poet puts it this way:

> They tell me, Lord, that when I seem
>   To be in speech with you,
> Since but one voice is heard, it's all a dream,
>   One talker aping two.
>
> Sometimes it is, yet not as they
>   Conceive it. Rather, I
> Seek in myself the things I hoped to say,
>   But lo!, my wells are dry.
>
> Then, seeing me empty, you forsake
>   The listener's role and through
> My dumb lips breathe and into utterance wake
>   The thoughts I never knew.
>
> And thus you neither need reply
>   Nor can; thus, while we seem
> Two talkers, thou art One forever, and I
>   No dreamer, but thy dream.9

And so we have the activity of the everlasting Trinity

focused around our frail prayers. God the Spirit is inter-
preting our sighs and groans before the throne of heaven.
God the Son is interceding on our behalf before the throne
of heaven. And God the Father, who sits upon the throne
of heaven, is using our prayers to form a perfect soliloquy
– God speaking to God.

With such divine aid, are we not able to relax our
tight-fisted hold on life? Are we not able to release our
urgent desire to succeed in prayer? Are we not able to
yield to the Divine Centre? Are we not able to trust him
to lead us into a richer, fuller communion? Are we not able
to come into the Prayer of Rest?

Three Classical Practices

There are three well-established practices designed to lead
us into the Prayer of Rest. The first is solitude. In Formation
Prayer we considered briefly how solitude changes us; here
we are looking at how solitude simplifies us. In solitude we
voluntarily abstain from our normal patterns of activity
and interaction with people for a time in order to discover
that our strength and well-being come from God alone.
"Solitude," writes Louis Bouyer, "serves to crack open and
burst apart the shell of our superficial securities."[10]

In experiences of solitude we gently press into the Holy
of Holies, where we are sifted in the stillness. Painfully,
we let go of the vain images of ourselves in charge of
everything and everybody. Slowly, we loosen our grip on
all those projects that to us seem so significant. Gently, we
become more focused and simplified. Joyfully, we receive
the nourishment of heavenly manna.

Have you ever noticed the many times Jesus experienced
solitude? The haunting words "in the morning, a great
while before day, he rose and went out to a lonely place"
describe a pattern of life more than a single event (Mark
1:35, RSV). Jesus needed frequent retreat and solitude to
do his work. Yet we somehow think we can do without
what he deemed essential.

Hesychia is the Greek word for "rest" and hesychasm refers to the spirituality of the desert fathers and mothers. Henri Nouwen observes, "The prayer of the hesychasts is a prayer of rest."[11] They discovered *hesychia*, this perfect rest of body and soul, in the solitude of the desert.

Few of us can – or would even want to – follow the desert fathers and mothers in any literal sense. We have families, and jobs, and social responsibilities. But we can experience solitude. This year, for example, I am engaging in a splendid new experiment. In order to give practical expression to my experience of solitude, I have scheduled into my calendar four private retreats, following the seasons of the year – winter, spring, summer, autumn. These are brief retreats of twenty-four to forty-eight hours, depending on my time constraints, but they keep me in a simple training programme of solitude. One group I know quite well takes an eight-hour retreat once a month. These are busy people – executives and secretaries and homemakers – but they have found that one Saturday a month makes good sense, spiritually and in every other way.[12] You too, I am sure, will discover creative ways to enter the solitude of the heart.

A second time-honoured practice is *silencio*, or the stilling of what the old writers called "creaturely activity". This means not so much a silence of words as a silence of our grasping, manipulative control of people and situations. It means standing firm against our co-dependency drives to control everyone and fix everything.

This agitated creaturely activity hinders the work of God in us. In *silencio*, therefore, we still every motion that is not rooted in God. We become quiet, hushed, motionless until we are finally centred. We strip away all excess baggage and non-essential trappings until we come into the stark reality of the kingdom of God. We let go of all distractions until we are driven into the Core. We allow God to reshuffle our priorities and eliminate unnecessary froth.

This silence of all creaturely activity enables us to hear God. François Fénelon writes, "We must silence every creature, we must silence ourselves, to hear in the deep hush of the whole soul the ineffable voice of the spouse. We must bend the ear, because it is a gentle and delicate voice, only heard by those who no longer hear anything else."[13]

Once I was attempting to solve a long-standing problem at the university where I have taught for many years. I brought the principal decision-makers together for lunch, assuming that face-to-face discussion would quickly settle the matter. As the hour ticked away, I watched as different ones hardened their respective positions. The meeting ended with no resolution in sight, and I walked back to my office, disheartened. "God," I complained, "we are no closer to solving this problem than before. This is going to take months of meetings and negotiations, and there is no guarantee we will reach a successful conclusion even then."

Then came the divine word: "I did not ask you to resolve this problem in the first place. Relax. When the time is right, changes will occur." I did indeed relax my frantic efforts and in doing so learned a little more about *silencio*.[14]

The third way we slip into the Prayer of Rest is what is called "recollection". Recollection means focus. It means tranquillity of mind, heart and spirit.

We will look at recollection more closely when we come to Contemplative Prayer. For now a brief word about its practice will be sufficient. What can we do? We can prayerfully cultivate a life of reflection. We can wrestle with existence clarification – who we are and what our purpose for being is. We can take a private retreat just to consider our direction in life. This is the stuff of recollection.

Cupping the Hands Lightly

Jean Vanier, the founder of the L'Arche communities for mentally handicapped people, often explains with a simple illustration his approach to those who live at L'Arche. He will cup his hands lightly and say, "Suppose I have a wounded bird in my hands. What would happen if I closed my hands completely?" The response is immediate:

"Why, the bird will be crushed and die." "Well then, what would happen if I opened my hands completely?" "Oh, no, then the bird will try to fly away, and it will fall and die." Vanier smiles and says, "The right place is like my cupped hand, neither totally open nor totally closed. It is the space where growth can take place."[15]

For us, too, the hands of God are cupped lightly. We have enough freedom so that we can stretch and grow, but also we have enough protection so that we will not be injured — and so we can be healed. This is the Prayer of Rest.

———————◆———————

Blessed Saviour, I am not good at resting in the hollow of your hand. Nothing in my experience has taught me this resting. I have been taught how to take charge. I have been taught how to be in control. But how to rest? No, I have no models, no paradigms for resting.

That is not exactly right. Jesus, when you walked among the Jerusalem crowds and in the Judean hills, you pioneered this way of living. You were always alert and alive. You lived utterly responsive to the will of the Father. Manifold demands were placed upon you, and still you worked in unhurried peace and power.

Help me to walk in your steps. Teach me to see only what you see, to say only what you say, to do only what you do. Help me, Lord, to work resting and to pray resting.

I ask this in your good and strong name.

— Amen

Sacramental Prayer

The true sacrament is holy personality.
— P. T. Forsyth

Sacramental Prayer is incarnational prayer. God in his great wisdom has freely chosen to mediate his life to us through visible realities. This is a great mystery. God, who is pure Spirit utterly free of all created limitations, stoops to our weakness and reveals himself to us through the physical and the visible. The eternal Son becomes an infant in a feeding trough. The bread and the wine are invested with sacramental power. We bow under the wonder of it all.

Over the centuries an unfortunate and, in my opinion, completely unnecessary division has arisen among Christians. On the one side are those who stress liturgy and sacrament and written prayer. On the other side are those who stress intimacy and informality and spontaneous prayer. And each group looks at the other in pious condescension.

It is here that we need the holy conjunction "and". We need not be forced to choose one above another. Both are inspired by the same Spirit. We can be lifted into high, holy reverence by the richness and depth of a well-crafted liturgy. We can also be drawn into breathtaking wonder through the warmth and intimacy of spontaneous worship. Ours is a spirituality that can embrace both.

Even now, many years later, I remember well my experiment with "religionless Christianity" — a popular notion of the times that had been inspired by the prison writings of Dietrich Bonhoeffer. Here was my experiment: I would seek to live in continuous communion with God for three months without any outward "props" whatever — no Bible, no liturgy, no Eucharist, no preaching, no worship services, no set times of prayer, nothing. God was gracious to me during those ninety days, but far and away the most important thing I learned was how badly I need those "props" to keep me pressing in to the Divine Centre. I discovered that regular patterns of devotion form a kind of skeletal structure upon which I can build the muscle and tissue of unceasing prayer. Without this outward structure, my internal heart yearnings for God simply do not hold together. These regular patterns – usually called rituals – are, in fact, God-ordained means of grace.

A Rite Riddled Book

What I did not know at the time of my little experiment, and what I imagine you already know, is that the Bible is full of rituals, liturgies, and ceremonies of all kinds. I am sure it is unnecessary to recount for you the details of tabernacle ceremonial laws and levitical priesthood and temple rituals.

The Psalms, of course, are rich with sacramental rites and temple liturgies. Since they were used frequently in worship settings, the titles of numerous Psalms – those phrases we today find so hard to understand – are actually directions for the temple musicians. The "alleluia" in the Psalter is a liturgical acclamation meaning "praise God!" A large number of the Psalms are written prayers for the use of the worshipping community.

Jesus most certainly participated in the liturgical life of his people at the earliest possible age. He went up to the synagogue on the Sabbath "as was his custom", says Luke (Luke 4:16). No doubt Jesus embraced the two disciplines of every faithful Jew: recite the *Shema* twice a day and observe the three hours of prayer – morning, afternoon and sundown. The *Shema* – "Hear, O Israel: the LORD our God is one LORD." – was (and is) a confession of faith (Deut. 6:4, RSV). At each of the hours of prayer a hymn, the *Tephilla*, was chanted. It consisted of a number of benedictions – eighteen by the end of the first century.

The epistles in the New Testament contain several of the early hymns and confessional statements that were undoubtedly used in the vibrant worship of the pristine Christian community. We can almost hear their shout of praise: "To the King of the ages, immortal, invisible, the only God, be honour and glory for ever and ever. Amen" (1 Tim. 1:17). Or their confessional witness to Christ: "He was revealed in flesh, vindicated in spirit, seen by angels, proclaimed among Gentiles, believed in throughout the world, taken up in glory" (1 Tim. 3:16b).

It is also easy to detect the joyous spontaneity of this faith- filled community. "Sing psalms and hymns and spiritual songs among yourselves, singing and making melody to the Lord in your hearts, giving thanks to God the Father at all times and for everything in the name of our Lord Jesus Christ" (Eph. 5:19–20). As I stated earlier, here is one place where it is completely possible to say "both/and" rather than "either/or".

The Freedom of Liturgical Prayer

While not all forms of Sacramental Prayer are liturgical, all liturgies are, rightly conceived, sacramental. Let me describe for you some of the freedoms of this more structured way of prayer.

First, liturgical prayer helps us articulate the yearnings of the heart that cry for expression. Sometimes it is hard for us to find the words to say what we feel. At other times we do not feel up to praying and the words of the liturgy "prime the pump", as we say. Who, for example, can improve upon the Spirit-empowered words of the General Confession from *The Book of Common Prayer*:

We have erred and strayed from thy ways like lost sheep, we have followed too much the devices and desires of our own hearts, we have offended against thy holy laws, we have left undone those things which we ought to have done, and we have done those things which we ought not to have done. But thou, O Lord, have mercy upon us, spare thou those who are penitent, according to thy promises declared unto mankind in Christ Jesus our Lord; and grant, O most merciful Father, for his sake, that we may hereafter live a godly, righteous, and sober life, to the glory of thy holy Name.[1]

Second, liturgical prayer helps us unite with the "communion of saints". The enterprise we are undertaking is far larger than us. While many of us differ over prayer *to* the saints, we all agree about prayer *with* the saints. Think of it: we are offering up to the throne of grace the very words that have been prayed by followers of the Way for many generations. What a thrill to add to the prayers of the saints throughout the ages our "own little twitter", as C. S. Lewis puts it.[2]

Third, liturgical prayer helps us stand against the temptation to be spectacular and entertaining. A charismatic personality is unnecessary. Clever words are useless. Brilliant insights are not needed. We pray the words that have always been prayed. Increasingly we focus more on God and less on the individual leader.

Fourth, liturgical prayer helps us resist the temptation of private religion. It is so very human of us to allow our petty concerns to be the whole burden of our prayer. Now, it is not wrong to pray over our own pressing needs, but that must never be the end of our prayer work. Through the liturgy we are constantly being brought back to the life of the whole community; we are constantly being confronted with sound doctrine; we are constantly being forced to hear the whimper of the poor and see the tumult of the nations.

Fifth, liturgical prayer helps us avoid the familiarity that breeds contempt. The intimacy of prayer must be always counterbalanced by the infinite distance of creature to

Creator. In the Bible it is common for those who encounter God to fall on their face as though dead. The stateliness and formality of the liturgy help us realize that we are in the presence of *real* Royalty.

Understandable Concerns

This approach to prayer may raise concerns in your mind. That is perfectly understandable. In one form or another I have had (and in some measure continue to have) all of the concerns that are often expressed about Sacramental Prayer.

One concern has to do with the sameness of set prayers and liturgies. Perhaps you have said or heard said things like: "Oh, you're just going through the motions. It's all rote. You're not really thinking about what you are praying."

The allegation is basically accurate, but far from being a drawback, I see it as primarily an asset. One of the great values of liturgical prayer is found precisely in our not having to think. If, when writing, I am constantly preoccupied with commas and split infinitives, I am not yet writing, only learning to write. It is the same with prayer. When I recite the words of the Morning Prayer — "O God, come to my assistance. Lord, make haste to help me" — I do not have to concern myself with how to express my need. Rather, I am free to enter into the depth of my need as well as the reality that God's resources are deeper still.

Another concern centres round relevance. The words of the liturgy are archaic. The litany seems old-fashioned and out of touch with the modern world.

Again, the supposed disadvantage is mostly asset. More often than not the demand for relevancy is simply a temptation of the devil that needs to be resisted. Liturgies are intended to conserve the best of Christian devotion, and in so doing they often save us from the latest fad. They do, of course, change with the changing of language, but

I hope not too quickly. For one thing, seldom in the life of the Church do we find sufficient literary skill to produce something even close to, say, *The Book of Common Prayer*. Besides, as C. S. Lewis once remarked, "The charge to Peter was Feed my sheep; not Try experiments on my rats."3

Another concern centres round whether liturgical forms of prayer are the "vain repetition" that Jesus criticizes so severely (Matt. 6:7, KJV). It is a valid concern. Sadly, I find that this is often exactly what happens. Our delight in literary finesse can easily become a fetish. The beauty and precision of the worship service can supersede heartfelt yearning for God.

That, of course, does not mean that "crude" and "spiritual" are necessarily bedfellows, but it should warn us loud and clear of the idolatry of sophistication. We can so easily "heap up empty phrases", as the Bible says, without the slightest drawings towards "righteousness and peace and joy in the Holy Spirit" (Matt. 6:7, Rom. 14:17).

I will mention one final concern. It is the fear that we will make Jesus "the prisoner of the Tabernacle", as the old pietists used to say. Again, I want to say that the concern is well taken. How easily we miss the import of Jesus' teaching that "God is spirit, and those who worship him must worship in spirit and truth" (John 4:24). How easily we lapse into sacred/secular dichotomies. How easily we think we can contain the movings of the Spirit, who always blows where he wills.

To take the concern seriously, however, should not hinder us from recognizing the special avenues of God's grace into our hearts and lives. The confession that the world is sacramental does not negate the fact that God ordains particular sacraments for imparting his mercy.

God is a God of means, says Jonathan Edwards. Edwards was right, and part of our spiritual growth comes in understanding and entering into these "means of grace".4 This is the task to which we now turn our attention.

A New Song in an Ancient Way

The Psalms have always been at one and the same time both hymn book and prayer book for the Church. The word Psalter originally referred to a musical instrument. The Hebrew title of the Psalms also means hymns. Psalm 72:20 describes all the preceding Psalms as "the prayers of David". The monastic communities that gather five times a day for prayers chant the Psalter, as do liturgical congregations who gather for vespers.

Not all Psalms are hymns or prayers, but the designation is still justified, for they all serve to glorify God, which is the goal of hymns, and to lead us into the will and way of God, which is the goal of prayer. By bringing together singing and praying, the Psalms do something genuinely significant. On a purely human level music is one of the most powerful of mediums because it appeals to both emotion and volition, both imagination and reason. When we tie music to prayer, we have a powerful combination. Singing also adds vivacity, buoyancy and gaiety to our prayers. You may know the old adage "the one who sings prays twice." In considering other prayer books Martin Luther remarks, "Ah, there is not the juice, the strength, the passion, the fire which I find in the Psalter."[5]

We can be glad for the many new efforts today to put various Psalms to music, some of them quite successful. I hope the trend continues. We can hope that some day we will have the whole Psalter set to music, as has been true in the past, or, short of that, at least a selection of Psalms from each of the subjects covered in the Psalter: the creation, the Law, sacred history, the Messiah, the Church, life, suffering, guilt, enemies, the end.[6] It is one of the best ways we have of praying the whole counsel of God, from lament to celebration.

One simple suggestion as you sing various Psalms: sing prayerfully, that is, filled with prayer. Allow the words to quiet you, settle you, deepen you. This is not hard to do, for the structure of many Psalms is geared to this end.

The *Sela*, which often occurs in the middle of a Psalm is meant to signal a meditative interlude. If you are creating a tune for a Psalm, you will want actually to put a musical interlude here so people can ruminate briefly on what they are singing. Martin Luther says that the *Sela* calls for "a quiet and restful soul, which can grasp and hold to that which the Holy Spirit there presents and offers".7 We are helped further by the Hebrew poetic structure of parallelism – repeating the same idea in slightly different words – which invites us to sing reflectively. By simple repetition we are being more and more deeply immersed into the prayer concern.

For those who are not accustomed to written prayers, the Psalter provides the best introduction possible. If we will commit various passages to memory, they will go deep into our heart and so inform and shape our more spontaneous expressions of prayer. In the early Christian communities it was not unusual to memorize "the entire David". St Jerome said that in his day one would frequently hear Psalms being sung in the fields and gardens. May the day come when we too can "sing to the LORD a new song" in this ancient way (Ps. 96:1).

The Most Complete Prayer

At the heart of all Christian prayer is the celebration of the Eucharist, or Holy Communion. Nearly every aspect of prayer is caught up in the eucharistic feast: examination, repentance, petition, forgiveness, contemplation, thanksgiving, celebration, and more. It most perfectly embodies the central core of prayer in that we are full participants in the action, but the grace that comes is all of God. All of the senses are employed. We see, we smell, we touch, we taste. We hear the words of institution, "This is my body . . . This is my blood." In short, eucharistic prayer is the most complete prayer we ever make this side of eternity.

Christian people of honest heart have long differed over

how the life of Christ is mediated to us through the Communion feast. Complicated words are used to make important distinctions: transubstantiation, consubstantiation, memorial, and the like. I believe these issues are significant and I have convictions on them, but I would be a fool to think I could shed much light on these complex matters here. Men and women of intellect far superior to mine have explored these issues in elaborate volumes. Besides, I have no desire to unsettle the convictions of any person, irrespective of the tradition by which he or she is able to enter fully into the Communion service.

Personally, I rather like the understanding of St Maximus the Confessor, the sacramental theologian *par excellence* of the patristic age. He calls the Body and Blood of Christ in the Eucharist "symbols," "images," and "mysteries".[8] It is his way of saying, "Christ is truly present among us, and his life is truly imparted to us, but how it all works is a holy mystery." It is here that our analysis gives way to doxology. In fact, in the Eastern Orthodox tradition the Eucharist is officially designated as one of the "holy mysteries". As C. S. Lewis wisely quipped, "The command, after all, was Take, eat: not Take, understand."[9]

We also differ among ourselves over frequency and style. Some celebrate often and simply. Jerome tells of a bishop whose love of poverty left him with only a wicker basket to hold the bread and a plain glass cup to contain the wine. At other times the eucharistic liturgy is more formal, even splendid. All these differences, however, are surface issues compared to what we hold in common. The Christian community overwhelmingly speaks with a single voice in understanding the eucharistic feast as a "visible means of an invisible grace".[10] God has freely chosen to take the most common elements of the Jewish meal – bread and wine – and somehow impart his life to us through them. This, in unison, we gladly confess.

In eucharistic prayer we are constantly reminded that the passion is the heart of the Gospel. It forces us to keep coming back to the Great Sacrifice. Jesus' body broken.

His blood poured out. This is how we live. This is how we are strengthened. This is how we are empowered. In eucharistic prayer we all come to the table on the same level: the articulate and the wise have no advantage over the illiterate and the immature. We all come with open hands, praying the prayer of the child – the prayer of receiving.

In eucharistic prayer our feelings are irrelevant. What a liberation! We do not have to conjure up some special pious emotion in order to be worthy to partake. Now, I know this is true with all forms of prayer, but it is easier to believe here. I come to the table "just as I am, without one plea, But that Thy blood was shed for me." You, too. It makes no difference how we feel about ourselves, or our performance before God. We come with empty hands as well as open hands. What happens is all of grace.

At this point I want to speak a word to any who may be troubled by Paul's teaching in 1 Corinthians about those who partake of the Supper in such a way that they bring "judgment" or, as the old version puts it, "damnation", upon themselves (1 Cor. 11:20–30). This may have frightened you, especially if you do not feel worthy of receiving the goodness and grace and bounty of God in the first place. Perhaps you worry that you have done things, or said things, or thought things that disqualify you from partaking of the table of the Lord. And if you do partake, you fear you will bring condemnation upon yourself.

If you have been troubled with such thoughts, I want to assure you that Paul is dealing with another kind of problem altogether. He is concerned about those who receive the Supper casually, even flippantly. His focus is on those who eat and drink "in an unworthy manner", who have no sense of or concern for the holy seriousness of what is happening.

You see, that is exactly the opposite problem of your situation. If anything, you are too serious, too concerned. Believe me, God receives you just as you are. You do not have to improve yourself, or increase your quota of good deeds, or do more adequate repenting, or anything. Do not hesitate because you feel unworthy; this Meal is expressly for the unworthy! Come! Eat! Drink! "For as often as you eat this bread and drink the cup, you proclaim the Lord's death until he comes" (1 Cor. 11:26).

The Sacrament of the Word

Martin Luther says that the Church is found wherever "the Word of God is preached in its truth and purity and the sacraments are administered according to the Word and institution of Christ."[11] The sacrament of the Supper is the Gospel through eyegate. The sacrament of the Word is the Gospel through eargate. P. T. Forsyth writes, "In the sacrament of the Word the ministers are themselves the living elements in Christ's hands — broken and poured out in soul, even unto death; so that they may not only witness Christ, or symbolize him, but by the sacrament of personality actually convey him crucified and risen."[12]

I hope you understand that when I speak of the sacrament of the Word, I am referring to more than preaching, though I certainly mean to include preaching. The Word means several things at once: the living, speaking voice of God; Jesus, the divine *Logos*; Scripture, the Word of God written; and the speaking forth of the truth of God by human beings under the power and inspiration of the Spirit.

Also, I hope you know that those who bring the sacrament of the Word are more than the officially recognized and properly ordained clergy, though they are certainly included. Jesus Christ, as the head of the Church, chooses and empowers those who bring forth the Word of life. Amazing as it may sound, God could use you, God could use me to speak his Word, which shall not return void but will accomplish that for which it was sent.

Then, too, I hope you recognize that the sacrament of the Word occurs in many places and circumstances besides the designated worship service, though certainly it should occur there. I have seen the Word spoken and the power descend on street corners and in hospital rooms and in business offices. This is the life of God flowing out to people, and God uses whatever means he wills to manifest his glory. We can be on the telephone with someone and utter anointed words that "speak truth to power", as the old writers loved to say. This is the sacrament of the Word.

Having said this, I want to underscore the preaching of the Word as one of the central, God-ordained means of grace into our lives. Without prayer-filled preaching and prayer-filled hearing, we are an anaemic Church and of all people most to be pitied. E. M. Bounds declares, "The character of our praying will determine the character of our preaching. Light praying will make light preaching. Prayer makes preaching strong, gives it unction, and makes it stick."[13]

In this statement Bounds uses an old word that describes what we need so desperately today – *unction*. Unction is the mystery of spiritual anointing that comes upon preaching and distinguishes it from every other kind of communication. It is more than earnestness; it is more than fervour; it is more than rhetorical skill. Unction is the divine in preaching. It gives preaching its point, sharpness and potency. It impregnates revealed truth with all the energies of God. It supports, soothes, cuts, confronts and brings dry bones to life.

I was once in a worship service I shall not soon forget. I had a friend with me who was unacquainted with Christian things. We arrived at the appointed hour of 10.30 a.m. but worship was already well under way. As we entered the doors of the worship room, a refurbished warehouse, both of us – we discussed it later – were physically jolted by the spiritual power and energy in the worshipping community. We literally caught our breath and pulled back half a step.

The pastor spoke with gentleness, compassion, authenticity, strength. There was no eloquence – the good man never dreamed of such a thing – but there was something far better: a godly disposition. We knew that he was speaking lived truth. It seemed as if between the mouth of the speaker and the ear of the hearer, the Word was animated with unusual life and power. The anointing of God rested on him with such grace and mercy that our hearts were softened and drawn towards obedience. The unction upon him had the feel of a heavenly consecration. The very air seemed vibrant and a holy hush fell upon everyone. For the two of us that preaching moment dispelled all doubts about God's activity in the affairs of human beings.

Such graces do not come automatically: "Prayer, much prayer, is the price of preaching unction; prayer, much prayer, is the one, sole condition of keeping this unction. Without unceasing prayer the unction never comes to the preacher. Without perseverance in prayer, the unction, like the manna overkept, breeds worms."[14]

How do you and I help? By steady prayer for the preacher, to be sure. But there is something even more vital: holy listening. As the preacher approaches the sacred desk, we deliberately take on a spirit of teachability. As the sacrament of the Word is being administered, we are in an inward posture of kneeling, of receiving. We are all the time listening for the *Kol Yahweh*, the voice of the Lord. We listen with the mind, and we listen with the heart. All of the time we are examining our lives and breathing prayers of acceptance and application.

"Yes, but you don't know the kind of preaching I have to endure week in and week out," you may be thinking. "It doesn't feel very sacramental to me!" I am well aware of the problem: preachers who preach a dead orthodoxy, preachers who prostitute the divine office for personal aggrandizement, preachers who traffic in the latest intellectual and cultural fashion. I know that many a sermon is poorly thought out, poorly prepared and poorly delivered. I am also acutely aware of the manifold pressures upon faithful pastors that hinder adequate preparation for the preaching task.

Still I say we must learn holy listening. We are listening,

always listening, for the Divine Whisper amid the human clatter, for, as P. T. Forsyth observes, the "sacrament of the Word is what gives value to all other sacraments."[15]

Body Prayer

I do not have a spirit: I am a spirit. Likewise, I do not have a body: I am a body. The same is true for you. Far too often though we pray as if we are disembodied spirits. It is high time we restore a Christian incarnational understanding of the body. God's grace is mediated to us through our bodies. We worship God with our bodies. We pray with our bodies.

The Bible is full of what could be called body prayer: Moses praying with his arms raised high as the Israelites battle the Amalekites; Elisha praying life back into the Shunemite boy as he lay on top of him; David dancing before the Lord as the Ark is carried into the holy city; Jesus laying his hands on multitudes of people; John falling prostrate before the glorified Christ while on Patmos. The list could be extended endlessly.

The most frequent prayer posture in the Bible is complete prostration with the hands stretched out. The second most common posture is with the hands lifted and the palms up.[16] The posture to which we are most accustomed – the hands folded and the eyes closed – is found nowhere in Scripture. This does not make the first two postures appropriate and the third inappropriate, but it should free us to use whatever body language *is* appropriate to the prayer experience we are entering into.

Allow me to offer a few suggestions. If we are drawn into confession and repentance, we may want to lie prostrate, face down, in contrition and heart sorrow. If we are drawn into a loving adoration of the Lord, high and lifted up, we may want to kneel with hands slightly raised, palms up, in silent thanksgiving and wonder. If we are drawn into active worship and praise, we may want to stand with hands raised, palms out, in song and supplication. Finally, if we are drawn to bless the Maker of heaven and earth, we may want to stand with arms stretched out before him, palms up, speaking forth the words of the Psalmist, "Bless the LORD, O my soul, and all that is within me, bless his holy name" (Ps 103:1).

Sacred dance is another form of body prayer that is once again being utilized in Christian celebration. One of the best things in this renewed emphasis is the mingling of liturgical forms with charismatic expressions of praise, adoration, and prophesy. I am delighted.

For a thousand years Christians did a dance called the *tripudium* to many of their hymns. As the worshippers sang, they would lock arms and take three steps forward, one step back, three steps forward, one step back. In doing this they were actually proclaiming a theology with their feet. They were declaring Christ's victory in an evil world, a victory that moves us forward, but not without setbacks.

Sacred dance can be done either as part of private prayer and worship or in corporate settings. Like the Psalmist, we praise God with lute and harp, with timbrel and dance, with strings and pipe. We celebrate the goodness of God with all our viscera!

I tell you all these things only to be suggestive. God will guide you and me into those forms of body prayer that are the most needful for us and that bring the most honour to him.

A full life of prayer contains infinite variety. We come before God in liturgical dignity and charismatic jubilee. Both are vital to an unabridged experience of prayer.

———————◆———————

Our Father who art in Heaven,
Hallowed be thy name.
Thy kingdom come,
Thy will be done,
On earth as it is in heaven.
Give us this day our daily bread.

And forgive us our trespasses,
  As we forgive those who trespass against us.
And lead us not into temptation,
  But deliver us from evil.
For thine is the kingdom, and the power, and the
  glory, forever.

— Amen.

Unceasing Prayer

*When the Spirit has come to reside in someone,
that person cannot stop praying; for the Spirit
prays without ceasing in him. No matter if he
is asleep or awake, prayer is going on in his
heart all the time. He may be eating or drinking,
he may be resting or working — the incense
of prayer will ascend spontaneously from his
heart. The slightest stirring of his heart is like a
voice which sings in silence and in secret to the
Invisible.*

— Isaac the Syrian

I want to tell you of a wonderful way of living always in
God's presence. I cannot witness that I have entered fully
into this life of perpetual communion with the Father, but
I have caught enough glimpses that I know it to be the best,
the finest, the fullest way of living.

Ordinary folk throughout the ages tell us it is possible.
Brother Lawrence shares simply, "There is no mode of
life in the world more pleasing and more full of delight
than continual conversation with God." St John of the
Ladder advises, "Let the memory of Jesus combine with
your breath." Juliana of Norwich says frankly, "Prayer
unites the soul to God." Kallistos, a Byzantine spiritual
writer, teaches, "Unceasing prayer consists in an unceasing
invocation of the name of God." It was said of St Francis
that he "seemed not so much a man praying as prayer itself
made man". And Frank Laubach reports, "Oh, this thing
of keeping in constant touch with God, of making him the
object of my thought and the companion of my conversa-
tions, is the most amazing thing I ever ran across."[1]

Maybe this sounds impossible, even undesirable, to you. At times I share the feeling. Life is complicated enough as it is. Why should we add another religious duty on to an already overcommitted schedule? Besides, it sounds unbelievably difficult. Nobody can think of God all the time. Who would even want to?

If you identify in any way with these sentiments, I want to encourage you. God does not expect you to dive immediately into the ocean of constant communion and swim from one continent to the other. We move into this way through a process of practised living that is both understandable and practical. And, while this "practise of the presence of God" is strenuous, everything else ceases to be so. We become increasingly focused, increasingly centred, increasingly synoptic. More and more we find ourselves going through the stresses and strains of daily activity with an ease and serenity that amaze even us . . . especially us.

Besides, steady, faithful communion is in some ways easier than our normal way of praying. It is harder to pray inconsistently than consistently in the same way that it is harder to play a good game of tennis when we practise only once in a while. Do we really think we can experience integration of heart and mind and spirit with an erratic prayer life? Do we really believe we can, like Moses, "speak face to face" with God as someone would a friend by our unpredictable prayers? No, we develop intimacy by regular association. We develop ease as well. Why ease? Because we are forming fixed habits of righteousness. In time these "holy habits" will do their work of integration so that praying becomes the easy thing, the natural thing, the spontaneous thing — the hard thing will be to refrain from prayer.

Unbroken Communion

The biblical writers are not silent about the possibilities of Unceasing Prayer. "Pray without ceasing," enjoins the

Apostle Paul (1 Thess. 5:17). To the Romans he says, "Rejoice in your hope, be patient in tribulation, be constant in prayer" (Rom. 12:12, RSV). To the Ephesians, "Pray in the Spirit at all times in every prayer and supplication" (Eph. 6:18). To the Colossians, "Continue steadfastly in prayer, being watchful in it with thanksgiving" (Col. 4:2, RSV). And to the Philippians, "Do not worry about anything, but in everything by prayer and supplication with thanksgiving let your requests be made known to God" (Phil. 4:6).

The writer to the Hebrews urges us to "continually offer a sacrifice of praise to God, that is, the fruit of lips that confess his name" (Heb. 13:15). Jesus gave us his parables on prayer to show us our "need to pray always and not to lose heart" (Luke 18:1). He modelled for us the reality of perpetual communion with the Father. "The Son can do nothing on his own, but only what he sees the Father doing; for whatever the Father does, the Son does likewise" (John 5:19); "I can do nothing on my own. As I hear, I judge" (John 5:30); "I am in the Father and the Father is in me (John 14:11). When Jesus told his disciples to abide in him like a branch abides in the vine, they instantly understood what he meant, for they had watched for years his abiding in the Father (John 15:1–11).

The Consuming Passion

I am sure you sense the desperate need for Unceasing Prayer in our day. We pant through an endless series of activities with scattered minds and noisy hearts. We feel strained, hurried, breathless. Thoughts dart in and out of our minds with no rhyme or reason. Seldom can we focus on a single thing for long. Everything and anything interrupt our sense of concentration. We are a distracted people.

Unceasing Prayer has a way of speaking peace to the chaos. We begin experiencing something of the cosmic patience of God. Our fractured and fragmented activities begin focusing around a new Centre of Reference.

We experience peace, stillness, serenity, firmness of life-orientation.

But this does not come automatically. We must want it, want it with a consuming passion. In some, writes William James, "Religion exists not as a dull habit, but as an acute fever."[2] Does not every cell within you cry out for this life? Is not there deep inside a longing for his continuous presence? Do not you crave an increase of God's love, God's joy, God's peace, God's power? My bet is that a little prayer sprinkled here and there is simply not enough for you. Oh no, you want more, much more. You long to burn the eternal flame of devotion on the altar of perpetual prayer. If only you knew how! Yes, if only we all knew how! This is the task to which we now turn our attention.

Breath Prayer

As Christians over the centuries have sought to follow the biblical injunction to "pray without ceasing", they have developed two fundamental expressions of Unceasing Prayer. The one is more formal and liturgical; the other is more conversational and spontaneous. The first has its origin in the Eastern Christian hesychastic tradition and is usually called aspiratory prayer or breath prayer.[3] The idea has its roots in the Psalms where a repeated phrase reminds us of an entire Psalm, for example, "O LORD, you have searched me and known me" (Ps. 139:1). As a result, the concept arose of a short, simple prayer of petition that can be spoken in one breath, hence the name "breath prayer". Gregory of Sinai says, "One's love of God should run before breathing."[4]

The most famous of the breath prayers is the Jesus Prayer: "Lord Jesus Christ, Son of God, have mercy on me, a sinner." As you can tell, this prayer is derived from Jesus' parable on self-righteousness, in which the tax collector beat his chest and prayed, "God, be merciful to me, a sinner!" (Luke 18:13). It came together in its present form and was used extensively in the sixth century and was then revived in the Eastern Church in the fourteenth century.

In the nineteenth century an anonymous Russian peasant tells the moving story of his search to pray without ceasing in *The Way of a Pilgrim*.5 Once he learned the Jesus Prayer, he prayed it continuously until the prayer moved from his mind into his heart and finally throughout his whole body – becoming so internalized that it was present with him at all times, whether he was awake or asleep. This particular book has had an influence upon Christians far beyond the borders of the Eastern Church.

But the Jesus Prayer is only one example. It is also possible to discover your own individual breath prayer. One evening some years ago I was out jogging, when a dozen or more breath prayers poured forth from my lips. Here are a few of those prayers that came tumbling out that summer evening: "O Lord, baptize me with love"; "Teach me gentleness, Father"; "Jesus, let me receive your grace"; "Gracious Master, remove my fear"; "Reveal my sin, O Holy Spirit"; "Lord Jesus, help me feel loved."

Notice the brevity of each of the prayers – seldom more than seven or eight syllables. Also, note the sense of near-ness and intimacy: God is addressed in a close, personal way. See too how the person praying expresses dependence, docility, trust – the opposite of self-reliance. Then notice that the prayers are all requests. This is self-focused prayer in the sense that we are asking something to be done in us or to us. But it is not self-centered prayer, for the requests of breath prayer are seasoned reflections on the will and ways of God.

Breath prayer is discovered more than created. We are asking God to show us his will, his way, his truth for our present need.

Here is one way you can discover a breath prayer for yourself. Find some uninterrupted time and a quiet place and sit in silence, being held in God's loving pres-ence. After a few moments allow God to call you by name: "Christy", "Nathan", "Joel", "Tess", "Carolynn",

"Richard", "Lynda", "Joy". Next, allow this question to surface: "What do you want?" Answer this question simply and directly. Maybe a single word will come to your conscious mind: "peace", "faith", "strength". Perhaps it will be a phrase: "to understand your truth", "to feel your love". Next, connect this phrase with the most comfortable way you have of speaking about God: "blessed Saviour", "Abba", "Immanuel", "Holy Father", "gracious Lord". Finally, you will want to write out your breath prayer, staying within what is comfortable to say in one breath.

Over the next few days allow God to adjust your breath prayer ever so slightly. You may have written down, "Help me understand your truth, Lord." But after a day or two of prayer, you realize that what you really need is not so much to understand God's truth as to live God's truth. Hence you begin praying, "Help me live your truth, Lord."[6]

Begin praying your breath prayer as often as possible. Allow God to plant it deep into the depths of your spirit. Do not rush or change prayers too quickly. Eight months ago I received a personal breath prayer and as yet I have no indication that the work is finished. Sometimes – not always, but sometimes – we reach a point beyond this prayer where we are stilled within and without. Christ is before us, Christ is behind us, Christ surrounds us and is through us. This is a point where we let go of our labour and *be* with God.

Commenting on breath prayers, Theophane the Recluse notes, "Thoughts continue to jostle in your head like mosquitoes. To stop this jostling you must bind the mind with one thought, or the thought of One only. An aid to this is a short prayer, which helps the mind to become simple and unified."[7]

The Practice of the Presence of God

The second major expression of Unceasing Prayer is associated with such practitioners of prayer as Brother Lawrence (*The Practice of the Presence of God*), Thomas Kelly (*A*

Testament of Devotion), and Frank Laubach (*Letters by a Modern Mystic*). Their profoundly simple approach is to go through all the activities of our days in joyful awareness of God's presence with whispered prayers of praise and adoration flowing continuously from our hearts. Brother Lawrence, who called himself "the lord of all pots and pans", crystallized this idea in his now famous comment "the time of business does not with me differ from the time of prayer; and in the noise and clatter of my kitchen, while several persons are at the same time calling for different things, I possess God in as great tranquillity as if I were upon my knees at the blessed sacrament."[8]

Lawrence urges us to "make a private chapel of our heart where we can retire from time to time to commune with him, peacefully, humbly, lovingly." He encourages us to make inward prayer the last act of the evening and the first act of the morning and in so doing discover that "those who have been breathed on by the Holy Spirit move forward even while sleeping."[9]

In the latter years of his short life philosopher Thomas Kelly tells us that "the wells of living water of divine revelation rise up continuously, day by day and hour by hour, steady and transfiguring." He writes:

> There is a way of ordering our mental life on more than one level at once. On one level we may be thinking, discussing, seeing, calculating, meeting all the demands of external affairs. But deep within, behind the scenes, at a profounder level, we may also be in prayer and adoration, song and worship and a gentle receptiveness to divine breathings.[10]

The many diary notations of Frank Laubach are radiant with the Shekinah of God: "This afternoon the possession of God has caught me up with such sheer joy that I thought I never had known anything like it. God was so close and so amazingly lovely that I felt like melting all over with a strange blissful contentment."

In 1930 on the tiny Philippine island of Mindanao he writes:

> This sense of cooperation with God in little things is what so astonishes me, for I never have felt it this way before. . . . My part is to live this hour in continuous inner conversation with God and in perfect responsiveness to his will. To make this hour gloriously rich. This seems to be all I need think about.

Several years later and on another continent he prays, "God, this attempt to keep my *will* bent towards your will is integrating me. Here in this Calcutta station, I feel new power such as I have not had for many years."[11]

I am at a loss to convey to you the sense of immediacy, of adventure, of breakthrough that is in the journals and letters not only of these three, but also of many other pioneers in the spiritual life. These people were alive to a reality that most of us miss. Their writings dance with the excitement of discovery. Thomas Kelly writes, "Life from the Center is a life of unhurried peace and power. It is simple. It is serene. It is amazing. It is triumphant. It is radiant. It takes no time, but it occupies all our time. And it makes our life programs new and overcoming."[12]

But can *you* live this way? Can *I* live this way? "No way!" we say. But wait, maybe it is more possible than we first imagine. To be sure, this life of unbroken fellowship is not automatic or effortless. This should not surprise us; anything worth anything always takes effort. Brother Lawrence admits that it took ten years before he fully entered into the practice of the presence of God. Laubach declares:

> The task to which you have called me is as hard to accomplish as scaling Mount Everest, but you can accomplish it if I can keep my will attuned to your will . . . That is *my* task, to hold my will to the current of power, and let you sweep through endlessly.[13]

Arduous, yes, but not impossible – and all the more so as we understand the process involved, one step at a time.

Steps into Unceasing Prayer

We do not leap into the dizzy heights of constant communion in a single bound. It comes over a period of time in measured, practical steps.

The first step is that of outward discipline. This is how we gain proficiency at anything. The accomplished pianist, who today spryly runs her hands up and down the keyboard, once had to agonize over the simplest scales. The same is true for us.

So we begin in simple, conspicuous, even artificial ways. Schoolteachers can use the ringing of the bell to remind them to lift their breath prayer into the arms of the Father. Those whose favourite colour is purple are reminded of God's continuous loving presence each time they see the colour purple. Surgeons can be prompted to prayer by each scrub down as they prepare for an operation. The bank teller can pray whenever someone comes to the window. We can put pressure-sensitive labels on the refrigerator and the bathroom mirror and the television set. Washing dishes, making beds, waiting in supermarket lines – all can call us to prayer. Jogging, swimming and walking can remind us as well.

The idea is surprisingly simple. Frank Laubach called it his *Game with Minutes*, and we too can turn it into a delightful game. How many minutes today can we turn into holy communion?

The second step is for this work to move into the subconscious mind. We say our prayer, and we are unaware of having said it. Breathed longings of wonder and adoration seem always underneath and in the background of everything – a little like a tune that we suddenly realize we have been humming all day long. Inward prayer bubbles forth at the oddest moments: in the midst of traffic, in the shower, in a crowded shopping mall. We begin to dream our prayer.

At this point we will begin to notice changes in our behaviour. We become less agitated in traffic. We endure the petty frustrations of home and office more easily. We are able to listen to others intently, quietly. We become more aware of children.

The third step occurs as prayer moves into the heart. In reality we are moving with the mind into the heart. Sentiment and reason act more in concert. Our prayer work becomes more and more tender, more and more loving, more and more spontaneous. It feels less like work and more like delight.

We now begin to think with love. Our decisions become increasingly bathed in a loving rationality. I do not quite have the words to explain it to you. We become, for example, more sensitive to the hurts and sufferings of others. We walk into a room and quickly know who is sad or lonely or dealing with a deep, inexpressible sorrow. In such a case we are able to slip over beside them and sit in silence, bringing comfort and understanding and healing, knowing that "deep calls to deep" (Ps. 42:7).

The fourth step comes as prayer permeates the whole personality. It becomes like our breath or our blood which moves throughout the entire body. Prayer develops a deep rhythm inside us.

Or so I am told, for I am now speaking beyond my own experience. But my sources are reliable. Saints throughout the ages have witnessed to this reality they often call "divine union". Madame Guyon declares that all of our prayers and all of our meditations are "merely preparations" for this deeper work: "*They are not the end*. They are a *way* to the end. The *end* is union with God."14

This last step is a little too big for me at the moment. Perhaps it is for you too. That says much more about the poverty of our spiritual experience today than about the reality of the step. At any rate, we will be looking at this matter more in a later chapter.

Two Problems

Before I end this chapter, I want to comment on one theoretical and one practical problem. The theoretical issue has to do with whether or not Unceasing Prayer falls under the umbrella of the vain repetition condemned by Jesus. You will remember that we considered this matter in the last chapter. Here we are actually in far less danger. Jesus was dealing with a specific practice in his day in which the Pharisees would make a public display of their piety by reciting their prayers in the marketplace. It was a repetition that was not only vain but also filled with vanity. But Unceasing Prayer is hidden prayer, the prayer of the closet. No one knows that we are engaged in it . . . except perhaps by noticing that we are happier and more fulfilled.

Repetition by itself in not wrong. Jesus recommends it in his parables of importunity and prayed this way himself in the Garden. Abraham prayed in this manner when he bargained with his supernatural visitor, as did Paul when he sought to have his "thorn in the flesh" removed. It is not repetition itself but the repetition that views prayer as a magical incantation that is the problem. The notion that we can say just the right combination of words in just the right sequence and thereby get God to espouse our cause is the repetition that the Bible rejects.

The second problem is more practical in nature. What I have said in this chapter is all well and good when we are feeling spiritual and wanting to pursue God. But what about those times that feel decidedly unspiritual – when we have a confrontation with the children or a disagreement with our spouse, for instance.

Frankly, beyond the desperation prayers we discussed in chapter 1 ("O God, help!"), I have found that I cannot pray during these times. So rather than try to fool myself by piously pretending constant communion, what I do in such situations is to ask God for a time out. He is gracious as always and understands our frailty. In time we can come back and try again. The question is not whether we fail again and again – that is a given; the question is whether over a period of time we are developing a practised habit of divine fellowship.

God waits for us in the inner sanctuary of the soul. He welcomes us there where we can experience in the words of Madame Guyon a "continuous inner abiding."15 And here is the joy: the results are always in excess of the work put in.

◆

"O Lord, my Lord, how excellent is your name in all the earth." The Pleiades and Orion sing your praise. Sparrows and chickadees mimic their song. All creation seems in harmony with you, the Master Conductor. All, that is, except me. Why? Why do I alone want to sing my own melody? I certainly am a stubborn creature. Forgive me.

I do desire to come into harmony with you more fully and more often. I do desire a fellowship that is constant and sustaining. Please nurture this desire of mine which seems so small and tentative right now. May I some day become like the trees which are "planted by streams of water, which yield their fruit in its season, and their leaves do not wither. In all that they do, they prosper".

For Jesus' sake.

– Amen.

The Prayer of the Heart

Heart speaks to heart.
> — John Henry Newman

The Prayer of the Heart is the prayer of intimacy. It is the prayer of love and tenderness of a child to Father God.* Like the mother hen, who gathers her chicks under her wings, we, through the Prayer of the Heart, allow God to gather us to himself — to hold us, to coddle us, to love us (Luke 13:34).

"I Want to Warm Their Hearts"

As I lay in the quilt-covered bed waiting for dawn to come, I thought over the past few days. I had just concluded a preaching mission that had gone well — people had been gracious and responsive, and the Spirit had rested upon us in tender ways. I had only one remaining task — to preach this Sunday morning in an area church — and then I would be on my way home.

"What, Lord, do you have for this congregation this morning? Is there anything special you want said or done?"

---

* The Prayer of the Heart is often called "abba prayer". I know that many find abba language painful because they have been inexpressibly hurt by their own human fathers. I grieve for those wounded by these terribly destructive experiences, and I pray, even as I write these words, that they may know grace and healing. Then, too, it may help all of us to remember that we are to receive our understanding of how human fathers are supposed to function by learning what God is like; not the other way round.

I queried. Even though my sermons are usually prepared well in advance, I frequently pray in this way, because often there are gentle nudgings that seem to provide just the right focus for individual needs. This particular morning the guidance was quite specific: "Tell them that I want to warm their hearts."

"Warm their hearts? What does that mean?" I thought to myself. I rose and jotted down a few ideas that tied into the message I planned to preach, but I really did not have a clue as to how God would warm our hearts. Over the years, however, I have learned that I do not need to know everything.

I met the choir before the service and shared this information with them as best I could, and a murmur of holy anticipation began to move throughout the group as we prayed for the worship experience to come.

The service flowed well, and when I finished preaching, I shared very simply that, as best I could discern, God wanted to warm the hearts of various ones in the room and so we should wait for him to touch us. We waited for some time with a gratifying response as perhaps a dozen individuals rose to speak of particular ways God was melting the coldness and softening the hardness of their hearts. I then asked those to stand who felt drawn to pursue a deeper life of discipleship to Jesus Christ. Perhaps half of the congregation stood, and I led an extended prayer of commitment – interspersed with times of silence – as we continued to wait upon God for the warming of our hearts. The time throughout was tender and encouraging. The process continued following the service. I was scheduled to speak at an adult forum, but instead the entire time was spent praying for individuals who wanted their hearts warmed in various ways: one who needed physical healing of a defective heart, another who needed emotional healing of a broken relationship, and so forth. Even the luncheon time that followed was graced by discernment into heart hurts, and I prayed silently for healing to continue.

In the afternoon I met the pastor of the church – a

young, energetic, rising star in his denomination. (Earlier I had been slightly irritated because I had to take a late flight home, but now I understood the reason, for we had ample time to be together in quiet and uninterrupted surroundings.) As he shared, he began to go deeper and deeper into the recesses of his heart. I could see that what this pastor was experiencing was a classic example of "the dark night of the soul". I listened for perhaps an hour, moved by what this highly successful pastor was going through.

I knew it was a holy moment, but what was I to do? Finally, I got up and stood at his left shoulder, placing one hand on his back and the other over his heart. He laid his head on my chest and began weeping quietly with deep sighs. I prayed over him for fifteen minutes or more, mostly in silence, but interspersed with a few words now and again. As I prayed, I gradually became aware of how extremely warm my hand on his chest was becoming. When we sensed that the work God wanted to do had been completed, we began chatting a little. I asked him if he noticed how warm my hand had become as we were praying. "Oh, yes!" he replied. "It could not have been any warmer if you had rubbed your hand hard on my bare skin." As he spoke, I placed my hand over his heart and immediately it grew extremely warm, almost hot, once again. I held my hand there as we talked on, both of us amazed at what was transpiring.

I thought of Richard Rolle's book *The Fire of Divine Love*, in which he describes such unusual experiences of intense heat around his heart that would cause him to reach down to feel his chest to be sure that it was not literally on fire.

Suddenly I realized the connection between what was happening to us and the message that had come to me that morning while I was in bed. (It had not occurred to me until that precise moment.) God's desire to warm the hearts of his people was for the congregation, to be sure, but it was most specifically for this good pastor.

As we stood there, God was warming his heart, and the physical manifestation of heat was a gracious indication to us of a much deeper work of healing love and grace-filled mercy that was going on inside. This faithful servant of Christ had not "felt" the presence of God for a very long time, and, as best we could tell, God was graciously confirming the reality that "I will never leave you nor forsake you" to him and healing deep wounds that had come from earlier years of ministry.

I share this story with you to underscore the longing God has to commune with us, heart to heart. Jean-Nicholas Grou says, "It is the heart that prays, it is to the voice of the heart that God listens and it is the heart that he answers."[1] We – like John Wesley so many years ago – need to have our hearts "strangely warmed".

The Touchstone

The Prayer of the Heart is abba prayer. The great Apostle Paul tells us that "God has sent the Spirit of his Son into our hearts, crying, 'Abba! Father!' " (Gal. 4:6). It is the abba experiences of Jesus that form the touchstone for the Prayer of the Heart.

One of the first things that strikes us when we read the Gospels is the deep, personal, intimate nearness of Father God that Jesus experienced and taught. Of course, the idea of God as Father is not new. The Psalmist declares, "As a father has compassion for his children, so the LORD has compassion for those who fear him" (Ps. 103:13). In Hosea God describes himself as a Father who takes his children into his arms, who leads them with "cords of compassion" and with "bands of love", and who bends down to feed them (Hos. 11:1–4).

Nor are we given only father pictures. Through the prophet Isaiah, for example, God uses the language of mother: "As a mother comforts her child, so I will comfort you" (Isa. 66:13).

No, it is not the parental image of God that startles us

as we read the Gospels; it is the invitation to *address God* in such a personal and intimate way that is entirely new. The disciples must have been stunned by the response to their request to be instructed about prayer, for Jesus says simply, "When you pray say: 'Father . . . '" (Luke 11:2). To the faithful Jew who even hesitated to speak the Divine Name, the childlike intimacy of Jesus' words must have been utterly shocking.

Abba and *imma* – daddy and mummy – are the first words Jewish children learn to speak. And *abba* is so personal, so familiar a term that no one ever dared to use it in address to the great God of the universe – no one until Jesus. Professor Joachim Jeremias declares, "There is not a single example of the use of *abba* . . . as an address to God in the whole of Jewish literature."[2]

It is Jesus' utter intimacy with Father God that startles us. Even as a twelve-year-old in the temple at Jerusalem, Jesus explains to his earthly parents, "I must be in my Father's house" (Luke 2:49). Eighteen years later, as he begins his public ministry, Jesus rises out of the baptismal waters to the heavenly words "You are my Son, the Beloved; with you I am well pleased" (Luke 3:22b). Again, at the Mount of Transfiguration, the voice coming out of the cloud declares, "This is my Son, the Beloved; listen to him!" (Mark 9:7). Jesus experienced the intimacy of Father God not only in the ecstasy of transfiguration but also in the agony of Gethsemane: "Abba, Father, for you all things are possible; remove this cup from me; yet not what I want, but what you want" (Mark 14:36).

These, of course, are only glimpses. This reality of deepest intimacy permeated everything Jesus said and did. As John Dalrymple observes, "The whole of Jesus' life was a prolonged 'abba experience'".[3]

Ontologically, Jesus' relationship with God the Father is, of course, absolutely unique, but experientially we are invited into the same intimacy with Father God that he knew while here in the flesh. We are encouraged to crawl into the Father's lap and receive his love and comfort

and healing and strength. We can laugh, and we can
weep, freely and openly. We can be hugged and find
comfort in his arms. And we can worship deep within
our spirit.

I was giving a series of lectures at a prominent seminary. The week had been filled with good theological
debate. Through the course of the time God reawak-
ened in one student her gifting in music and gave her
a song – "Abba's Lullaby". She gave me a handwritten
copy. As I read the words, my heart was quickened,
and I immediately called her on the phone, saying that
I believed God had given her not just a song but also
a very special word for the entire seminary community.
I asked if she would consider singing it in chapel the
next day – the last session of the series. She graciously
agreed.

Friday, after the customary introductions, I shared my
conviction that God had a special word for us, not from
me but from one of their own. I explained that this song
– which had been composed only the day before – was
a prayer, but a prayer in reverse. It was Jesus singing
over us, and it would help if our mode was one of
receptivity.

My student friend came to the microphone. Her beautiful
soprano voice was crystal clear, and we were all melted
into worship. The words she sang were overwhelmingly
simple and therefore exactly what this highly trained and
sophisticated audience needed:

> Sweet child, dear child, you know I care;
> Sweet child, dear child, you know I'm there.
> Sweet child, dear child, you know it's true;
> Sweet child, dear child, I love you.
>
> Got me a cradle, yes Lord,
> Big, strong cradle, my, my.
> Got me a cradle, yes Lord,
> God's hands my cradle, Mmm, Mmm.

Rock me gently Jesus,
Rock me gently all night long.
Rock me gently Mmm, Mmm,
In your hands I can be strong.4

These good men and women — people who had wrestled
long and hard with the arguments of Barth and Niebuhr
and Pannenberg and Tillich — absorbed these simple words
of love and intimacy like dry sponges. A holy hush covered
the auditorium, witnessing to the fact that our hearts had
been drawn close to the heart of God. We stayed in those
words for some moments and I am sure that long after all
my lectures are completely forgotten, this simple song will
remain because on that day Jesus sang his lullaby over us.

The Spirit Praying Within Us

What is it, this Prayer of the Heart? It is, very simply, the
Holy Spirit praying within us. The old writers spoke of
three stages in prayer: prayer of the lips, prayer of the
mind, and prayer of the heart.5 Whatever we may think of
this categorization, we can all agree with their assessment
that when we come to the Prayer of the Heart, we have
entered a realm where the Holy Spirit is the initiator. It is
the Holy Spirit who creates this prayer, and it is the Holy
Spirit who sustains it.

In the Prayer of the Heart we have come to the end of our
tether. We are trying to use words, but the words fail us.
We struggle to express our heart and are painfully aware
of how far the expression is from the reality. It is here that
the Holy Spirit steps in with "sighs too deep for words".
We receive from the Spirit the spirit of adoption, through
which we cry, "Abba! Father!" (Rom. 8:17–26).

In the Prayer of the Heart we experience "friendship held
in reverence", to use the phrase of George Buttrick.6 We
are ushered by the Spirit into the profoundest intimacy,
where we become "like a still pool of water able perfectly
to reflect the sun".7

Common Expressions

The ways that the Prayer of the Heart is expressed are as infinite and varied as the mind of God. We must never try to catalogue or categorize these winds of the Spirit too carefully. Even so, it is sometimes helpful to mention some of the more common ways the Holy Spirit moves among his people in the Prayer of the Heart.

Perhaps the most common way of all is through special revelatory impressions and words that the Spirit imparts to the individual. This is often called a *rhema*, Greek meaning simply "word". When Jesus observed that we live not by bread alone but by every word that comes from the mouth of God, he used the word *rhema* (Matt. 4:4). Likewise, when Paul spoke of the word of God as sharper than any two-edged sword, he used the word *rhema* (Eph. 6:17).

When reading the Bible, people commonly experience a special "word in the Word", in which a particular passage seems to apply to an individual situation in a new way. Sometimes I wonder if in such experiences God is working through the creative factor of the brain to bring to the conscious mind wonderful new combinations of ideas and insights. At any rate, this "quickening of the Word" encourages us that God is near and deeply interested in the particular circumstances of our lives.

A special *rhema* also comes to us frequently from other people, in which a divine revelation from God is applied to the specifics of our lives. The result of these experiences is to draw our hearts more and more deeply into the heart of God.

Glossolalia, or speaking in tongues is another expression of the Prayer of the Heart. This experience is quite common and has not been confined to the twentieth century. Nearly all generations and all groups have experienced this charism of the Spirit in some measure from the first century to the present.

There are many reasons and uses for glossolalia, but the most basic of all is for a release of our spirit into the Spirit of God whereby the Spirit prays through us. Spirit touches spirit. While we do not do violence to our rational faculties, we go beyond the rational. We enter the heavenlies by means of a heavenly language that condescends to the use of our feeble, stammering tongues to express the inexpressible.

My first introduction to a "prayer language", as some call it, was quite commonplace. It was many years ago in a simple prayer chalet, the "Quiet Place" at a retreat centre. I was with a trusted friend whom I had asked to teach me more about heart prayer. His main method of teaching was by praying, and so we sat quietly – listening to the Lord, he explained. Soon I was aware of a gentle murmuring of worship and adoration arising from my friend – syllables that made no sense to the conscious mind but that made perfect sense to the spirit.

I listened in reverence. My friend did not try to get me to pray in this way or to make me do anything. I am, by the way, profoundly grateful for this, for I would have avoided any contrived manipulation like the plague.

I spoke nothing audible at the time, but something had been released in my spirit that afternoon, and in the days that followed the charism of glossolalia came forth quite naturally as an ordinary part of my ongoing prayer life.

Another expression of the Prayer of the Heart is what is sometimes referred to as "resting in the Spirit". It is the experience of being taken up by the Spirit's power in such a way that the individual loses consciousness for a time. Some enter a trance-like state; and others lie quietly on the ground or floor.

To my knowledge, when this experience is uncontrived (and there are plenty of charlatans in this realm), it always seems to have beneficial results. Most report a penetrating interior communion and an increase of holy love. Some experience profound inner healing. While I have not personally been privileged to receive this grace, I have watched many who have – a few who simply slip to the floor while I am praying for them. In each case they seem to be perfectly at peace, perfectly at rest. It is as if the Shalom of God settles upon them. Evidently, interior prayer goes on throughout this time; Heart to heart, Spirit to spirit.

"Holy laughter" is still another expression of the Prayer of the Heart. The joy of the Spirit seems simply to well up within a person until there is a bursting forth into high, holy, hilarious laughter. It sometimes is given to the individual in personal prayer, but more frequently it comes upon the gathered community. That is as it should be, for laughter is, after all, a communal experience. To the uninitiated it might appear that these people are drunk, and so they are — with the Spirit. The experience can be stopped, I suppose, but who would want to? The Spirit is refreshing the soul and healing the heart. Often sadnesses and sorrows which have long bowed a person low are healed instantaneously.

Holy laughter is different in kind from good, old-fashioned belly laughter, but they *are* distant cousins! Real laughter, real hilarity — not the cheap stuff that comes at the expense of others — is always from God. It is given for our healing. It is given for our joy. It is given for our wholeness. It is nothing to fear. We know something of the psychology and physiology of ordinary laughter; the holy dimension only intensifies and deepens the reality. It is a grace to be received with joy and thanksgiving.

Some may be puzzled by my examples — *rhema*, glossolalia, resting in the Spirit, holy laughter, and the like. Are these really expressions of prayer? Ordinarily we think of prayer as something we do — something in which we are the initiators or at least active participants. Here it seems as if we are being acted upon more than participating in. How can we call it prayer when we do little beyond receiving?

It is a good question, and I will do my best to answer it. First of all, receiving is not a bad posture when we are entering into communion with the omnipotent Creator of the universe. To be sure, our participation is more passive, but at times that is all we can take. Besides, we are probably participating far more than we know. Even when a person is resting in the Spirit, there may well be a deep, inner communion going on that is much more active and participatory than at any other time. I imagine that our finite human spirit is completely alert and interacting with the infinite Spirit of the universe. We are praying, all right, perhaps praying more truly than ever before.

I must not, however, give the impression that the only expressions of the Prayer of the Heart are in the ecstatic realm, because many are not. Often there is a simple warming of the spirit towards the things of God. We feel more in love with God, more desirous of his presence, more eager to learn his ways. With God as our companion, we become all the more ready to face the demands of the day: looking forward to meetings with others, anticipating work with associates, eagerly awaiting time with children and spouse. This is the ordinary stuff of the Prayer of the Heart.

The Response of Love

In the Prayer of the Heart there is work for us to do, even though it is really only a reflex action to the Spirit's prior initiation upon the heart. But our responsiveness is important and worthy of our attention.

While I am going to share ways we can enter the Prayer of the Heart, I am not talking about methods or techniques. I am talking about nurturing a secret history with the Father. I am talking about developing a familiar friendship with Jesus. Madame Guyon writes, "Teach this simple experience, this prayer of the heart. Don't teach methods; don't teach some lofty way to pray. *Teach the prayer of God's Spirit*, not of man's invention."[8]

The first way of coming into the Prayer of the Heart is by simple love. Love is the response of the heart to the overwhelming goodness of God, so come in simply and speak to him in unvarnished honesty. You may be so awestruck and so full of love at his presence that words do not come. This is all right! It is enough to experience what Brennan Manning calls "the wisdom of accepted tenderness".[9]

You may be given a special love name for God that you can breathe quietly over and over as often as necessary to call you back into his loving presence. Such a love name could be simply, "Abba, Father" or you might use Spurgeon's favourite name for God, taken from the Song of Solomon: "My Well Beloved".

If you have disturbing thoughts, simply return to your special name for God, and the distractions will be driven out. If you must do this fifty times in an hour, you have made fifty beautiful acts of love towards God.

Speak words of love and compassion to the Father. It may feel strange and unnatural at first, for you are not used to loving God. However, in time you will find that love language is perfectly natural to those who are in love.

Falling asleep in prayer is no problem. You can rest in God's presence. Besides, to be next to the heart of God is a good place, a safe place, for sleeping. The anonymous author of The Cloud of Unknowing says to thank God if in prayer you fall asleep unawares.[10]

The prayer "Abba, I belong to you" is a perfect body rhythm prayer. It contains seven syllables that can be spoken easily in one breath. You will be led to other similar prayers.

We are, of course, commanded to love God with all our heart, soul, mind and strength. But you may find it difficult to love God. Every effort seems to leave you cold and hard of heart. You are not moved by God's grace and mercy. You are left untouched by his love and care. What are you to do?

I suggest that you begin by inviting God to kindle a fire of love within you. Ask him to develop an ache in your heart. Then when you are outside of his nearness for any length of time, this ache will begin again in you and will draw you back to his loving presence.

But even this may not be strong enough medicine for you.

Is there anything left to do? Yes, indeed! I commend to you the prayer of John Donne "Batter my heart, three-personed God."[11] This is the first line of a sonnet in which Donne is describing how the goodness and gentleness of God failed to move him to repentance. He pleads with God to use strong-arm tactics to bring him round: "Bend your force to break, blow, burn, and make me new." It is a strong prayer, to be sure, but one that can have startling results.

The Drenching Rain of the Father

I know I have only scratched the surface of the Prayer of the Heart. There is so much further to go, so much more to learn. But I also know that you have a far better Teacher than me, and he will lead you into all truth. The love of the Father is like a sudden rain shower that will pour forth when you least expect it, catching you up into wonder and praise and unspeakable speech. When this happens, do not put up an umbrella to protect yourself but rather stand in the drenching rain of the Father.

———◆———

Abba, dear Abba, you know that the language of love does not come easily to me. I can talk of courage and faith and a whole host of other things more readily than I can of love. In some ways it is easier to give up my body to be burned than to love.

O wine of my heart, intoxicate me with your love.

For Jesus' sake.

— Amen.

Meditative Prayer

Meditation is the tongue of the soul and the language of our spirit.

— Jeremy Taylor

Have you ever watched a cow chew the cud? This unassuming animal will fill its stomach with grass and other food. Then it settles down quietly and through a process of regurgitation reworks what it has received, slowly moving its mouth in the process. In this way it is able fully to assimilate what it has previously consumed, which is then transformed into rich, creamy milk.

So it is with Meditative Prayer. The truth being meditated upon passes from the mouth into the mind and down into the heart, where through quiet rumination — regurgitation, if you will — it produces in the person praying a loving, faith-filled response.

The Jogging Monk

Allow me to tell you the story of Jim Smith, a former student of mine. Genuinely bright Jim went on to do graduate work at a prestigious school on the East Coast of America. By the second year, however, he was struggling to maintain his spiritual life, and so he decided to take a private retreat.

He arrived at the retreat house and was introduced to the brother who was to be his spiritual director for the week. Instantly, Jim was disappointed, for under the brother's habit he noticed jogging shoes . . . Adidas jogging shoes! Jim was expecting a bearded sage filled with the wisdom of the ages, and instead he got a jogging monk!

The brother gave Jim only one assignment: to meditate on the story of the Annunciation in the first chapter of Luke's Gospel. That was it. Jim went back to his room and opened his Bible, muttering to himself, "Birth narrative, I've read it a thousand times." For the first couple of hours he sliced and diced the passage as any good exegete would do, coming up with several useful insights that could fit into future sermons. The rest of the day was spent in thumb-twiddling silence.

The next day Jim met the brother to discuss his spiritual life. He asked Jim how things had gone with the assigned passage. Jim shared his insights, hoping they would impress the monk.

They did not.

"What was your aim in reading the passage?" he asked.

"My aim? To arrive at an understanding of the meaning of the text, I suppose."

"Anything else?"

Jim paused. "No. What else is there?"

"Well, there is more than just finding out what it says and what it means. There are also questions, like what did it say to you? Were you struck by anything? And, most important, did you experience God in your reading?"

The brother assigned Jim the same text for that entire day, urging him to read it as much with his heart as with his head. All day Jim tried doing what his spiritual director had instructed, but he failed repeatedly. By nightfall he practically had the passage memorized, and still it was lifeless. Jim felt he would go deaf from the silence.

The next day they met again. In despair Jim told the brother that he simply could not do what was being asked of him. It was then that the wisdom behind the jogging shoes became evident: "You're trying too hard, Jim. You're trying to control God. Go back to this passage and this time be open to receive whatever God has for you. Don't manipulate God; just receive. Communion with him isn't something you institute. It's like sleep. You can't make yourself sleep, but you can create the conditions that allow sleep to happen. All I want you to do is create the conditions: open your Bible, read it slowly, listen to it and reflect on it."

Jim went back to his room and began reading. Nothing. By noon he shouted out to the ceiling, "I give up! You win!" There was no response, just as he expected. He slumped over the desk and began weeping.

A short time later he picked up his Bible and glanced over the text once again. The words were familiar but somehow different. His mind and heart were supple. The opening words of Mary's response became his words: "Let it be to me . . . let it be to *me*." The words rang round and round in his head. Then God spoke. It was as if a window had suddenly been thrown open and God wanted to talk friend to friend. What followed was a dialogue about the story in Luke, about God, about Mary, about Jim.

The Spirit took Jim down deep into Mary's feelings, Mary's doubts, Mary's fears, Mary's incredible faith-filled response. It was, of course, also a journey into Jim's feelings and fears and doubts, as the Spirit in healing love and gentle compassion touched the broken memories of his past.

Though Jim could barely believe it, the angel's word to Mary seemed to be a word for him as well: "You have found favour with God." Mary's perplexed query was also Jim's question: "How can this be?" And yet it was so, and Jim wept in the arms of a God of grace and mercy.

In the Scripture passage the angel had just informed Mary of her future destiny. What about Jim's future? They talked about this — God and Jim — what might be, what could be. Jim took a prayer walk with God, watching the sun play hide and seek behind the large oak trees to the west. By the time the sun had slipped below the horizon, he was able to utter the prayer of Mary as his own, "Let it be to me according to your word." Jim had just lost control of his life, and in the same moment had found it![1]

Bound to Scripture

Jim's story underscores the most fundamental form of Christian meditation – meditation that is bound to Scripture and also to the great devotional writings. In this chapter we shall focus our attention on this most basic approach to Meditative Prayer.[2] The reason for doing this is simple. We must first have our minds filled with and disciplined by Scripture before we can, with genuine profit, enter into the presence of the Holy in unmediated communion. We are to emulate the faithful described in the Psalm that introduces the Psalter whose "delight is in the law of the LORD, and on his law they meditate day and night" (Ps. 1:2). And throughout history all the devotional masters have viewed the *meditatio Scripturarum*, the meditation upon Scripture, as the central reference point by which all other forms of meditation are kept in proper perspective.

In Meditative Prayer the Bible ceases to be a quotation dictionary and becomes instead "wonderful words of life" that lead us to *the* Word of Life. It differs even from the study of Scripture. Whereas the study of Scripture centres on exegesis, the meditation upon Scripture centres on internalizing and personalizing the passage. The written Word becomes a living word addressed to us. This is a time not for technical studies or analysis or even the gathering of material to share with others. We are to set aside all tendencies towards arrogance and with humble hearts receive the word addressed to us. Often I find kneeling especially appropriate for this particular time. Dietrich Bonhoeffer says, "Just as you do not analyse the words of someone you love, but accept them as they are said to you, accept the Word of Scripture and ponder it in your heart, as Mary did. That is all. That is meditation."[3] When Bonhoeffer founded the seminary at Finkenwalde, everyone there practised a daily half-hour silent meditation upon Scripture.

It is important for us to resist the temptation to pass over many passages superficially. Our rushing reflects our internal state, and our internal state is what needs to be transformed. Bonhoeffer recommends spending a whole week on a single text! Therefore my suggestion is that we take a single event, or a parable, or a few verses, or even a single word and allow it to take root in us.

In meditation we experience what Søren Kierkegaard calls the "contemporaneity" of Scripture. The past does not merely parallel but actually intersects the present. In referring to this reality, the well-known Scottish preacher Alexander Whyte says that the Bible becomes "all over autobiographic of you".[4] In the meditation upon Scripture we cannot, for example, read the story of God's word to Abraham to sacrifice his son Isaac in total detachment, thankful that we are not in his shoes. We are, in point of fact, in his shoes! Along with Abraham we too struggle with the decision to sacrifice the one thing most precious to us. As Abraham did, so we are brought to the place of giving over to God our most cherished possession. And, like Abraham, we come down from the mountain with the meaning of the words my and mine for ever changed.

Sanctifying the Imagination

The simplest and most basic way to meditate upon the text of Scripture is through the imagination. In this regard Alexander Whyte speaks of "the divine offices and the splendid services of the Christian imagination".[5] Perhaps some rare individuals can experience God through abstract meditation alone, but most of us need to be more deeply rooted in the senses.

This is a wonderful aid as we come to the text of Scripture. We are desiring to see, to hear, to touch the biblical narrative. In this simple way we begin to enter the story and make it our own. We move from detached observation to active participation

We must not despise this simpler, more humble route into God's presence. Jesus himself taught in this manner, making constant appeal to the imagination in his parables. Many of the devotional masters likewise encourage us in this way. St Teresa of Avila says, "As I could not make reflection with my understanding I contrived to picture Christ within me. I did many simple things of this kind. I believe my soul gained very much in this way, because I began to practise prayer without knowing what it was."[6] Many of us can identify with her words, for we too have tried a merely cerebral approach and found it too mechanical, too detached.

Even more, the imagination helps to anchor our thoughts and centre our attention. Francis de Sales notes that "by means of the imagination we confine our mind within the mystery on which we meditate, that it may not ramble to and fro, just as we shut up a bird in a cage or tie a hawk by his leash so that he may rest on the hand."[7]

Using the imagination also brings the emotions into the equation, so that we come to God with both mind and heart. It is vitally important to understand the Scripture intellectually, but if we have not felt it emotionally, we have not fully understood it.

Some have objected to using the imagination out of concern that it is untrustworthy and could even be used by the evil one. There is good reason for concern, for the imagination, like all our faculties, has participated in the fall. But just as we believe that God can take our reason (fallen as it is) and sanctify it and use it for his good purposes, so we believe he can sanctify the imagination and use *it* for his good purposes. Of course, the imagination can be distorted by Satan, but then so can all our faculties. God created us with an imagination, and, as Lord of his creation, he can and does redeem it and use it for the work of the kingdom of God.

Another concern about the use of the imagination is the fear of human manipulation and even self-deception. After all, some people have an overactive imagination, and they can concoct all kinds of images of what they would like to see happen. Besides, does not the Bible warn against the vain imaginations of the wicked (Rom. 1:21)?

The concern is legitimate. It is possible for all of this to be nothing more than vain human strivings. That is why it is so vitally important for us to be thrown in utter dependence upon God in these matters. We are seeking to think God's thoughts after him, to delight in his presence, to desire his truth and his way. The more we live in this way, the more God utilizes our imagination for his good purposes. To believe that God can sanctify and utilize the imagination is simply to take seriously the Christian idea of incarnation. God so accommodates, so enfleshes himself into our world, that he uses the images we know and understand to teach us about the unseen world of which we know so little and find so difficult to understand.

Living the Experience of Scripture

In Christian meditation we seek to live the experience of Scripture. Alexander Whyte says:

> You open your New Testament. . . . And, by your imagination, that moment you are one of Christ's disciples on the spot, and are at his feet . . . with your imagination anointed with holy oil . . . at one time, you are the publican: at another time, you are the prodigal . . . at another time, you are Mary Magdalene: at another time, Peter in the porch.[8]

As a practical aid in living the experience of Scripture, Ignatius of Loyola encourages us to apply all our senses to our task. We smell the sea. We hear the lap of water along the shore. We see the crowd. We feel the sun on our heads and the hunger pangs in our stomachs. We taste the salt in the air. We touch the hem of his garment.

Suppose we want to meditate on Jesus' staggering statement "my peace I give to you" (John 14:27). Our task is not so much to study the passage as to be initiated into the reality of which the passage speaks. We brood on the truth that he is now filling us with his peace. The heart, the mind and the spirit are awakened to his inflowing peace.

We sense all motions of fear stilled and overcome by "a spirit of power and of love and of self-discipline" (2 Tim. 1:7). Rather than dissecting peace, we are entering into it. We are enveloped, absorbed, gathered into his peace.

The wonderful thing about such experiences is that the self is quite forgotten. We are no longer worried about how we can make ourselves more at peace, for we are attending to the impartation of peace within our hearts. No longer do we laboriously think up ways to act peacefully, for acts of peace spring spontaneously from within.

So many passages of Scripture provide a touchstone for Meditative Prayer: "Be still and know that I am God"; "Abide in my love"; "I am the good shepherd"; "Rejoice in the Lord always." In each case we are seeking to discover God near us and are longing to encounter his presence.

Remember, in Meditative Prayer God is always addressing our will. Christ confronts us and asks us to choose. Having heard his voice, we are to obey his word. It is this ethical call to repentance, to change, to obedience that most clearly distinguishes Christian meditation from its Eastern and secular counterparts. In Meditative Prayer there is no loss of identity, no merging with the cosmic consciousness, no fanciful astral travel. Rather, we are called to life-transforming obedience because we have encountered the living God of Abraham, Isaac and Jacob. Christ is truly present among us to heal us, to forgive us, to change us, to empower us.

There is a technical word for what I have been describing, and it might be helpful for you to know it – *lectio divina*, (divine reading). This is a kind of reading in which the mind descends into the heart, and both are drawn into the love and goodness of God. Henri Nouwen once pointed to a lovely picture hanging in his apartment, and said to me, "That is *lectio divina*." It depicted a woman with an open Bible in her lap, but her eyes were lifted upward. Do you get the idea? We are doing more than reading words; we are seeking "the Word exposed in the words", to use the phrase of Karl Barth. We are listening with the heart to the Holy within. This prayerful reading, as we might call it, edifies us and strengthens us.

The Wells That Nourish Us

While we always want to affirm Holy Scripture as the first and purest source for *lectio divina*, we can also draw from the great devotional writings that have nurtured Christians throughout the ages.

I almost hesitate to use the phrase devotional writings for some will think I am referring to the trite, fluffy, airy stuff that today passes for devotional writings. Far from it! It is here that we must exercise the wise use of the veto. It is a virtue to be ignorant of vast areas of today's "devotional book" field.

No, I am talking about the kind of writing that has come out of long experience in the desert and long experience in the confessional. It is writing that flows out of those who live on Mount Sinai and still speak to men and women on the level where they live.

The wells that nourish us are vast and deep. You might begin with Gregory of Nyssa's *The Life of Moses*. This book gives guidance in living the virtuous life. For Gregory – and we who follow him – virtue is discovered not so much in the attaining as in the trying, the struggling, the running of the race. We find virtue in the purity of our intentions. The final goal is to become friends with God: "We regard falling from God's friendship as the only thing dreadful and we consider becoming God's friend the only thing worthy of honour and desire. This . . . is the perfection of life."[9] Now that is a goal worth dedicating our lives to, is it not?

You might turn next to the *Confessions* of St Augustine. It is an adventure in itself just to follow Augustine's winding, tortuous path towards emancipation, complete with numerous detours and dead ends. Watch how personal disobedience, institutional evil, and social corruption all work their way into the warp and woof of his life – and ours. "Who," he writes, "can disentangle this most twisted and most inextricable knottiness? It is revolting; I hate to think of it; I hate to look at it."[10]

Study his intellectual pilgrimage from Cicero to the Manicheans, to "the Academics", to Plato, to the Apostle Paul. Notice the steady influence upon Augustine of sterling examples of virtue: Monica, the deceased friend of his youth, Victorinus, Anthony, Ambrose. Thrill to the grace-filled way God ultimately freed him from what he called "the whirlpools of vice" – pride, ambition, sensuality, laziness, prodigality, emulation, fear, vengeance.

After the rigour and struggle of St Augustine you may want to turn to the joyous simplicity of *The Little Flowers of St Francis*. Join Francis, in adoration of God, the Creator of all things, by singing his "Canticle of the Sun", with its celebration of Brother Sun and Sister Moon, Brother Wind and Sister Water. Enjoy the marvellous stories of Brother Bernard and Sister Clare, of Brother Masseo and, my favourite, Brother Juniper. Marvel at the wisdom and good sense in the "Sayings of Brother Giles". To one who was near despair at his dysfunctional behaviour, Giles advises, "You do right in grieving for your sin. However, I advise you to grieve moderately. For you must always believe that God's power to forgive is greater than your power to sin."[11] Whatever we may think about the historicity of the stories, we are better people for having read about these Friars Minor who called themselves God's Jugglers and went about humbly serving others, inebriated with the love of God.

Speaking of the love of God, you might want to turn next to the *Revelations of Divine Love* by Juliana of Norwich. This book contains her mature reflections upon sixteen visions that were given to her on May 8, 1373. It contains some of the most beautiful love language in all religious literature. "Our lover," she writes, "desires that our soul should cling to him with all its might, and that we should ever hold fast to his goodness." We today, who so easily gravitate to a passionless religion, need to hear her words of passion and zeal: "In his love he wraps and holds us. He enfolds us for love, and he will never let us go."[12]

You, of course, will not want to neglect the unchallenged masterpiece of devotional literature for half a millennium, *The Imitation of Christ*. Christians worldwide have been immensely enriched by this simple book which distils the insights of a dynamic spiritual movement in the fifteenth century known as the Brethren of the Common Life. Its surpassing popularity is witnessed to by the fact that it has been translated into more than fifty languages. The book is peppered throughout with pithy sayings that can be lived with for days with genuine profit. Consider this random sampling: "The person who has great peace of heart pays no attention to either praise or blame"; "It is greater work to resist our weaknesses than it is to sweat at manual labour"; "Do not be so quick to follow every good feeling, nor so eager to avoid every bad one"; "The old serpent will tempt you and entice you, but he will be sent packing by prayer, and if you do some useful work in the meantime, you will block his chief approach."[13]

One writer who will expand your horizons to the bruised and broken of humanity is John Woolman. Even though his *Journal* was penned in the eighteenth century, it pinpoints issues we still wrestle with today: racism, consumerism, militarism. After reading Woolman, we will never again be able to separate love of God from love of neighbour, for he rightly saw them as one commandment and not two. Woolman was at the head of a groundswell of anti-slavery conviction that was to assail and eventually abolish the practice of slaveholding among the Quakers nearly 150 years before the American Civil War. Most striking of all is how he blended compassion and courage, tenderness and firmness. Woolman's *Journal* is well worth patient, prayerful reading.

One of the most time-honoured ways of nurturing the spiritual life is by reading the stories of the saints throughout the ages. Through their stories we learn how great Christians walked with God and how we can follow their

lead. There are so many, many places to turn; from *The
Life of Anthony* in the fourth century, to Teresa of Avila's
Autobiography in the fourteenth, to *Toyohiko Kagawa* in
the twentieth. One of the really helpful introductions to
this faith-inspiring cloud of witnesses is James Gilchrist
Lawson's *Deeper Experiences of Famous Christians*.

I shall resist the temptation of going on endlessly with
these wonderful writings that nourish our hearts, in part
because I have yielded to that temptation elsewhere[14] but
also because it is quite possible to drown rather than swim
when first faced with a sea of options. It is far better to
find a few spiritual staples and feed on them until they
have moulded you.

One of the genuinely rewarding experiences in reading
the devotional masters for ourselves is discovering how
readily and how naturally they flow from precise description into the most passionate prayer and then on into
narrative again without the slightest artificiality. I believe
they did this because they experienced work and prayer as a
seamless robe. Pascal declared that his *Pensées* was written
"on his knees". Søren Kierkegaard said of his vocation as
a writer:

> I have literally lived with God as one lives with a Father,
> Amen. . . . I rise up in the morning and give thanks to
> God. Then I begin to work. At a set time in the evening
> I break off and again give thanks to God. Then I sleep.
> Thus do I live.[15]

No wonder St Benedict made *lectio divina* an integral
part of his *Rule* for daily life! Such prayer-filled reading is
given by God to strengthen and empower our lives. As we
read, we will do well to follow the counsel of Thomas à
Kempis: "Search for truth in holy writings, not eloquence.
All holy writing should be read in the same spirit with
which it was written. . . . Do not let the writer's authority
or learning influence you, be it little or great, but let the
love of pure truth attract you to read."[16]

God's Beams of Love

In Meditative Prayer God addresses us personally. This is not something we make happen. Indeed, even the desire to experience the living voice of God is a divine work upon the heart, for we automatically hide from the Hound of Heaven. Thomas Merton writes, "Anyone who imagines he can simply begin meditating without praying for the desire and the grace to do so, will soon give up. But the desire to meditate, and the grace to begin meditating, should be taken as an implicit promise of further graces."[17]

The desire has been given to you, I know, otherwise you would not be reading these words. Further graces will come as they are needed. May God grant you and me the ability to speak from our hearts the words of the Psalmist: "Oh, how I love your law! It is my meditation all day long. . . . How sweet are your words to my taste, sweeter than honey to my mouth!" (Ps. 119:97,103).

Lord, I seek now to meditate on your disturbing words "I came to bring fire to the earth" (Luke 12:49). What do they mean? What do they mean for me?

Are there things in me that need to be burned out . . . pride . . . fear . . . anger? Consume them, each one.

Are there things in this world that you want destroyed – the systems of religion we use to hide from you – the artificial lines we draw that separate us from each other: black from white, men from women, parents from children – the terrible injustices done to the weak and the helpless – the unspeakable violence done to women and to unborn children?

Forgive us O Lord.

For Jesus' sake.

– Amen.

Contemplative Prayer

O my divine Master, teach me this mute
language which says so many things.
                            — Jean-Nicholas Grou

Contemplative Prayer immerses us into the silence of
God. How desperately we in the modern world need
this wordless baptism! We have become, as the early
Church father Clement of Alexandria says, like old shoes
— all worn out except for the tongue. We live in a wordy
world with our sophisticated high-tech telecommunication
systems. We now have the dubious distinction of being able
to communicate more and say less than any civilization in
history.

Isaac of Nineveh, a Syrian monk, once observed, "Those
who delight in a multitude of words, even though they
say admirable things, are empty within."[1] We today stand
under the rebuke of this observation.

Contemplative Prayer is the one discipline that can free
us from our addiction to words. Progress in intimacy with
God means progress towards silence. "For God alone my
soul waits in silence," declares the Psalmist (Ps. 62:1). The
desert father Ammonas, a disciple of St Anthony, writes,

> I have shown you the power of silence, how thoroughly
> it heals and how fully pleasing it is to God. . . . Know that
> it is by silence that the saints grew, that it was because of
> silence that the power of God dwelt in them, because of
> silence that the mysteries of God were known to them.[2]

It is this recreating silence to which we are called in
Contemplative Prayer.

A Warning and a Precaution

At the outset I need to give a word of warning, a little
like the warning labels on medicine bottles. Contemplative
Prayer is not for the novice. I do not say this about any other
form of prayer. All are welcome, regardless of proficiency
or expertise, to enter freely into adoration and meditation
and intercession and a host of other approaches to prayer.
But contemplation is different. While we are all equally
precious in the eyes of God, we are not all equally ready
to listen to "God's speech in his wondrous, terrible, gentle,
loving, all-embracing silence".3

A baby is given milk rather than steak because steak
will do the baby no good. An apprentice electrician is not
allowed to do the tasks of a journeyman because he is not
ready for those tasks, and for him to undertake them could,
in fact, be dangerous.

So it is in the spiritual life. We must learn our multipli-
cation tables before we attempt calculus, so to speak. This
is simply a fact of the spiritual realm and it would be wrong
of me not to tell you about it.

C. S. Lewis tells his friend Malcolm how early in his
Christian experience he attempted wordless prayer with
little success. He writes:

> I still think the prayer without words is the best – if
> one can really achieve it. But I now see that in trying
> to make it my daily bread I was counting on a greater
> mental and spiritual strength than I really have. To pray
> successfully without words one needs to be "at the top
> of one's form".4

Lewis is correct. Contemplative Prayer is for those who
have exercised their spiritual muscles a bit and know
something about the landscape of the spirit. In fact, those
who work in the area of spiritual direction always look for
signs of a maturing faith before encouraging individuals
into Contemplative Prayer. Some of the more common

indicators are a continuing hunger for intimacy with God, an ability to forgive others at great personal cost, a living sense that God alone can satisfy the longings of the human heart, a deep satisfaction in prayer, a realistic assessment of personal abilities and shortcomings, a freedom from boasting about spiritual accomplishments and a demonstrated ability to live out the demands of life patiently and wisely.

It is not that we must be accomplished in these areas. It is that clear progress must be occurring. You may want to ask yourself several questions of examination to help evaluate your own readiness: "Am I becoming less afraid of being known and owned by God?" "Is prayer developing in me as a welcome discipline?" "Is it becoming easier for me to receive constructive criticism?" "Am I learning to move beyond personal offence and freely forgive those who have wronged me?" If, after this small experience of examen, you sense that you are not yet ready for unmediated communion with God, then feel perfectly free to pass over this chapter. Do not worry, a time will come when there will well up within you both a yearning and a readiness to "read the text of the universe in the original".[5]

I also want to give a word of precaution. In the silent contemplation of God we are entering deeply into the spiritual realm, and there is such a thing as supernatural guidance that is not divine guidance. While the Bible does not give us a lot of information on the nature of the spiritual world, we do know enough to recognize that there are various orders of spiritual beings, and some of them are definitely not in cooperation with God and his way!

I say these things not to make you fearful but to make you knowledgeable. You need to know that "like a roaring lion your adversary the devil prowls around, looking for someone to devour" (1 Pet. 5:8). You also need to know that "the one who is in you is greater than the one who is in the world" (1 John 4:4).

In a later chapter we will discuss in considerable detail the spiritual warfare we wage. But for now I want to encourage you to learn and practise prayers of protection. Here is the prayer that Luther used: "Shield us, Lord, with thy right arm. Save us from sin's dreadful harm."6 My own approach is to preface a time of contemplation by speaking this simple prayer: "By the authority of almighty God I surround myself with the light of Christ, I cover myself with the blood of Christ, and I seal myself with the cross of Christ. All dark and evil spirits must now leave. No influence is allowed to come near to me but that it is first filtered through the light of Jesus Christ, in whose name I pray. Amen." These, of course, are only suggestions – you are free to pray in whatever way is most comfortable to you.

A Loving Attentiveness to God

What is it, this experience Richard Baxter referred to as "the soul-rapturing exercise of heavenly contemplation"? Thérèse of Lisieux called it "dreaming of heaven". Nicholas of Cusa called it "the gaze of God". Madame Guyon called it "the prayer of reality".

In its most basic and fundamental expression, Contemplative Prayer is a loving attentiveness to God. We are attending to him who loves us, who is near to us, and who draws us to himself. In Contemplative Prayer talk recedes into the background and feeling comes to the foreground. Richard Rolle was sitting in chapel one day when he "suddenly felt within me an unwonted and pleasant fire".7 Bernard of Clairvaux, that towering religious and political figure of the twelfth century, described his experience of the presence of Jesus this way: "I have felt that he was present; I remember later that he has been with me; I have sometimes even had a presentiment that he would come; but I have never felt his coming or his leaving."8 And John Wesley exclaimed after the famous Moravian meeting at Aldersgate, "I felt my heart strangely warmed. I felt I did trust in Christ, Christ alone for salvation; and an assurance was given me that he had taken away my sins, even mine, and saved me from the law of sin and death."9

Note in each case the affective language. This kind of prayer is obviously more an experience of the heart than of the head. But this stress upon the feelings disturbs us. We have been trained throughout our lives to distrust our feelings, and the very idea that we could gain some knowledge of truth and reality by way of the feelings seems ludicrous.

We must not, however, be too quick to judge. In the first place, the witnesses who encourage us in this way are vast and reputable. Second, they are dealing with something far deeper than mere emotions. In using the language of feeling, contemplatives are referring to a deep experienced sense of God – a kind of inner hearing, if you will. They are seeking simply and faithfully to follow the command of Yahweh: "Incline your ear, and come to me; listen, so that you may live" (Isa. 55:3). It is the entering into this interior communion that contemplatives mean when they speak of feeling.

Besides, our feelings can be disciplined and sanctified by God just as fully as our reason and our imagination can be. Remember, Contemplative Prayer is for seasoned veterans in the life of faith. These are not people who are blown about by every wind of doctrine . . . or every wind of emotion. These are people who long ago walked away from the world, the flesh, and the devil. These are people who by extensive experience know the difference between the enthusiasm of a temporary spiritual high and a settled conviction given by the Spirit. These are people who by repeated trial and error have learned to distinguish the voice of Christ from that of human manipulators.

Union with God

What is the goal of Contemplative Prayer? To this question the old writers answer with one voice: union with God. Juliana of Norwich declares, "The whole reason why we pray is to be united into the vision and contemplation of him to whom we pray."[10] Bonaventure, a follower of St

Francis, says that our final goal is "union with God", which is a pure relationship where we see "nothing".[11] And Madame Guyon writes:

> We come now to the ultimate stage of Christian experience. Divine union. This cannot be brought about merely by your own experience. Meditation will not bring divine union; neither will love, nor worship, nor your devotion, nor your sacrifice. . . . Eventually it will take an *act of God* to make union a reality.[12]

This language reminds us of Jesus' great union statements in the Upper Room discourse: "Abide in me as I abide in you"; "I am the vine, you are the branches"; "I have said these things to you so that my joy may be in you, and that your joy may be complete"; "I ask . . . that they may all be one; as you, Father, are in me and I am in you, may they also be in us" (John 15:4, 5, 11; 17:21).

Union with God does not mean the loss of our individuality. Far from causing any loss of identity, union brings about full personhood. We become all that God created us to be. Contemplatives sometimes speak of their union with God by the analogy of a log in a fire: the glowing log is so united with the fire that it *is* fire, while, at the same time, it remains wood. Others use the comparison of a white-hot iron in a furnace: "Our personalities are transformed, not lost, in the furnace of God's love."[13]

Two Vital Preparations

How do we attain this goal of union with God? While union is entirely a work of God upon the heart, there are two vital preparations from our side of the equation: love of God and purity of heart.

Contemplative Prayer begins in love of God. It is, in fact, the engine that puts the entire enterprise into motion. Put simply, we receive his love for us and love him back in return. Thomas Merton writes:

The message of hope the contemplative offers you is not that you need to find your way through the jungle of language and problems that today surround God: but that ... God loves you, is present in you, lives in you, dwells in you, calls you, saves you, and offers you an understanding and light which are like nothing you ever found in books or heard in sermons.[14]

After we have worked our way through all the obscure, nearly unintelligible language of contemplatives who are struggling to describe the indescribable, we are reduced to the simple confession of Walter Hilton: contemplation is "love on fire with devotion."[15]

As love has its perfect way, it leads us into purity of heart. When we are perpetually bombarded by the rapturous experience of divine love, it is only natural to want to be like the Beloved. The Psalmist declares, "Who shall ascend the hill of the LORD? And who shall stand in his holy place? Those who have clean hands and pure hearts, who do not lift up their souls to what is false, and do not swear deceitfully" (Ps. 24:3–4). And Jesus seconds the motion, "Blessed are the pure in heart, for they will see God" (Matt. 5:8).

Impurity is fatal to union with God. The pure and the impure can never be united. For two things to become one, they need similar natures. For example, the impurity of dirt simply cannot be united with the purity of gold. Fire must be introduced in order to burn out the dross and leave the gold pure. So it is with us. "This is why God sends a fire to the earth," writes Madame Guyon, "to destroy all that is impure in you. Nothing can resist the power of that fire. It consumes *everything*. His Wisdom burns away all the impurities in a man for one purpose: *to leave him fit for divine union*."[16]

In earlier chapters we have explored some of the various pathways that lead to purity of heart, including such things as the disciplines that imitate the life of Christ and "the dark night of the soul". More, I am sure, could be added, but Søren Kierkegaard has brought this issue into its clearest focus with his famous phrase "purity of heart is to will one thing".

And so we do: we will one thing. We relinquish all competing loyalties. We become utterly responsive to the heavenly Monitor. We see only what the Father sees, say only what the Father says, do only what the Father does. We will one thing, which, as Kierkegaard reminds us, is the good, which is God. This is purity of heart.

Learning Recollection

There are three basic steps into Contemplative Prayer, and I find that often people are helped immensely by a simple description of them.

The first has been traditionally called *recollection*. It means a simple recollecting of ourselves until we are unified or whole. Basil Pennington uses the phrase *centring prayer*. Sue Monk Kidd calls it the *prayer of presence*. The old Quakers used the term *centring down*. They all refer to the same experience. The idea is to let go of all competing distractions until we are truly present where we are.

Here is one approach to recollection. Begin by seating yourself comfortably and then slowly and deliberately let all tension and anxiety drop away. Become aware of God's presence in the room. Perhaps you will want to picture Jesus sitting in the chair across from you, for he is indeed truly present.[17] If frustrations or distractions arise, simply lift them up into the arms of the Father and let him care for them. This is not suppressing our inner turmoil but letting go of it. Suppression implies a pressing down, a keeping in check, whereas in recollection we are giving away, releasing. It is even more than a neutral psychological relaxing. It is an active surrendering, a "self-abandonment to divine providence", to use the language of Jean-Pierre de Caussade.

Precisely because the Lord is present with us, we can relax

and let go of everything, for in his presence nothing really matters, nothing is of importance except attending to him. We allow inner distractions and frustrations to melt away before him as snow before the sun. We allow him to calm the storms that rage within by saying, "Peace, be still." We allow his great silence to still our noisy hearts.

I must warn you that this centredness does not come easily or quickly in the beginning. Most of us live such fractured and fragmented lives that collectedness is foreign to us. The moment we try to be genuinely centred we become painfully aware of how distracted we really are. Romano Guardini notes, "When we try to compose ourselves, unrest redoubles in intensity, not unlike the manner in which at night, when we try to sleep, cares or desires assail us with a force that they do not possess during the day."

We must not be discouraged at this. We must be prepared to devote the entire time of contemplation to this recollection without any thought for result or reward. We willingly "waste our time" in this manner as a lavish love-offering to the Father. God will then take what looks like a foolish waste and use it to bring us further into his loving presence. Perceptively Guardini comments, "If at first we achieve no more than the understanding of how much we lack in inner unity, something will have been gained, for in some way we will have made contact with that centre which knows no distraction."[18]

The Prayer of Quiet

As we grow accustomed to the unifying grace of recollection, we are ushered into a second step in Contemplative Prayer, what Teresa of Avila calls "the prayer of quiet". We have through recollection put away all obstacles of the heart, all distractions of the mind, all vacillations of the will. Divine graces of love and adoration wash over us like ocean waves. As this is happening, we experience an inward attentiveness to divine motions. At the centre of our being we are hushed. The experience is more profound than mere silence or lack of words. There is stillness, to be sure, but it is a listening stillness. We feel more alive, more active, than we ever do when our minds are askew with muchness and manyness. Something deep inside us has been awakened and brought to attention. Our spirit is on tiptoe – alert and listening.

There is an inward steady gaze of the heart sometimes called beholding the Lord. We bask in the warmth of his presence. We sense his nearness and his love. James Borst says, "He is closer to my true self than I am myself. He loves me better than I love myself. He is 'Abba', Father, to me. *I am* because HE IS." [19]

On the Mount of Transfiguration the word of God came out of the overshadowing cloud saying, "This is my Son, the Beloved; with him I am well pleased; listen to him." (Matt. 17:5). And so we listen, really listen. We listen with the mind, the heart, the spirit, the bones and muscles and sinew. We listen with the whole being.

François Fénelon says:

> Be silent, and listen to God. Let your heart be in such a state of preparation that his Spirit may impress upon you such virtues as will please him. Let all within you listen to him. This silence of all outward and earthly affection and of human thoughts within us is essential if we are to hear his voice. [20]

This listening does indeed involve a hushing of all "outward and earthly affection". St John of the Cross used the graphic phrase "my house being now all stilled". In that single line he helps us to see the importance of quieting all physical, emotional and psychological senses.

As we wait before the Lord, we are graciously given a teachable spirit. I say "graciously" because without a teachable spirit any word of God that may come to guide us into truth will only serve to harden our hearts. We will resist any and all instruction unless we are docile. But if we are truly willing and obedient, the teaching of the Lord is life and light. The goal, of course, is to bring this stance of listening prayer into the course of everyday experience. This does not come to us immediately. However, over time we experience more and more an inward attentiveness to the Divine Whisper throughout all life's motions – balancing the cheque book, vacuuming the floor, visiting neighbours or business associates.

Spiritual Ecstasy

The final step into Contemplative Prayer is spiritual ecstasy. Ecstasy is quite different from the other two steps I have mentioned in that it is not an activity we undertake but a work that God does upon us. Our responsibility here is to have a continuous openness and receptivity for the Spirit to rest upon us. Beyond this, the matter of ecstasy is God's business and not ours.

No doubt you remember the Apostle Paul's experience of being caught up into the third heaven where he heard things that he was not permitted to share (2 Cor. 12:1–5). But you may not be as well acquainted with the lovely experience of St Augustine and his mother, Monica, while at the city of Ostia on the Tiber river. Allow me to share it with you.

The two of them were leaning out of a window, looking at a beautifully manicured garden and discussing the goodness of life in the kingdom of God. Augustine writes, "With the mouth of our heart we panted for the heavenly streams of your fountain, the fountain of life." As they were talking, however, words failed them, and they were raised

higher and step by step passed over all material things, even the heaven itself from which sun and moon and stars shine down upon the earth. And still we went upward, meditating and speaking and looking with wonder at your works, and we came to our own souls, and we went beyond our souls to reach that region of never-failing plenty where *Thou feedest Israel* forever with the food of truth.

After describing this unusual experience of spiritual ecstasy, Augustine notes, "We sighed and left captured there the firstfruits of our spirits and made our way back to the sound of our voices, where a word has both beginning and end."[21]

Augustine's experience, while certainly unusual, is not unique. Listen to this witness of Theodore Brakel, a Dutch Pietist in the seventeenth century:

> I was . . . transported into such a state of joy and my thoughts were so drawn upward that, seeing God with the eyes of my soul, I felt one with him. I felt myself transported into God's being and at the same time I was so filled with joy, peace, and sweetness, that I cannot express it. With my spirit I was entirely in heaven for two or three days.[22]

Ecstasy is Contemplative Prayer taken to the nth degree. Even the recognized authorities in the contemplative life found it a fleeting experience rather than their staple diet. And it may be just a little more than you – or I – would bargain for, and that is all right, for this is not really something we do but something God gives – and then only when he knows we are ready. Besides, it could well be that all this lofty talk of contemplation is discouraging to you. Perhaps you feel miles away from such experiences. Rather than attempting to scale the heights of spiritual ecstasy, you are hoping just to be able to get through the next week.

If that in some measure describes your feelings, do not be disheartened. I had some of those very feelings writing this chapter, for I feared I was on the edge of unlived truth. Many times we all fall miserably short of our goal. Often our attempts at listening prayer never seem to get past our frustration over the unwashed dishes in the sink or the chemistry exam tomorrow. But what little we have experienced encourages us, for we have glimpsed the loving heart of God, all full of grace and mercy, welcoming us to the Communion table of the Spirit.

One final note of encouragement about Contemplative Prayer. One of its great values comes when we are at the sunset of life and our rational faculties begin to falter. A time may come when we are no longer able to utter words, but – and here is the glory – we are still able to pray, to pray without words. At the end of life, as at the beginning, we find ourselves, in the words of Gerhard Tersteegen, "looking at God, who is ever present, and letting him look on us".[23]

My Lord and my God, listening is hard for me. I do not mean exactly hard for I understand that this is a matter of receiving rather than trying. What I mean is that I am so action-oriented, so product driven, that doing is easier for me than being. I need your help if I am to be still and listen. I would like to try. I would like to learn how to sink down into the light of your presence until I can become comfortable in that posture.

Help me to try now.

Thank you.

– Amen.

PART III

Moving Outward
Seeking the Ministry We Need

Transformation and intimacy both cry out for ministry. We are led through the furnace of God's purity not just for our own sake but for the sake of others. We are drawn up into the bosom of God's love not merely to experience acceptance, but also so we can give his love to others.

The world writhes under the pain of its arrogance and self-sufficiency. We can make a difference, if we will.

In earlier days we tried to serve out of our spiritual bankruptcy, and we failed. We now know that ministry must flow out of abundance.

Bernard of Clairvaux writes,

> If then you are wise, you will show yourself rather as a reservoir than as a canal. For a canal spreads abroad water as it receives it, but a reservoir waits until it is filled before overflowing, and thus communicates, without loss to itself, its superabundant water. In the Church at the present day, we have many canals, few reservoirs.

We have determined to be reservoirs.

Praying the Ordinary

*Do not forget that the value and interest of life is
not so much to do conspicuous things . . . as to
do ordinary things with the perception of their
enormous value.*

— Teilhard de Chardin

Many of us today live in a kind of inner apartheid. We
segregate out a small corner of pious activities and then
can make no spiritual sense out of the rest of our lives. We
have become so accustomed to this way of living that we fail
to see the contradiction in it. The scandal of Christianity in
our day is the heresy of a 5 per cent spirituality.

We overcome this modern heresy by Praying the Ordinary. We pray the ordinary in three ways: first by turning
ordinary experiences of life into prayer; second by seeing
God in the ordinary experiences of life; and third by praying
throughout the ordinary experiences of life.

The Sanctity of the Ordinary

I would like to tell you of the death of my mother, Marie
Temperance Foster. I was a teenager and she at midlife, or
so we thought. Her death, however, was far from sudden or
dramatic. At first no one knew what was wrong — Mum just
had difficulty walking. In time her condition was diagnosed
as multiple sclerosis, though no one seemed really certain.
She grew slowly worse. I sometimes discovered her up at
5 a.m., trying to vacuum the floor. She would struggle to
clean a small patch of carpet and then slump on to the sofa,
exhausted. After a brief rest she was up and working on
another patch.

As her condition worsened, we three brothers took over the duties of daily life. Actually, it wasn't so bad because Mum always cheered us on, and complaint did not seem to be in her vocabulary. When she became bedridden, we set up a hospital bed in the living-room. I had become a Christian by this time, and one of my earliest prayers was for her healing. It was not to be.

Soon I was off to college a thousand miles away. Mum was now in the hospital. Three times in that first year I rushed home because the medical staff called saying the end was near. But each time she would rally a bit, and the dark tragedy of death would be replaced by the untheatrical regularity of the uneventful. Finally, my elder brother and I made the hard practical decision that I was not to be notified until Mum had died.

As it turned out, I was home on summer break. Did she know somehow? I was the last one to visit her. For months we were not sure she recognized any of us when we visited, since all speech and physical response was mute. But on that last visit she squeezed my hand. I'm glad for that.

But I was not there when she slipped into eternity. She had been so close for so long that the idea of a vigil was simply not reasonable. It was 2 a.m., and she was completely alone ... except possibly for the angels of God. She simply stopped breathing. That is what the medical staff said. Actually her leaving was so quiet, so uneventful, that they did not discover it until later.

Perhaps that is as it should be. So much about my mother was uneventful and ordinary. There was no spectacular drama, no newspaper headline, no high adventure. She lived an ordinary life and died an ordinary death.

But she did both well. She loved my father well, and she loved us kids well. She lived through the drab terrain of the ordinary with grace and gentleness. She accepted her slowly deteriorating condition with a noble faith. She received death as she had life and disability: with patience and courage. My mother understood the sanctity of the ordinary.

The Holiness of Created Things

The Bible is almost casual in its assertion that "God created the heavens and the earth ... and indeed, it was very good" (Gen. 1:1, 31). Then, in the fullness of time, God reinforced and intensified this reality by choosing birth in a stable as his ultimate revelation. How the shepherds must have wondered at the twofold sign by which they were to identify Messiah — swaddling cloths and a manger. How unimpressive! How commonplace!

But think of this: in the creation and the incarnation the great God of the universe intertwined the spiritual and the material, wedded the sacred and the secular, sanctified the common and the ordinary. How astonishing! How wonderful!

The discovery of God lies in the daily and the ordinary, not in the spectacular and the heroic. If we cannot find God in the routines of home and shop, then we will not find him at all. Ours is to be a symphonic piety in which all the activities of work and play and family and worship and sex and sleep are the holy habitats of the eternal. Thomas Merton urges us to have an "unspeakable reverence for the holiness of created things".[1]

Prayer in Action

Jesus, we must remember, spent most of his earthly life in what we would call a blue collar job. He did not wait until his baptism in the Jordan to discover God. Far from it! Jesus validated the reality of God over and over in the carpentry shop before speaking of the reality of God in his ministry as a rabbi.

Many today see their vocation as a hindrance to prayer. "If only I had some time free from the distractions of work, then I could pray" is a common sentiment. But prayer is not another duty to add to an already over-committed schedule. In Praying the Ordinary, our vocation, far from being a hindrance, is an asset.

How is this so? Is it that we learn the secret of praying as we work? Certainly this is important, but it is not why our work is such an asset to prayer. Our vocation is an asset to prayer because our work *becomes* prayer. It is prayer in action. The artist, the novelist, the surgeon, the plumber, the secretary, the lawyer, the homemaker, the farmer, the teacher – all are praying by offering their work up to God.

"Whether you eat or drink, or whatever you do, do everything for the glory of God" is St Paul's counsel (1 Cor. 10:31). I came into a fuller understanding of this counsel when, as a teenager, I was privileged to spend a summer among the Eskimo people of Kotzebue, Alaska. The Eskimo Christians I met there had a deep sense of the wholeness of life with no break between their prayer and their work.

I had come to Kotzebue on the adventure of helping to "build the first high school above the Arctic Circle", but the work itself was far from an adventure. It was hard, backbreaking labour. One day I was trying to dig a trench for a sewer line – no small task in a world of frozen tundra. An Eskimo man whose face and hands displayed the leathery toughness of many winters came by and watched me for a while. Finally he said simply and profoundly, "You are digging a ditch to the glory of God." He said it to encourage me, I know. And I have never forgotten his words. Beyond my Eskimo friend no human being ever knew or cared whether I dug that ditch well or poorly. In time it was to be covered up and forgotten. But because of my friend's words, I dug with all my might, for every shovelful of dirt was a prayer to God. Even though I did not know it at the time, I was attempting in my small and unsophisticated way to do what the great artisans of the Middle Ages did when they carved the back of a piece of art, knowing that God alone would see it.

Anthony Bloom writes, "A prayer makes sense only if it is lived. Unless they are 'lived,' unless life and prayer become completely interwoven, prayers become a sort of polite madrigal which you offer to God at moments when you are giving time to him."[2] The work of our hands and of our minds is acted-out prayer, a love offering to the living God. In what is perhaps the finest line in the movie *Chariots of Fire*, Olympic runner Eric Liddell tells his sister, "Jenny, when I run, I feel his pleasure." This is the reality that is to permeate all vocations whether we are writing a novel or cleaning a latrine.

It is at the latrine cleaning that many have a problem. It is not hard to see how a Michelangelo or a T. S. Eliot is giving glory to God — theirs are creative vocations. But what about the boring jobs, the unimportant jobs, the mundane jobs. How are those prayer?

Here we must understand the order in the kingdom of God. It is precisely in the "slop-bucket job" — the work that we abhor — where we will find God the most. We do not need to have good feelings or a warm glow in order to do work for the glory of God. All good work is pleasing to the Father. Even the jobs that seem meaningless and mindless to us are highly valued in the order of the kingdom of God. God values the ordinary. If, for the glory of God, you are putting an endless supply of nuts on an endless line of bolts, your work is rising up as a sweet-smelling offering to the throne of God. He is pleased with your labour.

"Aren't you glorifying work a bit too much — you know, Protestant work ethic and all?" you may be wondering. I think not. Work came before the fall, and the curse of the fall was that work would be "by the sweat of your brow" — that is, the results would not be commensurate with the labour put in. In fact, one of the clearest signs of the grace of God upon us is when the results of our labour are far in excess of the amount of work we do. We glorify God in our labour because we most closely approximate the Creator when we engage in the creative activity of work.

"But what about those who have no jobs, the unemployed and the retired? How do they Pray the Ordinary?" you may ask. We can all work whether we have employable skills or not. Remuneration is not a factor in deciding the value of labour in the kingdom of God. If our abilities or opportunities allow for nothing more than picking up sticks, we are to do so with all our might to the glory of God and the good of our neighbour.

"Can a person live a full, satisfying life that glorifies God without work?" you may question. I do not know how. Certainly all things are possible with God, but I am sure such a thing would be the exception and not the rule. In fact, I value labour as a reflection of the image of God within us so much that my personal conviction is that part of the bliss of heaven will be joyous, creative, productive work.

The Prayer of Action

We are also Praying the Ordinary when we engage in what Jean-Nicholas Grou calls "the prayer of action". "Every action performed in the sight of God because it is the will of God, and in the manner that God wills, is a prayer and indeed a better prayer than could be made in words at such times."[3]

Each activity of daily life in which we stretch ourselves on behalf of others is a prayer of action – the times when we scrimp and save in order to get the children something special; the times when we share our car with others on rainy mornings, leaving early to get them to work on time; the times when we keep up correspondence with friends or answer one last telephone call when we are dead tired at night. These times and many more like them are lived prayer. Ignatius of Loyola notes, "Everything that one turns in the direction of God is prayer."[4]

Then, too, we are Praying the Ordinary when we see God in the ordinary experiences of life. Can we find meaning in the crayon marks on the wall made by the kids? Are they somehow the finger of God writing on the wall of our hearts?

Waiting is part of ordinary time. We discover God in our waiting: waiting in checkout queues, waiting for the telephone to ring, waiting for graduation, waiting for a promotion, waiting to retire, waiting to die. The waiting itself becomes prayer as we give our waiting to God. In waiting we begin to get in touch with the rhythms of life – stillness and action, listening and decision. They are the rhythms of God. It is in the everyday and the commonplace that we learn patience, acceptance and contentment. St Benedict's criterion for allowing a visitor to stay at the monastery is that "he is content with the life as he finds it, and does not make excessive demands . . . but is simply content with what he finds".[5]

I am attracted to this "contentment without excessive demands" because it is the way I would really like to live. In a world in which *Winning Through Intimidation* is the order of the day, I am attracted to people who are free from the tyranny of assertiveness.[6] I am drawn to those who are able simply to meet people where they are, with no need to control or manage or make them do anything. I enjoy being around them because they draw the best out in me without any manipulation whatsoever.

Another way of Praying the Ordinary is by praying throughout the ordinary experiences of life. We pick up a newspaper and are prompted to whisper a prayer of guidance for world leaders facing monumental decisions. We are chatting to friends in a school corridor or a shopping precinct, and their words prompt us to lapse into prayer for them, either verbally or silently as the circumstances dictate. We jog through our neighbourhood, blessing the families who live there. We plant our garden, thanking the God of heaven for sun and rain and all good things. This is the stuff of ordinary prayer through ordinary experience.

Holiness is Homemade

Prayers arising out of the context of the family are perhaps the most common expression of Praying the Ordinary. Edward Hays, in *Prayers for the Domestic Church*, provides a whole host of prayers that can be participated in by the

entire family, whether large or small. It includes everything
from "Blessing Prayer for an Automobile" to "Prayer for
Protection in a Time of Storm or Danger" to "Prayer of a
Single Parent".7 As we pray in the context of the family, we
learn that holiness is homemade. The earliest altar was the
hearth whose open fire burned in the centre of the home.
Even today the family table can be a significant altar where
meals are celebrated and all the great and small events of
our personal histories can be recounted. Here mothers and
fathers fulfil the priestly role.

We can also establish a "hermitage" in our home. A
hermitage is a house specially set aside for silence and
solitude. In old Russia every village had its hermitage, or
poustinia. We today lack such a religious sanctuary in the
community, which argues all the more for having one in
the home. It could be a den or a study or an attic room. It
could be almost any quiet place in the home, which, when
being used as a hermitage, remains off limits to the rest of
the family.

Single-parent households often need different kinds of
community structures to make these things work. It sometimes helps for various households to gather for periodic
meals and activities. In this way single people, single parent
families, couples without children, and nuclear families can
all be enriched by the presence of one another.

Some families have been helped and strengthened by
experiences of a "family altar" – gathered times of Bible
reading and prayer. Others have found such a practice
extremely difficult, if not impossible, to maintain, and they
experience considerable guilt over the omission. The guilt
is unnecessary, for these things, by and large, represent a
change in cultural patterns more than a lack of piety in the
family. When farming communities and large families were
predominant and gathering for meals and evening activities
was common, this kind of family altar made perfect sense.
For most of us, however, those days are gone. We live in
urban surroundings and belong to small families. We eat
out at fast food restaurants much of the time and have

to contend with ballet lessons and football practice and PTA meetings all in the same evening.

Question: what are we to do? Answer: the best we can! Try "blessing prayers" as the kids run out of the door and "thank-you prayers" as they return. Before the teen years it is especially appropriate to pray over them at night. This can be done both before they go to sleep and again after they are asleep. We can pray for the healing of any emotional traumas of the day; and we always add prayers of protection for the long night and the day to come.

One ancient custom that can be traced back to the early days of the Christian Church was for the children to ask the father for a blessing every evening before retiring. We may find the patriarchal character of that custom hard to swallow, but parents – and grandparents – can bless little ones. Let them jump into your lap, read them a story, and give them – each and every one – a well-thought-out blessing. On occasion you may want to rock your child to sleep, all the while singing your blessing.

The teen years demand adjustments. Usually teenagers do not want you in their room, they do not want to be touched, and they do not like family prayers! Even though the nature of demonstrative prayer must often be changed, you can pray for them always in your heart. Also you will find that the content of what you pray will change. More and more you will be speaking prayers of release for they are trying to cut the emotional umbilical cord, and you must help them.

Often these are times of tension for teenagers are struggling to define themselves. They may have to reject your beliefs for a time in order to reclaim them as their own. In our case, for example, both boys went to different churches from us during their teenage years in order to have the emotional space to explore their own faith experience.

If you have teenagers, I want to offer you a word of encouragement. I know these years are often turbulent – a little like a rubber raft going through a series of rapids. And I know it feels as if the rapids are heading straight to a disastrous waterfall. But more often than not there is no waterfall on this river, and the water is smooth and calm on the other side. Regardless, we pray for our children as they go through the rapids, and we pray for our children for what comes after the rapids. In so doing we are Praying the Ordinary.

The Common Ventures of Life

All of us share in what D. Elton Trueblood calls "the common ventures of life" – birth, marriage, work, death.[8] Jesus, in his life and in his teaching, gave sacramental significance to these ordinary experiences of daily life. In his own birth the common and the sacred have been for ever united. He rejoiced in the wedding of a couple in Galilee and added wine to the sacred festivities. He rubbed shoulders with fishermen and tax collectors and other entrepreneurial types. And he stared-out death without flinching so that we can face our own death with hope.

Because of this rock-solid foundation, we know that all work is holy work and all places are sacred places. Therefore we lift our voices in joyful song, declaring, "This is holy ground, We're standing on holy ground; For the Lord is present, And where he is is holy. These are holy hands, He's given us holy hands; He works through these hands, And so these hands are holy."[9]

Almighty, most holy, most high God, thank you for paying attention to small things. Thank you for valuing the insignificant. Thank you for being interested in the lilies of the field and the birds of the air. Thank you for caring about me.

In Jesus' name.

– Amen.

Petitionary Prayer

Whether we like it or not, asking is the rule of the Kingdom.

– C. H. Spurgeon

Do you know why the mighty God of the universe chooses to answer prayer? It is because his children ask. God delights in our asking. He is pleased at our asking. His heart is warmed by our asking.

Our Staple Diet

When our asking is for ourselves it is called petition; when it is on behalf of others it is called intercession. Asking is at the heart of both experiences.

We must never negate or demean this aspect of our prayer experience. Some have suggested, for example, that while the less discerning will continue to appeal to God for aid, the real masters of the spiritual life go beyond petition to adoring God's essence with no needs or requests whatever. In this view our asking represents a more crude and naïve form of prayer, while adoration and contemplation are a more enlightened and high-minded approach, since they are free from any egocentric demands.

This, I submit to you, is a false spirituality. Petitionary Prayer remains primary throughout our lives because we are for ever dependent upon God. It is something that we never really "get beyond" nor should we even want to. In fact, the Hebrew and Greek words that are generally used for prayer mean "to request" or "to make a petition".[1] The Bible itself is full of Petitionary Prayer and unabashedly recommends it to us.

When the disciples requested instruction about prayer, Jesus gave them the greatest prayer ever uttered – what we today call The Lord's Prayer – and it is mainly petitionary. He urged his disciples to "ask, and it will be given you; search, and you will find; knock, and the door will be opened for you. For everyone who asks receives, and everyone who searches finds, and for everyone who knocks, the door will be opened" (Matt. 7:7–8).

I know that many of our petitions seem immature and self-absorbed. In one sense it would be less problematic to stay with worship and adoration and contemplation. These things feel elevated, stately, noble. And Christianity would be, intellectually, a far easier religion if it kept us on this "lofty" plane. Then we would not have to be dealing constantly with the frustration of unanswered prayer and the embarrassment of those who seek to engineer God for their own ends. Yes, we might like the less crude realms of adoration and contemplation, but as P. T. Forsyth observes, "Petitions that are less than pure can only be purified by petition."[2] Besides, Jesus keeps drawing us into the most basic relationship of child and parent, to asking and receiving. Hans Urs von Balthasar writes, "It is quite wrong to subordinate *oratio* to *contemplatio*, as if vocal prayer were more for beginners and contemplative prayer more for the advanced, for each pole determines and presupposes the other; the one leads directly to the other."[3]

Petition, then, is not a lower form of prayer. It is our staple diet. In a childlike expression of faith we bring our daily needs and desires to our heavenly Father. None of us would give our children a stone if they asked for bread, says Jesus. None of us would give them a snake if they requested fish. No, even we who are filled with our own self-centred agendas respect the most fundamental codes of parent-child relationships. All the more, then, God who lovingly respects us and joyfully gives to us when we ask (Matt. 7:9–11).

Two Common Problems

By focusing on this basic parent–child relationship, we get
light on two of the most common problems in Petitionary
Prayer. The first is the very reasonable question of why
we should ask God for things when he already knows our
needs. The most straightforward answer is simply that God
likes to be asked. We like our children to ask us for things
that we already know they need because the very asking
enhances and deepens the relationship. P. T. Forsyth notes,
"Love loves to be told what it knows already. . . . It wants
to be asked for what it longs to give."4

Besides, I am not so sure that God knows everything
about our petition. It seems that God has freely chosen to
allow the dynamic of the relationship to determine what
we will eventually ask. The fact that God is all-knowing –
omniscient, as we say – does not preclude his withholding
judgment on matters in which the decision depends on the
give and take of the relationship. More will be said about
this in a later chapter. For now, be encouraged that God
desires authentic dialogue, and that as we speak what is
in our hearts we are sharing real information that God is
deeply interested in.

A second problem with Petitionary Prayer arises from
those of tender heart. It is the deference of spirit that says,
in effect, "I shouldn't bother God with the petty details of
my life. There are issues of far greater consequence in the
world than my little needs."

But here we must see the Abba heart of God. In
one important sense nothing is more important to him
than the anxiety we feel over the surgery we must face
tomorrow and the exasperation we feel today over our
child's irresponsibility and the desperation we feel over
the plight of our ageing parents. These are matters of
great magnitude to him because they are matters of great
magnitude to us. It is a false humility to stand back and
not share our deepest needs. His heart is wounded by our
reticence. Just as we long for our own children to share

with us the petty details of their day at school, so God longs to hear from us the smallest matters of our lives. It delights him when we share.

The Perplexity of Unanswered Prayer

We now come to what has to be one of the most troubling issues of Petitionary Prayer, namely unanswered prayer. We must not rush too quickly here to solve this problem with glib talk about God answering with "yes, no, or wait," and the like. If we are honest, and not just trying to cover up our insecurity, we must all admit to deep perplexity over these things. C. S. Lewis notes, "Every war, every famine or plague, almost every death-bed, is the monument to a petition that was not granted."5

The problem is intensified when we consider the lavish promises to answers contained in the New Testament, especially in the words of Jesus. Consider, for example, his startling statement found in Mark 11:24: "I tell you, whatever you ask for in prayer, believe that you have received it, and it will be yours." The gloriousness of the promise is tempered by the empirical data of our personal prayer lives. What can we say to this vexing problem?

The first thing we must confess is that we have a genuine, not an imagined, problem. Any supposed solutions that I or anyone else, give are only partial and will not make the problem go away. I do not know why the heartfelt petition of a terminally ill person or a homeless person goes unanswered. Frankly I wish it were otherwise. We stand here under the mystery of the ways of God, and we are peering through a glass darkly. Only in the age to come will we understand fully, even as we are fully understood (1 Cor. 13:12).

Actually it is from the vantage point of the age to come – to the extent that we can understand that perspective – that we get our first hint of a solution to the problem of unanswered prayer. P. T. Forsyth observes perceptively, "We shall come one day to a heaven where we shall gratefully know that God's great refusals were sometimes the true answers to our truest prayer."6 Many times in our shortsightedness we ask for things that are not in our best interests. At other times the answer to our prayers would be detrimental to others, or mean the refusal of their prayers, or both. Then there are times when our prayers are simply self-contradictory, a "grant me patience quickly" kind of prayer. And finally, sometimes our prayers, if answered, would do us in. We are not yet prepared for what we have asked.

In such cases, and many others like them, it is God's grace and mercy that prevent our prayers from being answered. God withholds his gifts from us for our good. We could not handle what might come if our requests were granted. So we must thank God that many of our prayers go unanswered. C. S. Lewis writes, "If God had granted all the silly prayers I've made in my life, where should I be now?"7

Another reality to keep in mind is the simple fact that many times our prayers are indeed answered, but we lack the eyes to see it. God understands the deeper intent of our prayers and so responds to this greater need which, in its time and in its way, solves our specific prayer concern. We may ask for greater faith so that we can heal others, but God, who understands human need far better than we do, gives us greater compassion so that we can weep with others. A part of our petition must always be for an increasing discernment so that we can see things as God sees them.

We must also confess how little we know of the ways and timing of God. Sometimes we, like the disciples of old, want to rain down fire from heaven upon God's enemies. (Of course they always turn out to be our enemies too, which works out quite well for us.) But Jesus makes it abundantly clear that fire from heaven is simply not God's way (Luke 9:54). On other occasions our finger-tapping anxiety is simply out of timing with the ever-patient mercy of the Eternal.

Then, too, we must remember that, since Petitionary

Prayer centres on us and our needs, we are not disinterested parties. It is far easier to pray with clarity regarding matters that have no direct impact upon us than regarding our infected toe. This must never keep us from praying for our own needs, for we are commanded to do so, but it should remind us that we are capable of infinite self-deception.

There is one further thing I want to say about unanswered prayer though I hesitate to mention it for fear of being misunderstood. It is the fact that sin hinders our prayers. By saying this I am not endorsing the highly misleading cliché, "God never hears a sinner's prayer." If that were actually the case, we would all be in real trouble! Nor do I mean that we must attain some special level of holiness before the Almighty will respond to our pleas. Simple observation alone will show that God is quite lavish in his answering mercy to all kinds and sorts of people irrespective of their sanctity. My own personal history confirms as much.

No, I mean something quite different when I say that sin hinders our prayers. I mean that our sin, by its very nature, separates us from God, rupturing the intimate fellowship and dulling our spiritual sensitivities. We become nearsighted and we develop thickened eardrums, if you will. The result is an inability to discern the heart of God and an asking that is askew. We ask wrongly, to spend it on our passions, as James reminds us (James 4:3). Therefore our prayers are hindered.

God tells me, for example, to act lovingly towards my neighbour, perhaps inviting him over for dinner. I decide against it mainly because I am annoyed with him because his tree dropped leaves in my garden! God reminds me about my resentment towards my neighbour more than once. I do nothing. In time, I do not hear God speaking to me about my neighbour any more, and I think to myself, "Good, I got away with that one!" Oh no, I didn't. Deafness has come, in part. Blindness has come, in part. The dulling of our spiritual sensitivities is something I hope we will come to fear.

I know that these few comments will not erase the dilemma you feel over unanswered prayer. Many times I too stand in perplexity at prayers that seem to be ignored. It may encourage us to know that we have a Saviour who, in the darkness of Gethsemane, shouldered the weight of unanswered prayer and in his moment of greatest agony shared our confused question: "Why?"

The Paternoster

For sheer power and majesty no prayer can equal the Paternoster, the "Our Father" (Matt. 6:9–13). As I mentioned earlier, today we call it the Lord's Prayer, though that distinction more rightly belongs to the high priestly prayer of Jesus in the Upper Room (John 17). The Paternoster is the prayer given by the Lord for disciples of the Lord, namely you and me.

The Paternoster is really a total prayer. Its concerns embrace the whole world, from the coming of the kingdom to daily bread. Large things and small things, spiritual things and material things, inward things and outward things – nothing is beyond the purview of this prayer.

It is lifted up to God in every conceivable setting. It rises from the altars of the great cathedrals and from obscure shanties in unknown places. It is spoken both by children and by kings. It is prayed at weddings and death-beds alike. The rich and the poor, the intelligent and the illiterate, the simple and the wise – all speak this prayer. As I prayed it this morning at my spiritual formation group, I was joining with the voices of millions around the world who pray in this way each day. It is such a complete prayer that it seems to reach all people at all times in all places.

The Lord's Prayer is essentially petitionary – asking. Adoration is present at the beginning and the end, but petition is present through the main body of the prayer. Of its seven perfectly crafted requests, three relate to personal petition. These three entreaties can be gathered up into three words: give, forgive, and deliver. Together they form a paradigm for Petitionary Prayer by which we can conjugate all the verbs of our individual asking.

Give

If we were not so familiar with the Lord's Prayer, we would be astonished at the petition for daily bread. If it had come from the lips of any other than Jesus himself, we would consider it an intrusion of materialism upon the refined realm of prayer. But here it is smack in the middle of the greatest of prayers: "Give us this day our daily bread."

When we think about it for a moment though, we realize that this prayer is completely consistent with Jesus' pattern of living, for he occupied himself with the trivialities of humankind. He provided wine for those who were celebrating, food for those who were hungry, rest for those who were weary (John 2:1–12; 6:1–14; Mark 6:31). He went out of his way to find the "little people": the poor, the sick, the powerless. So it is fully in order that he invites us to pray for daily bread.

In doing so Jesus has transfigured the trivialities of everyday life. Try to imagine what our prayer experience would be like if he had forbidden us to ask for the little things. What if the only things we were allowed to talk about were the weighty matters, the important things, the profound issues? We would be orphaned in the cosmos, cold and terribly alone. But the opposite is true: he welcomes us with our 1001 trifles, for they are each important to him.

We pray for daily bread by taking to God those trifles that make up the bulk of our days. Are we unable to find a babysitter to care for the children while we are at work? Well then, we pray for daily babysitters. Do we need a little space to think things out? Then we pray for daily solitude and rest. Is it a warm sweater or gloves that we need because of the bitter cold? We ask for clothing, day by day. Are we struggling with a relationship at work or at home? We ask for patience and wisdom and compassion – daily, hourly. This is how we pray for daily bread.

Forgive

I am constantly amazed that the petition "give" precedes the petition "forgive" and not vice versa. It is as if God's graciousness in giving to us allows us to see the enormous debt we owe and leads us to cry out, "Forgive us our debts."

The debts are enormous indeed. It is not just the things that we do, though those by themselves are enough. It is also the things we leave undone. We commit sins of commission and sins of omission. The mountain of offences grows too high for us – its very weight threatens to crush the life out of us.

It is just when we are gasping for breath that Jesus invites us to pray: "Forgive us our debts." He teaches us in this way because he knows how very much God loves to forgive. It is the one thing he yearns to do, aches to do, rushes to do. At the very heart of the universe is God's desire to give and to forgive.

But in this petition we are faced with a quandary. We are taught to pray: "forgive us our debts, as we also have forgiven our debtors." It is a conditional request. We are forgiven as we forgive. And, as if to intensify the problem, this is the only petition that Jesus feels compelled to amplify upon, "For if you forgive others their trespasses, your heavenly Father will also forgive you; but if you do not forgive others, neither will your Father forgive your trespasses" (Matt. 6:14–15). Why is this? It is not that God begrudges his forgiveness, nor is it so hard to get God to forgive that we must demonstrate good faith by showing how well we can first forgive others. No, not at all. It is simply that by the very nature of the created order we must give in order to receive. I cannot, for instance, receive love if I do not give love. People may try to offer me love, but if resentment and vindictiveness fill my heart, their offers will roll off me like water off a duck's back. If my fists are clenched and my arms folded tightly round myself, I cannot hold anything.

But once I give love, I am a candidate for receiving love. Once I open my hands, I can receive. As St Augustine says, "God gives where he finds empty hands."[8]

So it is with forgiveness. As long as the only cry heard among us is for vengeance, there can be no reconciliation. If our hearts are so narrow as to see only how others have hurt and offended us, we cannot see how we have offended God and so find no need to seek forgiveness. If we are always calculating in our hearts how much this one or that one has violated our rights, by the very nature of things we will not be able to pray this prayer.

In the affairs of human beings there is a vicious cycle of retaliation: you gore my ox and I'll gore your ox, you hurt me and I'll hurt you in return. Now the giving of forgiveness is so essential because it breaks this law of retribution. We are offended, and, instead of offending in return, we forgive. (Be assured that we are able to do this only because of the supreme act of forgiveness at Golgotha, which once and for all broke the back of the cycle of retaliation.) When we do, when we forgive, it unleashes a flood of forgiving graces from heaven and among human beings.

If forgiving is so important, we really need to ask the question: what is forgiveness? There is great confusion on this matter today, and therefore we must first understand what forgiveness is not.

Forgiveness does not mean that we will cease to hurt. The wounds are deep, and we may hurt for a very long time. Just because we continue to experience emotional pain does not mean that we have failed to forgive.

Forgiveness does not mean that we will forget. That would do violence to our rational faculties. Helmut Thielicke, a German pastor who endured the darkest days of the Nazi Third Reich, says, "One should never mention the words 'forgive' and 'forget' in the same breath."[9] No, we will remember, but in forgiving we no longer use the memory against others.

Forgiveness is not pretending that the offence did not

really matter. It did matter, and it does matter, and there is no use pretending otherwise. The offence is real, but when we forgive, the offence no longer controls our behaviour.

Forgiveness is not acting as if things are just the same as before the offence. We must face the fact that things will never be the same. By the grace of God they can be a thousand times better, but they will never again be the same.

What then is forgiveness? It is a miracle of grace whereby the offence no longer separates. If a husband ignores his wife, valuing business and all other things above her, he has sinned against her. The offence is real and the hurt is real. A sacred trust has been broken. We speak rightly when we say that something has come between them. She will never forget this violation of respect. Even in old age she may feel an icy chill at the memory of this disregard.

But forgiveness means that this real and horrible offence shall not separate us. Forgiveness means that we will no longer use the offence to drive a wedge between us, hurting and injuring one another. Forgiveness means that the power of love that holds us together is greater than the power of the offence that separates us. That is forgiveness. In forgiveness we are releasing our offenders so that they are no longer bound to us. In a very real sense we are freeing them to receive God's grace. We are also inviting our offenders back into the circle of fellowship.

One final word regarding the petition directly: God has bound himself to forgive when we forgive. Perhaps you have felt deeply the load of guilt at your offence against heaven. You have been uneasy and unsure of your pardon from God. You long for some assurance that will give you peace. Well, here is assurance given by the highest authority. Jesus Christ, the eternal Son, guarantees your acquittal: "If you forgive others their trespasses, your heavenly Father will also forgive you" (Matt. 6:14).

Deliver

This third petition is perhaps the most important of them all. It contains both a negative (lead us not into temptation), and a positive (but deliver us from evil).

The first part of the petition has disturbed many. How can God tempt us or lead us into temptation? The Greek word itself means "trials" or "trying circumstances", and the only time God tries us is when there is something in our hearts that needs revealing. For example, Judas was a man who had difficulty with money which was precisely why Jesus made him the treasurer of the apostolic band. In time, what was in the heart of Judas came to light.

Therefore the prayer "lead us not into temptation" means this: "Lord, may there be nothing in me that will force you to put me to the test in order to reveal what is in my heart." We want to be progressing in the realms of transformation with no hidden sins so that God will not be forced to put us to the test.

We must not here be thinking of the temptations of childhood, what Martin Luther called "puppy-sins".[10] No, it is the adult sins with which we must concern ourselves. We, like Jesus in the wilderness, will be tempted with power and influence and the opportunity to help others without reference to God. How much good we could accomplish if we only had those things, we may think. These desires in our heart are the seeds of destruction. In the Lord's Prayer we are asking God to remove them from our hearts so that he will never have to put us to the test.

Now with regard to the petition "deliver us from evil": as much as we might like it otherwise, the original text is quite clear that Jesus is urging us to pray for rescue not from evil in a generic sense, but from the evil one, namely Satan. I know that does not sit well in our modern and post-modern understanding of reality, but it is there nevertheless.

Helmut Thielicke preached on this very passage right after the Allied occupation of his home town of Stuttgart near the end of the Second World War. Commenting on

the modern "properly spiritualized 'concept of evil'",
he wrote:

> Dear friends, in our time we have had far too much
> contact with demonic powers;
>   we have sensed and seen how men and whole move-
> ments have been corrupted and controlled by mysteri-
> ous, abysmal powers, leading them where they had no
> intention of going;
>   we have observed all too often how an alien spirit
> can ride people and change the very substance of men
> who before may have been quite decent and reasonable
> persons, driving them to brutalities, delusions of power,
> and fits of madness of which they never appeared to be
> capable before;
>   year by year we have seen an increasingly poisonous
> atmosphere settling down upon our globe and we sense
> how real and almost tangible are the evil spirits in the air,
> seeing an invisible hand passing an invisible cup of poison
> from nation to nation and throwing them into confusion.[11]

And in the intervening decades have we not seen enough of
the hideous and the horrible to speak without embarrassment the phrase of Martin Luther, "The prince of darkness
grim"? You may remember that Luther continues, "We
tremble not for him/ His rage we can endure,/ For lo, his
doom is sure:/ One little word shall fell him."[12] This is the
outcome of the prayer for deliverance.

The Cambridge professor Herbert Farmer reminds us that
"if prayer is the heart of religion, then petition is the heart
of prayer."[13] Without Petitionary Prayer we have a truncated
prayer life. May I remind us all once again how very much
God delights in our asking, looking for an excuse to give.

◆

*Dear Father, I don't want to treat you like Santa
Claus but I do need to ask things of you. Give*

*me, please, food to eat today. I'm not asking
for tomorrow, but I am asking for today.
Please forgive me for the infinite offences to
your goodness that I have committed today . . .
this hour. I'm not even aware of most of them.
I live too unaware. That in itself is a sin against
heaven. I'm sorry. Increase my awareness.*

*And in my ignorance if I have asked for
things that would really be destructive, please,
do not give them to me — do not lead me into
temptation. Do protect me from the evil one.*

For Jesus' sake.

— Amen.

Intercessory Prayer

Intercessory prayer is the purifying bath into which the individual and the fellowship must enter every day.

— Dietrich Bonhoeffer

If we truly love people, we will desire for them far more than it is within our power to give them, and this will lead us to prayer. Intercession is a way of loving others.

When we move from petition to intercession we are shifting our centre of gravity from our own needs to the needs and concerns of others. Intercessory Prayer is selfless prayer, even self-giving prayer. In the ongoing work of the kingdom of God nothing is more important than Intercessory Prayer. People today desperately need the help that we can give them. Marriages are being shattered. Children are being destroyed. Individuals are living lives of quiet desperation, without purpose or future. And we can make a difference . . . if we will learn to pray on their behalf.

Intercessory Prayer is priestly ministry, and one of the most challenging teachings in the New Testament is the universal priesthood of all Christians. As priests, appointed and anointed by God, we have the honour of going before the Most High on behalf of others. This is not optional; it is a sacred obligation – and a precious privilege – of all who take up the yoke of Christ.

A Magnificent Model

Moses was one of the world's great intercessors, and one particular incident in his life provides a magnificent model for us in our continuing work of intercession. On this occasion the Amalekites had engaged the children of Israel in battle (Exod. 17:8–13). The military strategy of Moses was strange and powerful. He ordered Joshua to`lead the army into the valley to fight the battle. Moses himself went to the top of a hill overlooking the battleground with his two lieutenants, Aaron and Hur. While Joshua engaged in physical combat, Moses engaged in spiritual combat by raising hands of prayer over the conflict. Evidently Moses had the harder task for he was the one who got tired. Aaron and Hur had to step in and hold up Moses' arms until the sun set.

In the military annals Joshua was the general who won the victory that day. He was the person up front and in the thick of the conflict. But you and I know the rest of the story. Back behind the scenes the battle of intercession was won by Moses and Aaron and Hur. Each role was essential for victory. Joshua was needed to lead the charge. Moses was needed to intercede on behalf of the children of Israel. Aaron and Hur were needed to assist Moses as he grew weary.

What Moses and Aaron and Hur did on that day is the work all of us are called upon to undertake. We are not all asked to be public leaders, but all of us are to engage in Intercessory Prayer. And as P. T. Forsyth reminds us, "The deeper we go down into the valley of decision the higher we must rise . . . into the mount of prayer, and we must hold up the hands of those whose chief concern is to prevail with God."[1]

The Interceding One

We are not left alone in this interceding work of ours. Our little prayers of intercession are backed up and reinforced by the eternal Intercessor. Paul assures us that it is "Christ Jesus, who died, yes, who was raised, who is at the right hand of God, who indeed intercedes for us" (Rom. 8:34). As if to intensify the truth of this, the writer to the Hebrews declares Jesus an eternal priest after the order of Melchizedek who "always lives to make intercession" (Heb. 7:25).

In the Upper Room discourse recorded in John's Gospel, Jesus made it unmistakably clear to his disciples that his going to the Father would catapult them into a new dimension of prayer. He explained to his mystified band: that he is in the Father and the Father is in him, that he is going to the Father in order to prepare a place for them, that they will be enabled to do greater works because he is going to the Father, that they will not be left orphaned but that the Spirit of Truth will come to guide them, that they are to abide in him as branches abide in the vine, that he will do anything they ask in his name, and so much more (John 13–17).

What is it about Jesus going to the Father that so radically changes the equation? Why would that make such a difference in their – and our – prayer experience? The new dimension is this: Jesus is entering his eternal work as Intercessor before the throne of God, and, as a result, we are enabled to pray for others with an entirely new authority.

What I am trying to say is that our ministry of intercession is made possible only because of Christ's continuing ministry of intercession. It is a wonderful truth to know that we are saved by faith alone, that there is nothing we can do to make ourselves acceptable to God. Likewise, we pray by faith alone – Jesus Christ our eternal Intercessor is responsible for our prayer life. "Unless he intercedes," writes Ambrose of Milan, "there is no intercourse with God either for us or for all saints."[2]

By ourselves we have no entrée to the court of heaven. It would be like ants speaking to humans. We need an interpreter, an intermediary, a go-between. This is what Jesus Christ does for us in his role as eternal Intercessor – "There is one mediator between God and men, the man Christ Jesus" (1 Tim. 2:5, RSV). He opens the door and grants us access into the heavenlies. Even more: he straightens out and cleanses our feeble, misguided intercessions and makes them acceptable before a holy God. Even more still: his prayers sustain our desires to pray, urging us on and giving us hope of being heard. The sight of Jesus in his heavenly intercession gives us strength to pray in his name.

In the Name of Jesus

Now that the topic of prayer in the name of Jesus has been raised, I would like to make a few comments about it. We are urged repeatedly in the Gospels and elsewhere to pray in this way. And wonderful results are promised as a result of doing so. "Until now you have not asked for anything in my name," says Jesus. "Ask and you will receive, so that your joy may be complete" (John 16:24).

I know that this notion seems rather provincial and intolerant to some. Perhaps you are wondering, "Isn't it possible to be a bit more broad-minded and accept all sincere prayers in whosoever's name and by whatever authority?" Well, first of all, it is not my business or yours to accept or reject anyone's prayer. That is a matter that, thank God, belongs to him. My guess is that God is far more accepting of prayers than even the most broad-minded among us. (Often we are terribly narrow in our broad-mindedness.) We who are people of the Way, however, have been asked to pray by virtue of the authority given to us by Jesus Christ, who claimed to be the unique revelation of God to us. And so we do.

But here we are faced with the practical question of how we pray in the name of Jesus. Any thoughtful person knows that this means far more than just tacking on a rote formula to the end of our prayers. But what exactly does it mean?

Two things, at least. The first we have already been discussing. To pray in the name of Jesus means to pray in full assurance of the great work Christ accomplished – in his life, by his death, through his resurrection and by means of his continuing reign at the right hand of God the Father. Donald Bloesch writes:

To pray in the name of Christ means to pray in the awareness that our prayers have no worthiness or efficacy apart from his atoning sacrifice and redemptive mediation. It means to appeal to the blood of Christ as the source of power for the life of prayer. It means to acknowledge our complete helplessness apart from his mediation and intercession. To pray in his name means that we recognize that our prayers cannot penetrate the tribunal of God unless they are presented to the Father by the Son, our one Saviour and Redeemer.[3]

This is the objective, forensic side of prayer in Jesus' name. But there is also the subjective, experiential side. To pray in the name of Jesus means that we are praying in accord with the way and nature of Christ. It means that we are making the kinds of intercessions he would make if he were among us in the flesh. We are his ambassadors, commissioned by him. We have been given his name to use with his full authority. Therefore the content and the character of our praying must be, of necessity, in unity with his nature.

When Simon Magnus asked to have the power to lay hands on people so they could receive the Spirit, he was wanting to use the power of God for his own ends (Acts 8:14-24). He was not praying in Jesus' name, and Peter, recognizing this, rebuked Simon for it. The seven sons of the Jewish high priest, Sceva, had seen Paul cast out demons in the name of Jesus, and so they gave it a try, saying, "I adjure you by the Jesus whom Paul proclaims." But the evil spirit replied to them, "Jesus I know, and Paul I know; but who are you?" You see, even though they used the proper formula, they were not praying out of the life and power of Jesus, and so they failed. In an almost comical aside Luke tells us that the evil spirit leaped on these seven pseudo-exorcists and overpowered them, and they ran out of the house "naked and wounded" (Acts 19:11-16).

So how do we pray in Jesus' name, that is, in conformity to his nature? Jesus himself says, "If you abide in me, and my words abide in you, ask for whatever you wish, and it will be done for you" (John 15:7). This "abide in me" is the all-inclusive condition for effective intercession. It is the key for prayer in the name of Jesus. We learn to become like the branch which receives its life from the vine: "Abide in me as I abide in you. Just as the branch cannot bear fruit by itself unless it abides in the vine, neither can you unless you abide in me" (John 15:4). Nothing is more important to a life of prayer than learning how to become a branch.

As we live this way, we develop what Thomas à Kempis calls "a familiar friendship with Jesus." We become accustomed to his face. We distinguish the voice of the true Shepherd from that of religious hucksters in the same way professional jewellers distinguish a diamond from glass imitations – by acquaintanceship. When we have been familiar with the genuine article long enough, the cheap and the shoddy become obvious.

When we have immersed ourselves long enough in the way of Christ, we can smell Gospel. So we ask and do as we know he would ask and do. How do we *know* what Jesus would ask and do, you may ask? Well, how does a couple who have been married many loving years know what each other thinks and wants and feels? We know, even as we are known. This is how we pray in Jesus' name.[4]

Persistence That Wins

When we begin praying for others, we soon discover that it is easy to become discouraged at the results which seem frustratingly slow and uneven. This is because we are entering the strange mix of divine influence and human autonomy. God never compels, and so the divine influence always allows a way of escape. No one is ever forced into a robot style of obedience.

This aspect of God's character – this respect, this courtesy, this patience – is hard for us to accept because we operate so differently. Some people frustrate us so much that sometimes we wish we could open up their heads and tinker around inside a bit. This is our way, but it is not God's way. His way is higher than our way. His way is like the rain and the snow that gently fall to the earth, disappearing into the ground as they nourish it. When the time is right, up springs new life. No manipulation, no control; perfect freedom, perfect liberty. This is God's way (Isa. 55:8–11).

This process is a hard one for us to accept, and we can easily become disheartened by it. I think Jesus understood this, and, as a result, he gave more than one teaching on our need for persistence – what we today call the parables of importunity. He even specifies his reason for telling these stories, namely that we would "pray always and not . . . lose heart" (Luke 18:1).

These parables have been a special grace to me, for how quickly I lose heart. Perhaps you know what I mean. We pray once or twice, and when nothing seems to move, we go on to other matters, or sulk in self-pity, or even give up on prayer altogether. Our quick-fix approach is a little like turning on a light switch, and, if the lights do not come on immediately, declaring, "Well, I didn't believe in electricity anyway!"

But Jesus gives us an altogether different vantage point from which to view our prayer work. Prayer, he says, is a little like a helpless widow who refuses to accept her helplessness and instead stands up to injustice, and her persistence wins the day (Luke 18:1–8). It is something like forcing a neighbour to help provide food for a stranger – even though to do so is terribly inconvenient – because otherwise the whole village will be disgraced for not caring for the stranger in their midst (Luke 11:5–13). In each case the point of the teaching is persistence. We keep asking, we keep seeking, we keep knocking.

There is a religious word for what I have been describing: supplication. Supplication means to ask with earnestness, with intensity, with perseverance. It is a declaration that we are deadly serious about this prayer business. We are going to keep at it and not give up. John Calvin writes,

"We must repeat the same supplications not twice or three times only, but as often as we have need, a hundred and a thousand times . . . We must never be weary in waiting for God's help."5

This is an important teaching to hear, for we live in a generation that eschews commitment. One of the old cardinal virtues was fortitude, but where today do we find such courageous staying power? We must admit that it is in short supply everywhere we look. Jesus, however, makes it foundational to real effectiveness in Intercessory Prayer.

Do you, do I exhibit this patient determination in our prayers for others? How easily we fall short! In the levitical legal code the fire on the altar was to be kept burning perpetually; it was never to go out (Lev. 6:13). As God builds stamina and grit into our spirituality, we today must learn to burn the eternal flame of prayer on the altar of devotion.

Organized, Corporate, Intercessory Prayer

Intercession is done individually; it is also done corporately. Jesus promises to be present in great power whenever the community of faith is truly gathered in his name (Matt. 18:20). When enough faith, hope and love are found in any given community, the blessings are multiplied, for then organized, corporate, intercessory prayer is possible.

Drawing upon the prophet Isaiah, Jesus declares, "My house shall be a house of prayer" (Isa. 56:7; Luke 19:46). I would love to see our churches become houses of prayer. I know you would, too. All too often, however, they are places for everything and anything except prayer. I say this with sorrow, for I believe it saddens the heart of God. True, we need to have our business meetings and our committee meetings and our Bible studies and our self-help groups and our worship services, but if the fire is not hot at the centre, these things are only ashes in our hands.

In the seventeenth century Jonathan Edwards wrote a slender book with a bulky title: *A Humble Attempt to*

Promote Explicit Agreement and Visible Union of All God's People in Extraordinary Prayer for the Revival of Religion and the Advancement of Christ's Kingdom on Earth, Pursuant to Scripture Promises and Prophecies Concerning the Last Time. Edwards understood it so well. We must have both "explicit agreement" and "visible union" for this kind of prayer to go forward. It is not an easy combination to come by, but when it occurs, "extraordinary prayer" is not too strong a description.

Recently a student of mine, Jung-Oh Suh – a Korean pastor on a study sabbatical – learned of my research on prayer and brought me a newspaper article (complete with his excellent translation, for it was written in Korean) that describes the story of the Myong-Song Presbyterian Church, in the south-eastern part of Seoul. The Korean churches are well-known for their early morning prayer meetings, but even so this story is unusual. This is a group that began about ten years ago with forty people, and today twelve thousand gather each morning for three prayer meetings – at 4 a.m., 5 a.m., and 6 a.m. Jung-Oh explained to me that they must shut the doors at 4 a.m. to begin the first service, and so if people arrive a little late, they must wait until the 5 a.m. meeting. Then he added, "This is a problem in my country because it gets cold in the winter! So everyone brings a little pot of tea or coffee to keep warm while they wait for the next service."[6] This is organized, corporate, intercessory prayer.

There are indications that, as we approach the twenty-first century the greatest prayer movement in living memory is already under way. In much smaller but still significant ways the story of Myong-Song Presbyterian Church can be repeated many times over. One congregation I know has forty prayer meetings per week involving a total of a thousand people. I am acquainted with churches in which anywhere from 15 per cent to 24 per cent of the congregation are engaged in organized, corporate, intercessory prayer weekly. I have met with national prayer leaders, and none of them has seen anything like what is now beginning to occur. It is too early to tell how significant this new awakening towards prayer will be, but the signs are encouraging.

It is God's desire to bring individuals and families into saving faith. It is God's desire to bring people off addictions to drugs, sex, money, status. It is God's desire to deliver people from racism, sexism, nationalism, consumerism. It is God's desire to harvest cities, bringing whole communities into Gospel fidelity. Organized, corporate, intercessory prayer is a crucial means for the fulfilment of these yearnings in the heart of God.

For the Well-Being of Others

If you are part of a community where corporate prayer is the serious business of the church, I hope you are rejoicing in this gracious gift of God. Many are not as fortunate. A very large number of us find ourselves in situations where the Christian leaders simply do not lead in this realm, but that must not stop our work of intercession. We are responsible before God to pray for those God brings into our circle of nearness. With Samuel of old we say, "God forbid that I should sin against the LORD in ceasing to pray for you" (1 Sam. 12:23, KJV). We do this individually and in little bands of two and three. Some small instruction may be helpful for these situations.

There are as many ways to go about the work of intercession as there are people. Some like to keep lists of people they are concerned to pray for with regularity. I once visited a very holy lady who was confined to a bed. She showed me her "family album" of some two hundred photographs of missionaries and others she was concerned to hold before the throne of heaven. She explained how she worked her way through this entire album each week, flipping the pages and praying over the pictures. I was a teenager at the time, but even at that young age I knew that the place where I stood beside that bed was holy ground.

Another approach comes from the great preacher and

pray-er George Buttrick. He recommends that we begin with prayer for our enemies: "The first intercession is, 'Bless So-and-so whom I foolishly regard as an enemy. Bless So-and-so whom I have wronged. Keep them in Thy favour. Banish my bitterness.'" He next encourages us to go on to leaders in "statecraft, medicine, learning, art, and religion; the needy of the world, our friends at work or play, and our loved ones".7 The great value of Buttrick's counsel is that it keeps us moving beyond our provincial little concerns and into a broken and needy world.

Here is my own approach. After prayer for my immediate family, I wait quietly until individuals or situations spontaneously rise to my awareness. I then offer these to God, listening to see if any special discernment comes to guide the content of the prayer. Next I speak forth what seems most appropriate in full confidence that God hears and answers. After spoken intercession I may remain for a while, inviting the Spirit to pray through me "with sighs too deep for words". I will stay with any given individual or situation until I feel released from the prayer concern. Throughout the time I may jot down brief notes in a small prayer journal as I sense the Spirit giving instruction. These notes are often extremely helpful, for over time a pattern sometimes emerges that holds the key to the person's need. This then informs the direction of future intercessions.

When it is possible and appropriate, it helps to go direct to the person to whom we are drawn to pray. This was Jesus' normal, though not exclusive, pattern. A simple question such as, "What would you like prayer for?" can at times be tremendously revealing. Remember, prayer is a way of loving others, and so courtesy, grace and respect are always in order.

One caution: none of us is to shoulder the burden of prayer for everyone and everything. We are finite human beings, and it is an act of humility to recognize our limitations. Often people will come to us with a glib "pray for me", and they have no idea what they are asking of us. In such cases we are to take the matter under advisement and wait until there are promptings from a higher source. God will make it clear who and what are to be our prayer concerns, and the other situations we are to leave with him.

Your situation, however, may be just the opposite. Far from getting overcommitted, perhaps you find it hard to get up much enthusiasm to pray for others. The desire simply is not there. What can you do?

There can be many causes for such a lack, but I suggest that you begin by praying for an increase in your love for others. As God grows your capacity to care, you will very naturally begin working for the good of your neighbours, your friends, even your enemies. Doing this, you will quickly reach the end of your tether. You will want them to enter into things and receive things that you cannot give them. This will cause you to pray. "Prayer," writes Augustine, "is to intercede for the well-being of others before God."[8] By means of Intercessory Prayer God extends to each of us a personalized, hand-engraved invitation to become intimately involved in labouring for the well-being of others. In the following chapters we will turn our attention to several specific forms of intercession. It is my hope that each one will play a part in helping us to accept this divine invitation freely to give even as we have freely received.

--------◆--------

Gracious Holy Spirit, so much of my life seems to revolve around my interests and my welfare. I would like to live just one day in which everything I did benefited someone besides myself. Perhaps prayer for others is a starting point. Help me to do so without any need for praise or reward.

In Jesus' name.

— Amen.

Healing Prayer

*Many great and wonderful things were wrought
by the heavenly power in those days; for the
Lord made bare his omnipotent arm, and mani-
fested his power, to the astonishment of many,
the healing virtue whereby many have been
delivered from great infirmities.*

— George Fox

Healing Prayer is part of the normal Christian life. It should
not be elevated above any other ministry in the community
of faith, nor should it be undervalued; rather, it should be
kept in proper balance. It is simply a normal aspect of what
it means to live under the reign of God.

This should not surprise us, for it is a clear recognition
of the incarnational nature of our faith. God cares as much
about the body as he does the soul, as much about the
emotions as he does the spirit. The redemption that is in
Jesus is total, involving every aspect of the person — body,
soul, will, mind, emotions, spirit.

Infinite Variety

God joyfully employs an infinite variety of means to bring
health and well-being to his people. We are glad for
God's friends, the doctors, who with skill and compassion help our bodies fight against disease and sickness.
We rejoice for every advance of modern psychiatry and
psychology as better ways are discovered to promote
the healing of the deep mind. We also celebrate the
growing army of women and men and children who
are learning how to bring the healing power of Christ

to others for the glory of God and the good of all concerned.

Furthermore we can be grateful for every co-operative effort of the many branches of healing. After all, the distinction between priest and psychologist and physician is of recent vintage. Always before, the physician of the body, the physician of the mind, and the physician of the spirit were the same person. The ancient Hebrews, in particular, saw persons as a unity, and for them it would be unthinkable to minister to the body without ministering to the spirit and vice versa. The Pentateuch contained detailed stipulations about going to the priest whenever disease was suspected (Lev. 13ff.). Jesus used well-known first-century medical techniques in his ministry (Mark 7:33; John 9:6; and so on). Even in many "primitive" cultures today the doctor and the priest are one and the same person. So it is with enthusiasm that we applaud the demise of the heretical tendency to fragment and compartmentalize human beings.

There may be times when God asks us to rely upon prayer alone for healing, but this is the exception, not the rule. The refusal to use medical means to promote healing may be a gesture of faith – more often it is a gesture of spiritual pride.

It is just as possible to err in the opposite direction, of course. Many trust in medical means exclusively and turn to prayer only when all available medical technology has failed. This only betrays the materialistic base of so much of our thinking. Normally the aid of prayer and the aid of medicine should be pursued at the same time and with equal vigour, for both are gifts from God.

Small Beginnings

My initial interest in Healing Prayer began out of a concern for emotional, not physical, healing. At the time, I worked at a family counselling centre, and I was acutely aware of my seeming inability to bring the healing power of Christ to bear on emotional and mental illness. The only success I had was completely explainable by human techniques of psychological manipulation. While I never felt any need to reject these professional tools, I came to believe that Healing Prayer could greatly enhance the good that was being accomplished.

My first experience was with a man who had lived in constant fear and bitterness for twenty-eight years. He would wake up at night, screaming and in a cold sweat. He lived in constant depression, so much so that his wife said that he had not laughed for many years.

He told me the story of what had happened those many years before that had caused such a deep sadness to hang over him. He was in Italy during the Second World War and was in charge of a mission of thirty-three men. They became trapped by enemy gunfire. With deep sorrow in his eyes, this man related how he had prayed desperately that God would get them out of that mess. It was not to be. He had to send his men out two by two and watch them get killed. Finally in the early hours of the morning he was able to escape with six men – four seriously wounded. He had only a flesh wound. He told me that the experience turned him into an atheist. Certainly, his heart was filled with rage, bitterness and guilt.

I said, "Don't you know that Jesus Christ, the Son of God who lives in the eternal now, can enter that old painful memory and heal it so that it will no longer control you?" He did not know this was possible. I asked if he would mind if I prayed for him – never mind that he was an atheist; I would have faith for him. He nodded his consent. Sitting beside him with my hand on his shoulder, I invited the Lord Jesus to go back those twenty-eight years and walk through that day with this good man. "Please, Lord," I asked, "draw out the hurt and the hate and the sorrow and set him free." Almost as an afterthought I asked for peaceful sleep to be one of the evidences of this healing work, for he had not slept well for all those years. "Amen."

The next week he came up to me with a sparkle in his eyes and a brightness on his face I had never seen before. "Every night I have slept soundly, and each morning I have awakened with a hymn on my mind. And I am happy . . . happy for the first time in twenty-eight years." His wife concurred that it was so. That was many years ago, and the wonderful thing is that although this man has had the normal ups and downs of life since then, the old sorrows have never returned. He was totally and instantaneously healed.[1]

In time, this led me to the inescapable conclusion that the healing ministry of Jesus is intended for the total person, and so my prejudices against physical healing began to crumble. But my early experiences in praying for the sick were dismal failures. First I prayed for a cancer patient – he died. Next I prayed for a lady severely crippled with arthritis – she continued to be crippled.

I guessed I had a few things to learn! "Teach me," I prayed. Within a few days the answer came through an elderly lady who did not know me or my question. She said to a group of us, "When you are first learning to pray for healing, do not start with the most difficult cases . . . *like cancer or arthritis*. Instead begin more simply."

I nearly fell out of my seat. It was utterly fundamental – this principle of progression – I used it in every other field of endeavour, but somehow I had failed to apply it to the spiritual life. That elementary teaching opened up a whole new world to me. I began to pray for small things like earaches, and headaches, and colds – whatever needs arose among my family and friends. And slowly, one step at a time, I began discovering the ways of Healing Prayer.

Since those early days, I have learned many things. While some I pray for today are still not healed, many others are, especially when I am praying with a team or in a loving community.

The Perplexing Question

But what about the fact that not everyone who receives prayer is healed. I call this a "fact" because simple observation shows to us that Jesus is the only one of whom it can be said, "He cured all of them" (Matt. 12:15). Certainly not everyone I pray for is healed. I imagine you experience the same. And sometimes the lack of healing can take on tragic dimensions that precipitate a genuine crisis of faith. Why then are some not healed?

The most straightforward answer to this perplexing question is "I don't know." I wish – desperately so – that every single person who sought Healing Prayer were instantaneously and totally healed. But it simply does not happen that way. Some are, and we thank God. Many others evidence substantial improvement, though not total healing. But others show no change whatsoever. I even know of people who have effective healing ministries in their own right and are themselves crippled by some persistent physical malady.

In one sense Healing Prayer is incredibly simple, like a child asking her father for help. In another sense it is incredibly complex involving the tangled interplay between the human and the Divine, between the mind and the body, between the soul and the spirit, between the demonic and the angelic. As Kenneth Swanson reminds us, "We all live in a fallen world, where illness, suffering, and pain are part of the fabric of existence."[2]

Sometimes we make a faulty diagnosis of the problem and pray, for example, for physical healing when the real need is for emotional healing. Sometimes we neglect the natural means of health such as diet and exercise and sleep. Sometimes we refuse to see medicine as one way God heals. Sometimes we do not pray specifically enough or do not get down to the root problem. Sometimes we are not an adequate conduit for the flow of God's love and power, the faith and compassion in us are not yet sufficiently developed. Sometimes there is sin in our lives that hinders

God's work. I could go on, for the reasons healing does not occur are labyrinthine, but whatever the reasons, the sad fact is that sometimes we stand face to face with one for whom we have prayed and he or she is not well.

What are we to do? Well, first of all, let me tell you what we are *not* to do. In no circumstances are we to tell those receiving prayer that it is their fault: that they lack the faith, or that there must be some sin in them that is hindering the prayer, or any such thing. This will only redouble the burden they must carry. It has been painful enough for them to seek us out. If we must place blame somewhere, let's place it on ourselves as the pray-ers; perhaps it is *our* lack of faith or *our* sin that is hindering the flow of God's grace and mercy.

Actually the matter of blame is simply not the issue. When the disciples got into the blaming game – "Rabbi, who sinned, this man or his parents, that he was born blind?" – Jesus dismissed their speculations as irrelevant (John 9:1–12). The simple fact is that we are learning about the prayer that heals, and there is much that we do not understand. Often we must stand under the imponderable mysteries of the divine. On occasion Jesus' disciples also failed in their attempts at Healing Prayer (see, for example, Mark 9:14–29).

The one thing we are to do is show compassion. Always! The Gospel writers frequently mention that Jesus was "filled with compassion" for people. In one story a leper came to Jesus, begging to be healed. When Jesus looked at the leper, he was moved with compassion. The Hebrew and Aramaic roots of compassion are *inward parts*, what the old King James Version used to call *bowels of mercy*. It comes from the same source as the word "womb", and so we could speak of the womblike heart of Jesus which brought healing mercy to the leper. Now, Jesus could have kept his distance and ordered the man to be well, but instead, he touched him. Jesus' touch of compassion was comparable to our taking hold of a person with AIDS, stopping the bleeding with our bare hands, and putting our own life in jeopardy. This is the compassion of Jesus.

The Laying on of Hands

Since I have mentioned the touch of compassion, this might be a good time to discuss the laying on of hands. This is a teaching found throughout the Bible, and it is a valid ministry ordained by God for the benefit of the community of faith. It is not an empty ritual but a clear understanding of the law of contact and transmittal. It is one means through which God imparts to us what we desire or need, or what God in his infinite wisdom knows is best for us. It is one of the elementary matters of the Gospel without which we cannot go on to maturity (Heb. 6:1–6).

The laying on of hands is used in Scripture in a number of ways such as the tribal blessing, the baptism in the Holy Spirit, and the impartation of spiritual gifts,[3] but one of its most pre-eminent uses is in Healing Prayer. Jesus laid hands on the sick at Nazareth and healed them (Mark 6:5). He laid his hands on the blind man at Bethsaida twice before he fully recovered his sight (Mark 8:22–25). On the island of Malta the Apostle Paul laid hands on the sick, and they were healed (Acts 28:7–10). In the longer ending of Mark's Gospel ordinary believers are encouraged in this ministry (Mark 16:18).

The laying on of hands in itself does not heal the sick – it is Christ who heals the sick. The laying on of hands is a simple act of obedience that quickens our faith and gives God the opportunity to impart healing. Often people will add the accompanying means of anointing with oil, following the counsel of James 5:14. Like many others I have discovered that, when praying for people with the laying on of hands, I sometimes detect a gentle flow of energy. I have found that I cannot make the flow of heavenly life happen, but I can stop it. If I resist or refuse to be an open conduit for God's power to come into a person, it will stop. Also, a spirit of hate or resentment arrests the flow of life immediately. Unforgiveness on the part of the person receiving ministry is also a roadblock.

Obviously common sense and a respect for the integrity of others will keep us from engaging in this work lightly or carelessly. We simply do not go around plopping our hands on anyone we please. Paul cautions about laying hands on people indiscriminately because it might bring them into things for which they are not ready (1 Tim. 5:22).[4] Sanctified common sense will teach us what is appropriate at any given time.

I might add that while we adults struggle with this idea of the laying on of hands, children have no difficulty with it whatever. I was once called to a home to pray for a seriously ill baby. Her four-year-old brother was in the room and so I told him I needed his help in praying for his baby sister. He was delighted to help and I was delighted to have him, for I know that children can often pray with unusual effectiveness. He climbed up into the chair beside me. "Let's play a little game," I suggested. "Since we know that Jesus is always with us, let's suppose that he is sitting over in that chair across from us. He is waiting patiently for us to focus our attention on him. When we see him and the love in his eyes, we start thinking more about his love than about how sick Julie is. He smiles, gets up, and comes over to us. When that happens, we both put our hands on Julie, and as we do, Jesus puts his hands right on top of ours. He releases his healing light right into your little sister like a whole bunch of soldiers who go in and fight the bad germs until they are all gone. Okay!" Seriously the boy nodded. Together we prayed just as I had described it to him, and then we thanked God that this was the way it was going to be. Amen. While we prayed, I sensed that my small prayer partner had exercised unusual faith.

The next morning Julie was perfectly well. Now, I cannot prove to you that our little prayer game made Julie well. All I know is that Julie was healed, and that was all I needed to know.

Straightforward Steps

I doubt that anyone who reads these words will ever have a healing ministry in large auditoriums before thousands of people. But we will all have numerous opportunities through the course of our routine days to bring the healing light of Christ to those who are around us. Therefore I would like to provide you with a simple approach to Healing Prayer that I hope will be helpful in ordinary situations. It has four straightforward steps.

First, we listen. This is the step of discernment. We listen to people, and we listen to God. Sometimes people share their deepest needs in the most casual offhand way. But if we are listening, really listening, there is often a rise within us, an inner "yes" which is a divine invitation to prayer. So we ask politely if they would like prayer for the situation. In over twenty years of praying for people in this manner, I have yet to have one person turn me down – and I have done this in airports and shopping malls and crowded halls. It is the most natural thing in the world to show love and concern in this way.

We are also listening to God, asking him to show us the key to the problem. This sometimes comes by direct revelation, sometimes by hearing the words beneath the words, and sometimes by a combination of both. A friend of mine was listening to a well-dressed woman share in rapid-fire monologue a sad tale of emotional illnesses, psychiatric treatment and mental hospitals. All the time there was rising within him the counsel, "Tell her her sins are forgiven her." But she never seemed to stop long enough even to catch her breath. Finally he said, "Lady, your sins are forgiven you." She kept right on with her story of this illness and that hospital stay. Again he said, "Lady, your sins are forgiven you," and again, she kept right on with her monologue. Finally he held her by the shoulders and looked her directly in the eye and said, "Look at me. I'm trying to tell you that your sins are forgiven you!"

The woman stopped in mid-sentence as if her breath had been taken away. "What did you say?" she asked.

He said, "Your sins are forgiven you."

Tears came to her eyes. "They are?"

My friend answered simply and lovingly, "Yes, they are."

The dam broke, and the flood gushed forth from her eyes. She turned to her husband and announced through her tears, "My sins are forgiven me!" It was the breakthrough that was needed and the key to substantial healing. This good woman has needed ongoing counselling, to be sure, but in the dozen years since that encounter, she has not had to return to the mental hospitals and has been functioning in a relatively normal way. We listen.

Second, we ask. This is the step of faith. As we come to clearness about what is needed, we invite God's healing to come. We speak a definite, straightforward declaration of what is to be. We do not weaken our request with ifs, ands or buts. We speak with the boldness of Martin Luther when he prayed for his sick friend Melanchthon: "I besought the Almighty with great vigour . . . quoting from Scripture all the promises I could remember, that prayers should be granted, and said that he must grant my prayer, if I was henceforth to put faith in his promises."[5]

I was once visiting a young boy, whom I shall call Franky, who was in hospital, suffering from a deteriorating eye condition. Each time I visited, we got a little better acquainted, but his eyesight continued to degenerate. The parents told me that the doctors feared the worst. Then one day I walked into his hospital room to find the shades pulled down and the lights off. Franky could not recognize me, though he knew by the shadows that someone had come into the room.

I stood there, trying to decide how to counsel Franky, and for an instant I entertained the demonic notion that perhaps blindness was the will of God for him. But immediately there was a rise of faith in me, and I murmured to myself, "No! Now is not the time to counsel acceptance of his disability. We must still fight this thing." To Franky I said quietly, "We both know that your eyes are not getting better, but somehow I think we should ask God to help. Would you let me put my hands on your eyes and invite Jesus' healing light to come into them? I can't promise anything will happen, but I'm sure it won't do any harm." Franky quickly agreed, and together we asked for what up to this point I had not dared to ask.

The next week when I came to see Franky, sunlight was streaming through the window, and Franky, ball and glove in hand, was preparing to check out of the hospital. His parents told me that wondrously the deterioration had been reversed somehow, and Franky's eyesight was now almost normal. Now, I do not know what kind of medical treatment the doctors had given him, but I am glad for their efforts. I am also glad that on one dark afternoon Franky and I together dared to ask for his sight. We ask.

Third, we believe. This is the step of assurance. We believe with the whole person: body, mind, spirit. At times we must confess with the father of the demonized child, "I believe; help my unbelief!" (Mark 9:24). But regardless of whether we feel strong or weak, we remember that our assurance is not based upon our ability to conjure up some special feeling. Rather, it is built upon a confident assurance in the faithfulness of God. We focus on his trustworthiness and especially on his steadfast love. Francis MacNutt writes, "Personally I prefer to concentrate on the love of God made visible in Jesus, from which flows his healing power."[6]

I was new at the university and it was the second week of term. I went into the classroom early for a course on spiritual formation that I was teaching. One student – I shall call her Maria – was already there, and so we got acquainted. Later that day I was walking across a part of the campus I had not seen before and I noticed a crowd gathering in one corner. As I went over to see what was going on, an ambulance pulled up, siren blaring. A bystander told me that a student had fallen out of the back of a pickup lorry as it was turning the corner and that her head had struck the concrete pavement. As they lifted the student into the ambulance, I recognized her as the young woman I had met earlier in the classroom. I knew our meeting that morning was for this moment.

Quickly I jumped into the ambulance, explaining to the medical staff that I was her "pastor". I did this so I could begin praying for her immediately at close range. I held Maria's hand as the medical technicians worked on her. She was unconscious, and blood was oozing from one ear.

Student friends of Maria began to gather in the hospital emergency room. "You can help me," I told them. Briefly I gave them a crash course on Healing Prayer. "The brain is bleeding and swelling from the impact of the injury," I went on to explain. "So our initial prayer efforts must focus on seeing the injured capillaries in the brain begin to heal and for the swelling of the brain to slow down." They took their prayer assignment quite seriously, some of them staying in the hospital throughout the night. They actually believed that their prayer work could make a difference in Maria's condition.

The doctor asked me to call Maria's parents who lived in Texas some eight hours' drive away. "Tell them to come as quickly as they can," he instructed. "We may have to operate."

Maria's parents arrived about midnight, and I updated them on her condition. "Yes, she is still unconscious, but they have not taken her into surgery yet. They may not need to if the bleeding and swelling stop in time." I then explained how we were praying for Maria and gave them a few suggestions on how they too could help in prayer. Normally parents are not very helpful in such prayer efforts because of understandable fears, but Maria's parents were exceptional in this regard and prayed with unusual faith.

This was in stark contrast to a meeting I had had earlier in the evening with a few of the faculty who wanted to pray for Maria. One prayed, "We place Maria into your hands; there is nothing else we can do." I understood the sentiment, but he was completely wrong, for there was a great deal we could do in bringing the healing light of Christ into Maria.

Another prayed, "Lord, help Maria to get well, if it be thy will." That was enough for me. I knew that my colleagues, while well-intended, did not believe Maria would get better, and their prayers hindered faith. I left the room as quickly as possible and returned to my students at the hospital, who were filled with faith, hope and love.

Eventually I went home to get some sleep, and so I learned from the students what happened about six the next morning. The parents were in a motel near the hospital and decided to pray as I had taught them, picturing in their mind's eye Maria awakening from her unconscious state. At precisely that moment a student was in the intensive care unit at the hospital, and Maria opened her eyes and smiled at her. Within a week Maria was released from the hospital, completely restored, due in large measure, I think, to the faith-filled belief of those students and parents. We believe.

Fourth, we give thanks. This is the step of gratitude. Simple courtesy leads us to express our thanks for what we have asked to happen. Now, I have never been able to pray in quite the way some do, with their bold pronouncements of accomplished fact. What I do say is something like this: "Thank you, Jesus, that what we have seen and what we have said is the way it is going to be. Amen." What am I doing? With the eyes of faith I am just looking ahead a little bit – a few weeks or months or years, it does not matter – and giving thanks for what can be . . . what will be, by the mercy of God.

Gratitude itself is often very powerful. A psychiatrist in England was teaching about the history of inherited traits in the family tree and the need to pray for healing so that the negative characteristics would not come down upon future generations. The next week one member of the class – an elderly woman far into her seventies – began looking over her family tree, but she was unable to find any problems to pray over. Her family had a godly history with many pastors and other relatives who truly loved and served God. She could find no major inherited sicknesses or tragic deaths. As she read of her ancestry, great waves of gratitude swept over her, and she began thanking God for her wonderful heritage.

This good woman had not seen her own situation as needing Healing Prayer. As a child she had been stricken with polio and as a result had a withered leg. She needed to use a brace in order to walk. But this was something she had lived with all her life; she never dreamed of praying about it. And so she went to bed, praising and thanking God for the women and men she had never met but to whom she was so deeply indebted. The next morning when she woke up she discovered her leg completely healed – the result of a heart of gratitude. We give thanks.

Healthy Scepticism and Wholesome Faith

I wish I had space to go into other matters, for there is so much to learn. You may remain sceptical about Healing Prayer. That is not all bad – there are some people in our day who could profit from a little healthy scepticism.

St Augustine was that way. He doubted the validity of Healing Prayer, stating in his early writings that Christians should not look for the continuance of the healing gift.

But in AD 424 a brother and sister came to his town of Hippo, seeking healing of convulsive seizures. They came every day to Augustine's church to pray for healing. Nothing happened until the second Sunday before Easter. The young man was in the crowded church, praying. Augustine was still in the vestibule, ready for the processional, when the young man fell down as if dead. People nearby were seized with fear, but the next moment he got up and stood staring back at them, perfectly normal and fully cured.

Augustine took the young man home for dinner, and they talked at length. Slowly Augustine's scepticism began to crumble before the witness of this young man. Finally, on the third day after Easter, Augustine told the brother and sister to stand on the choir steps, where the whole congregation could see them – one quiet and normal, the other still trembling convulsively – while he read a statement from the young man. He then told everyone to sit down and began a sermon on healing. However, Augustine was interrupted by shouts from the congregation, for the young woman had also fallen to the ground and was instantaneously healed. Once more she stood before the people, and, in Augustine's own words, "Praise to God was shouted so loud that my ears could scarcely stand the din."[7]

All this happened while Augustine was writing his magnum opus, *The City of God*, so he devoted one of the final sections to the miracles of healing occurring in his own diocese. He described how he set up a process for recording and authenticating miracles, for:

> once I realized how many miracles were occurring in our own day . . . [I saw] how wrong it would be to allow the memory of these marvels of divine power to perish from among our people. It is only two years ago that the keeping of records was begun here in Hippo, and already, at this writing, we have nearly seventy attested miracles.[8]

May we, like Augustine, be able to trade in our healthy scepticism for wholesome faith as we witness the humble testimony of those who receive the healing touch of God.

———————◆———————

My Lord and my God, I have a thousand arguments against Healing Prayer. You are the one argument for it. . . . You win.

Help me to be a conduit through which your healing love can flow to others.

For Jesus' sake.

– Amen.

The Prayer of Suffering

It is the prayer of agony which saves the world.
— St Mary of Jesus

We now come to a topic that is not at all popular. I would hesitate even mentioning it if it were not for my conviction that you are quite serious about the life and work of prayer. I am speaking, of course, about the Prayer of Suffering.

If in all the pantheon of prayer there is one form that is totally other-centred, we have now come to it. In the Prayer of Suffering we leave far behind our needs and wants, even our transformation and union with God. Here we give to God the various difficulties and trials that we face, asking him to use them redemptively. We also voluntarily take into ourselves the griefs and sorrows of others in order to set them free. In our sufferings those who suffer come to see the face of the suffering God.

No Greater Image

There is no greater image of this suffering love that redeems than Jesus pinned to Golgotha's tree, uttering the words of absolution: "Father, forgive them; for they do not know what they are doing" (Luke 23:34). This is the unrepeatable, supreme act of redemption, and in this we cannot in any way be Christ's companions. He had to walk this path alone.

But he has invited us to share in his sufferings and so participate with him in the redemption of the world. Paul understood this. "I am now rejoicing in my sufferings for your sake," writes the great Apostle, "and in my flesh I am completing what is lacking in Christ's afflictions for the sake of his body, that is, the church" (Col. 1:24).[1] Paul's idea is not that something is missing in the sufferings of Christ as if there were some deficiency in his substitutionary atonement for the salvation of the world. Far from it. It is rather that we are invited to be partners with Christ by sharing in the "fellowship of his sufferings" (Phil. 3:10).

Redemptive Suffering

But before you think I am leading you into some kind of strange religious masochism, let's back up a bit and see if we can get a clearer picture on all this. I am talking about a form of suffering, to be sure, but it is redemptive suffering. We are all acquainted with the unredemptive negative variety — suffering that is utterly cruel and completely meaningless. This we must fight against with all our might for it is always opposed to life in the kingdom of God.

But there is a kind of suffering that has purpose and meaning. It is the kind that enriches the lives of others and brings healing to the world. On a purely human level we understand this instinctively with regard to our children. We are glad to deprive ourselves of many things so that they may have a better chance in life. (This, by the way, is one reason why their teenage rebellion is so hard for us — we fear that all our sacrifices will be for nothing.)

It is hard for us to grasp the idea of redemptive suffering because our whole culture militates against any form of discomfort or inconvenience. It is the same reason we find it difficult to reconcile Jesus' words about bearing our cross with his promise of life abundant. But the entire life of Jesus shows us the compatibility of grace and suffering. And Paul, whose sufferings were abundant and well documented, declared, "I consider that the sufferings of this present time are not worth comparing with the glory about to be revealed to us" (Rom. 8:18). Pope Paul VI writes, "The Christian can have at the same time two different, opposite experiences — sorrow and joy — which become complementary."[2]

In redemptive suffering we stand with people in their sin and in their sorrow. There can be no sterile, arm's-length purity. Their suffering is a messy business and we must be prepared to step smack into the middle of the mess. We are "crucified" not just *for* others but *with* others. We pray in suffering, and as we do, we are changed. Our hearts are enlarged to receive and accept all people. The language of "they" and "them" is converted into "we" and "us". All supposed superiority – whether intellectual, cultural or spiritual – simply melts away. Together we stand under the cross.

Joy, not misery, is the compelling energy behind redemptive suffering. It is not that we love pain or are trying to find ways to be martyrs. This is not misery for misery's sake. It is that God is using us for the greater good of all – which is a rather amazing notion once we stop to think about it. This is why it could be said of Jesus that he "for the sake of the joy that was set before him endured the cross" (Heb. 12:2). This is why we today can resonate with Peter's words, "Rejoice insofar as you are sharing Christ's sufferings, so that you may also be glad and shout for joy when his glory is revealed" (1 Pet. 4:13).

Finding Value

The values of the Prayer of Suffering are legion. To begin with it saves us from a superficial triumphalism. Perhaps you have had the experience of hearing someone talk about faith and confidence and victory. In one sense all the words are right and the stories certainly sound good, but somehow something does not ring quite true. The problem is that you are listening to someone who is living on the fluff side of faith, someone who has not been baptized into the sacrament of suffering. Augustine notes wryly, "How deep in the deep are they who do not cry out of the deep."[3]

But we have a Saviour who was "a man of sorrows, and acquainted with grief" (Isa. 53:3, RSV). Jesus, we are told, "offered up prayers and supplication, with loud cries and tears" (Heb. 5:7). I ask you: is the servant any better than the Master? There is a triumph that is in Christ, but it goes *through* suffering, not around it. The triumphant note of the Apostle Paul is no triumphalism. His "we are more than conquerors" comes on the other side of hardship and distress and persecution and famine and nakedness and peril and sword (Rom. 8:35b-39).

The trenchant words of William Penn ring true to life: "No Cross, no Crown". For disciples of Jesus suffering simply comes with the territory. Thomas Kelly notes, "God, out of the pattern of His own heart, has planted the cross along the road of holy obedience."4

But here is the wonder: the suffering is not for nothing! God takes it and uses it for something beautiful, something far beyond anything we can imagine. At the moment we catch only glimpses here and there, the moon's reflected light. But a day is coming when the blinders will be removed and the scales will fall off and then we will see a glory in our sufferings that will blaze like the noonday sun. Jesus tells us frankly, "In this world you will have trouble." But he goes on to add, "Take heart! I have overcome the world" (John 16:33, NIV).

Another value: our hearts are enlarged and sensitized by suffering. We become "wounded healers", as Henri Nouwen has taught us to say. Gone for ever are the pat answers that – zip, zap – make everything fine. We endure the agony that prepares us to enter into the anguish of others. "The more love sandpapers our hearts," writes Glenn Hinson, "the more it quickens us to suffering."5 We come to recognize the suffering of our time in our own hearts, and that becomes the starting point for ministry.

I once prayed for a young woman whose father was a pastor. There were many wonderful things about this good pastor, but on this occasion the daughter's heart was heavy with the losses: the multiplied times he was gone because of the demands of the ministry; the tight budget, which meant few toys, skimpy holidays, no special things; the snooping, sniping parishioners who found fault with anything and everything. I know these are garden-variety losses, but that does not make them hurt any less.

I wondered to myself if she was telling a story my own children might recite some day, for I was a young pastor, and for me too the hours were long, the money short and the parishioners picky.

After she finished her sharing, I stood behind her, gently placing my hands on her head in a ritual form of the laying on of hands. I wanted to pray for the healing of the little girl still inside this woman, the little girl who had suffered all these losses. But I could speak only a few words, for I felt a deep sorrow welling up within me for her emotional pain. I prayed forgiveness for the father who did not know what he had done. But by then I could no longer speak, for a great brokenness came over me, and I quietly sobbed on her behalf. Emotion does not come to me quickly, and so you can understand that what was happening was unusual, to say the least. There I was, standing behind her with great tears falling to the floor as I entered into her pain, repented for her father and sought healing for her inner child. Evidently the tears did what the words could not, for she left substantially healed. This way of prayer we learn only in the school of suffering.

Shall I go on enumerating the values of redemptive suffering, ticking them off like items on a grocery list? I think not, for though they are all true — each and every one — they can actually become like those pat answers that we use to protect us from the raw nerves of sorrow. No, I think it is better if we turn our attention to the practice of the Prayer of Suffering.

What Do We Do?

Our task — yours and mine — would be so much easier if we were, for example, dissecting the problem of evil. Then we could debate all the theories in a properly detached fashion. Our question, however, is not, "Why is there suffering in the world?" but "How do I enter into the suffering that is in the world in a way that is redemptive and healing?" We must ask the question of practice.

What do we do? We do the kind of thing Moses did. After he leads the children of Israel out of Egyptian bondage, they thank him by rebelling, making a golden calf. Yet Moses refuses to give them up, saying, "I will go up to the LORD; perhaps I can make atonement for your sin" (Exod. 32:30b). And this is exactly what he does, boldly standing between God and the people, arguing with God to withhold his hand of judgment. Listen to the next words Moses speaks: "But now, if you will only forgive their sin — but if not, blot me out of the book that you have written" (Exod. 32:32). What a prayer! What a reckless, mediatorial, suffering prayer! It is exactly the kind of prayer in which we are privileged to participate.

What do we do? We do the kind of thing Daniel did. Daniel had lived all his adult life in the Babylonian courts, but now he reads in the writings of Jeremiah the prophet that the days of Jerusalem's devastation are complete. This leads to one of the most beautiful prayers ever recorded in Scripture, surpassed only by Jesus' Upper Room prayer. It is a prayer of repentance: "I prayed to the LORD my God and made confession" (Dan. 9:4). But Daniel is not confessing his sins; he is confessing the sins of his people, Israel. And note that he refuses to stand off at a safe, self-righteous distance but instead identifies intimately with the sins of the people. Listen: "*We* have sinned and done wrong . . . *we* have not listened . . . *we* have sinned against you" (Dan. 9:5–19, italics mine). On it goes: Daniel standing with his people; Daniel repenting on behalf of his people; Daniel mediating between God and his people. Finally, he closes his prayer with exactly the right perspective: "We do not present our supplication before you on the ground of our righteousness, but on the ground of your great mercy." What a prayer! This is what we are to do.

There were so many who lived and who prayed in this way. Think of Joseph and his exile. Think of Mary and her Calvary vigil. Think of Stephen and his stoning. Think of

Paul and his tribulations. Think of the list of those suffering giants of the faith in Hebrews 11 and the appropriate epitaph, "of whom the world was not worthy" (Heb. 11:38).

I reiterate: this is not suffering for suffering's sake. There is no hankering for martyrdom here. This is a conscious shouldering of the sins and sorrows of others in order that they may be healed and given new life. George MacDonald notes, "The Son of God suffered unto the death, not that men might not suffer, but that their sufferings might be like his."[6]

The Passive Side and the Active Side

There is a passive side and there is an active side to the Prayer of Suffering. The passive side involves the many trials that come into the course of our daily lives. These can be merely irritating or genuinely tragic. Sometimes they come because of disobedience or wrong living and, when this is the case, we are to change the way we live. But there are other times when we are caught in the whirlpool of a good world gone bad: a collapsing economy that eats up our life savings, a personality feud at the office that adversely affects our position, a terrible accident that changes our lives for ever.

When we suffer these things – for which we are not responsible and over which we have no control – we are to endure them patiently, putting our trust in God. Few of us today have much capacity for despair and destitution, and the Prayer of Suffering increases this capacity. Barrenness of soul sometimes comes to us for this very purpose. Jean-Nicholas Grou writes, "Let your suffering be borne for God; suffer with submission and patience and suffer in union with Jesus Christ and you will be offering a most excellent prayer."[7]

We can be assured of this: God, who knows all and sees all, will set all things straight in the end. Even better, he will dry every tear. In the meantime he mysteriously takes our sorrows and uses them to heal the world.

I know the danger inherent in the counsel I have just given. People can wrongly turn it into a passivity towards injustice and evil. This we must never do. We are under divine orders to fight against evil in every form. Passivity, however, is seldom *our* problem. We tend to fight and struggle over every minor inconvenience that comes our way. With spiritual maturity comes the ability to discern between the trials that are a normal part of living under the cross and the injustices of an evil world that demand correction.

The active side of suffering involves those times when we voluntarily take into ourselves the griefs and sorrows of others in order to set them free. A woman I shall call Anne once came to my wife, Carolynn, for prayer counselling. Anne's outward problem of depression was easy enough to see. In a short time the inner cause came to the surface as well – a sudden and tragic loss of her child. Carolynn has the gift of burden bearing, and so, as she began praying, she took on Anne's grief vicariously. Wave after wave of deep sobs, even wailing, came over Carolynn as she mourned the death of Anne's child. She asked God to take Anne's emotional pain and redeem it through the cross of Jesus Christ. When she did this, the sobbing subsided and was replaced with a settled peace.

Later, Carolynn received a letter from Anne, describing the new life that had been breathed into her during that prayer session. The healing Anne received on that day was significant though not total, for the roots of these matters go very deep and have many branches. Certainly Anne's depression had lifted enough that she could function normally once again. Through Carolynn's redemptive suffering, God had opened up a healing conduit into Anne's past so that she could mourn for herself the loss of her child.

I must add one small counsel to this story. We need not continue shouldering the burdens of others but rather we release them into the arms of the Father. Without this releasing the burdens will become too much for us, and depression will set in. Besides, it is not necessary. Our task in reality is a small one: to hold the agony of others just long enough for them to let go of it for themselves. Then together we can give all things over to God.

Repenting on Behalf of Others

The Prayer of Suffering stands out in all its naked reality when we are given the grace to repent on behalf of others, especially our enemies, forgiving them and setting them free. Dietrich Bonhoeffer says that when we pray for our enemies, "we are taking their distress and poverty, their guilt and perdition upon ourselves, and pleading to God for them. We are doing vicariously for them what they cannot do for themselves."[8]

In the Ravensbruck Nazi concentration camp – where an estimated 92,000 men, women and children were murdered – a piece of wrapping paper was found near the body of a dead child. On the paper was written this prayer:

> O Lord, remember not only the men and women of good will, but also those of ill will. But do not only remember the suffering they have inflicted on us; remember the fruits we bought, thanks to this suffering: our comradeship, our loyalty, our humility, the courage, the generosity, the greatness of heart which has grown out of all this. And when they come to judgment, let all the fruits that we have borne be their forgiveness.[9]

This idea of repenting on behalf of others may be new to you. "Do people not have to repent for themselves?" you may wonder. You are correct, of course. Each of us must turn for ourselves in heart sorrow for our offences to Divine Mercy. But – and here is the wonder – our repenting prayers on behalf of others somehow seem to make it easier, more possible for them to turn on their own. How this works I do not know. That it does work I am quite certain. Not that everyone we pray for is instantly transformed into some sort of saint. (Not even Jesus' sacrifice produced that kind of result — a result we would not even want once we fully understood it.) No, it is more like the releasing of little droplets of grace and mercy — droplets that perhaps can be shaken off but certainly cannot be ignored.

The Groanings of a Struggling Faith

This standing between God and people involves a kind of wrestling with God. That is part of our suffering, a little like arguing with our best friend. Tertullian calls it "a kind of holy violence to God".[10] Like Jacob of old, who wrestled all night with the angel, we refuse to let go until we receive a blessing, not for us, but for others. We argue with God so that his justice may be overcome by his mercy. It is only because of our intimacy with God that we can thus wrestle with him.

This intense interaction is not unlike God himself, for, as Donald Bloesch tells us, "God even wrestles with himself, seeking to reconcile his holiness, which cannot tolerate sin, with his infinite love for a sinful human race."[11] Even so, this wrestling is a hard image for us to accept. We much prefer the image of restful harmony. Our difficulty is due, in part, to our culture's inability to reconcile struggle with love. We assume that a loving relationship by its very nature must be peaceful and harmonious, and yet, even on a human level, those things we care about the most deeply we argue for the most passionately. Struggle is consistent with love, for it is an expression of our caring.

This is not anger. It is not whining. It is, as Martin Luther puts it, "a continuous violent action of the spirit as it is lifted up to God".[12] We are engaging in serious business. Our prayers are important, having effect with God. We want God to know the earnestness of our heart. We beat on the doors of heaven because we want to be heard on high. We agonize. We cry out. We shout. We pray with sobs and tears. Our prayers become the groanings of a struggling faith. As Charles Spurgeon reminds us, "Prayer is able to prevail with heaven and bend omnipotence to its desires."13

Fasting is one expression of our struggle. Fasting is the voluntary denial of a normal function for the sake of intense spiritual activity. It is a sign of our seriousness and intensity. When we fast we are intentionally relinquishing the first right given to the human family in the Garden – the right to eat. We say no to food because we are intent upon others receiving a far greater nourishment. We are committed to breaking every yoke and setting the captives free. Our fasting is a sign that nothing will stop us in our struggle on behalf of the broken and oppressed.

In *Celebration of Discipline* I provide detailed instruction in the practice of fasting, and there are many other good books to guide you. Here I want to underscore fasting as a means of helping us to suffer joyfully. We are depriving ourselves for the sake of a greater good. Our fasting has weight with God and effect upon others. Pastor Hsi of China was so concerned to see his wife set free from her deep depression and mental torment that he "called for a fast of three days and nights in his household, and gave himself to prayer. Weak in body, but strong in faith, he laid hold on the promises of God."14 His subsequent prayer for her was completely successful, restoring her to full health. In time she became an effective companion in his remarkable ministry.

This is no excessive, unhealthy asceticism. It has nothing to do with the extremes of torture and self-mortification, which are a perversion of genuine sacrifice. We do not take pleasure in pain, nor do we seek it out unnecessarily. Our fasting is part of our wrestling with God. It is part of the birth pangs we endure in order to see new life come forth.

The wrestling may be painful, but the net result is worth the struggle, for, as Søren Kierkegaard reminds us, we win – and so does God: "The righteous man strives in prayer with God and conquers – in that God conquers."15

Suffering with the Body of Christ

The Bible tells us that we are "the body of Christ". This description of the community of faith is not some romantic metaphor but is a genuine reality. Jesus Christ through the Spirit continues to live within his Church, and our sufferings are his sufferings. John Calvin writes, "As, therefore, Christ has suffered *once* in his own person, so he suffers *daily* in his members."[16] And these sufferings are redemptive; they are actually used of God to change and transform and draw people into the way of Christ.

As our sufferings are his, so his sufferings are ours. Every now and then we are given the privilege of sharing in the sufferings of Christ over some special need in his Body. A minister in Africa once woke up in the middle of the night in tears. A strange name came to him over and over, a name he did not know. He sensed it was a call to pray, but for whom, for what? He did not know. Still he prayed in the Spirit over this name that he did not know, suffering intense pain as he did so. After several hours the burden lifted, and he knew his intercessory work was complete. The next day the newspapers carried the sad story of a Christian village whose inhabitants had been massacred during the night. The village had the same name the minister had been weeping over.[17] In some way that we do not understand, this minister was allowed to share in the sufferings of the village people and so share in the sufferings of Christ. Our prayer privilege may never be this striking, but it will be just as important.

———————◆———————

O Holy Spirit of God, so many hurt today. Help me to stand with them in their suffering. I do not really know how to do this. My temptation is to offer some quick prayer and send them off rather than endure with them the desolation of suffering. Show me the pathway into their pain.

In the name and for the sake of Jesus.

— Amen.

Authoritative Prayer

God has instituted prayer so as to confer upon his creatures the dignity of being causes.
— Blaise Pascal

In Authoritative Prayer we are calling forth the will of the Father upon the earth. Here we are not so much speaking *to* God as speaking *for* God. We are not asking God to do something; rather, we are using the authority of God to command something to be done.

There is personal prayer and there is devotional prayer, but the kind of prayer we are discussing is in a different category. Many times we have personal needs, so we ask of God, and he answers. At other times we sense the nearness of God and are encouraged by the intimate friendship. But there is also prayer that God uses to invade enemy territory and establish his kingdom. This is the kind of prayer that is under consideration here.

When the children of Israel had their backs to the Red Sea and the armies of Pharaoh were pressing in, the Bible tells us they "cried out to the LORD". But God said to Moses, "Why do you cry out to me? Tell the Israelites to go forward. But you lift up your staff, and stretch out your hand over the sea and divide it" (Exod. 14:15–16a). On this occasion prayer, as we normally understand it, was not appropriate. In essence God was saying, "Stop praying to me and start exercising the authority I have given you!" God was telling Moses to take control of the situation, which is precisely what he did. And that is precisely what we do in Authoritative Prayer.

Venturing Out

In my own experience I stumbled on this way of prayer almost by accident many years ago. Our eldest son, Joel, frequently had ear infections as a baby despite our most watchful attention. They were extremely painful, and we would often be up with him all night. On one of those nights when it was my turn to stay up, I prayed every prayer I could think of, but nothing seemed to help. It was about 4 a.m. and I had been pacing the floor, holding his ear against my shoulder, hoping against hope that the pain would subside enough for him to stop the heartbreaking whimpering and fall asleep. I was tired and frustrated.

All of a sudden I was struck by the notion that I should speak directly to the pain. The idea seemed a bit strange, but quietly I addressed the pain: "Thank you for letting us know that there is an infection in Joel's ear. We are providing the best medical attention for it we can. We have received the message, and so you do not need to keep sending pain signals to his ear. So in Jesus' name stop it, now!" Instantaneously Joel's whining and fussing ceased; he laid his head on my shoulder and fell fast asleep. It happened so abruptly and so completely that it startled me. When he awoke later in the day, his ear infection was completely gone. (I might add that a few months later we had his tonsils removed, for the doctor felt they were the source of his constant infections.)

Authority Wedded to Compassion

Actually, I almost wish I did not have to tell you about Authoritative Prayer. It is one area that has been terribly abused and misused today. The old adage that "power corrupts and absolute power corrupts absolutely" has a lot of truth in it. This way of prayer can be extremely dangerous, which is one reason why I waited until nearly the end of this book to bring up the subject. Hopefully by now we have experienced enough of the transforming graces of God that the old passion to run roughshod over the lives of others has been effectively defeated or at least clearly identified.

I have discovered that the excesses in Authoritative Prayer come most frequently when people fail to match the exercise of the power of Christ to a clear understanding of the compassion of Christ. Dostoevsky, in *The Brothers Karamazov*, depicts this problem well in his portrayal of two monks, Father Ferapont and Father Zosima. In the novel Father Ferapont is the cold, rigid ascetic, but he has power, real spiritual power. Everyone trembles when Father Ferapont comes into the room. Father Zosima, on the other hand, is the epitome of the compassionate, kind, caring priest. Everyone loves Father Zosima.[1]

Now, in our practice of the prayer of authority we have a lot better chance of being a blessing if we combine the power of a Father Ferapont with the compassion of a Father Zosima. Far too often we see power and compassion as mutually exclusive, but in Jesus they were beautifully united. Authority needs compassion to keep it from becoming destructive. Compassion provides the environment in which authority can function.

The Guard-Rails of Discernment and Prudence

But compassion alone is not enough. We also need the spiritual gift of discernment and the cardinal virtue of prudence to provide guard-rails for the right exercise of Authoritative Prayer. Discernment is a supernatural charism of the Spirit, and prudence has been universally recognized as a central virtue for those seeking to live uprightly. The two balance and play off one another a little like a gyroscope, the heart of a gyrocompass, which was once used to keep ships and planes on course. Discernment is like the rotating axis of the gyroscope and prudence is akin to its horizontal plane, the combination of which gives freedom of movement within the context of balance and direction.

Discernment is the divine ability to see what is actually going on and to know what needs to be done in any situation. As John Woolman says, we "feel and understand the spirits of people".[2] This charism of the Spirit is critical because accurate diagnosis is necessary for effective ministry. We need, for example, to be able to discern between multiple personalities caused by emotional wounds and those caused by demonic activity. We must never become so enamoured of the spiritual world that we think every jot and tittle of life is caused by supernatural activity, nor should we be so taken in by the naturalistic assumptions of modern society that we fail to see the markings of the transcendent.

The best way to learn about the spiritual gift of discernment is to be close to those who move in this realm. Look for them − they are not hard to spot, even though they seldom call attention to themselves. They are the ones people seek out when needing help or guidance. Comments are made about these people, comments like "She is just so wise"; "I don't know how he knew, but he said exactly what I needed to hear"; "Every time I see her I feel as if I understand things so much better." When you discover such people, find ways to be with them and learn from them.

"Prudence," says C. S. Lewis, "means practical common sense, taking the trouble to think out what you are doing and what is likely to come of it."[3] It is a virtue that is in short supply today. Some people, once they understand the authority they have in Christ, seem to lose all good sense . . . and good manners. They go round ordering this and that to happen in the most unkind and destructive of ways. Jesus never did that. He knew when to speak and when to be silent. He was always appropriate to the situation in which he found himself. Even his teachings are filled with good, ordinary "horse sense". When he told us not to cast our pearls before swine, for example, it was not to be mean, but because he knew that swine cannot digest pearls; they do them no good (Matt. 7:6). We too should have the good sense to refrain from giving people truth that they are not ready to receive, for it will do them no good. This practical common sense pervaded everything Jesus said and did.

Most often discernment and prudence operate hand in glove. I have an acquaintance I shall call Derek who went to the hospital to visit a friend who was nearing death. As Derek went up in the lift, he thought he might just tell the disease to go away, but when he got into the room he saw that his friend was asleep. Derek then did an unusual thing; he went to the foot of the hospital bed and prayed the prayer for guidance; "Lord, how do you want me to pray?" Immediately he sensed an inward check about "telling the disease to go away". In fact he felt no prompting to pray. It seemed best simply to visit his friend.

So Derek went over to his friend, touching him on the shoulder to wake him, and said, "Good morning. I just came to see you for a bit."

Derek's friend responded weakly but gratefully, "Oh, I'm so glad. Everyone has been coming in and laying their hands on me and trying to make me well, and all I want to do is go home to heaven. And I was hoping someone would come and just visit me." Therefore we must be both wise and sensitive so that we speak forth the command of faith *only* when it is right and good.

The Lead of Our Leader

We must also be confident to speak the authoritative word when it *is* right and good. We simply cannot get beyond the fact that Jesus prayed in this way and urged his followers to do likewise. In one significant passage Jesus says, "Truly I tell you, if you say to this mountain, 'Be taken up and thrown into the sea,' and if you do not doubt in your heart, but believe that what you say will come to pass, it will be done for you" (Mark 11:23).

Notice that he is not telling us to speak to God about the mountain; he is telling us to speak directly to the mountain.

This is not prayer as we normally think of it, but it is most certainly prayer.

On one occasion Jesus' disciples tried to heal a child who evidenced signs of demonic oppression. They failed miserably. Finally Jesus took over the situation. He got a brief history of the child's situation, and then, upon seeing the faith of the boy's father, rebuked the demonic spirit, saying, "You spirit that keeps this boy from speaking and hearing, I command you, come out of him, and never enter him again!" The child went into terrible convulsions and then, as the evil spirit left him, he fell to the ground as though dead. In fact, everyone thought he was dead until Jesus took him by the hand and lifted him up perfectly whole.

The disciples were understandably amazed at all this, and could hardly wait to get Jesus alone so they could ask the reason for *his* success and *their* failure. Jesus' response was simple and direct: "This kind can come out only through prayer" (Mark 9:14–29). But notice, in the situation Jesus did not pray as we ordinarily think of prayer. He did not talk to God at all. Instead he spoke direct to the demonic spirit, commanding it to leave.

This is prayer, all right, but it is the prayer of command. This kind of prayer is peppered all through Jesus' ministry. He compelled the wind and the waves to stop, saying, "Quiet, be still!" He commanded the lepers, "Be clean." He touched blind eyes, saying, "Be opened." To deaf ears he said the same; "Be opened." To the paralytic he ordered, "Get up." At the grave of his friend Lazarus he commanded, "Come forth." To demonic spirits he ordered, "Come out."

Not only did Jesus exercise the prayer of command; he also delegated this same authority to others. When he sent out the twelve, he "gave them power and authority over all demons and to cure diseases, and he sent them out to proclaim the kingdom of God and to heal" (Luke 9:1–2). In essence, he told them to declare the availability of the kingdom and to demonstrate its presence with works of power. And that is exactly what they did: "They departed and went through the villages, bringing the good news and curing diseases everywhere" (Luke 9:6).

When he sent out the seventy, it was with the same commission: "Cure the sick who are there, and say to them, 'the kingdom of God has come near to you'" (Luke 10:9). They returned from their mission ecstatic, saying, "'Lord, in your name even the demons submit to us!'" (Luke 10:17). Jesus was thrilled, for now he knew that the heavenly power could be delegated to ordinary human beings: "Jesus rejoiced in the Holy Spirit and said, 'I thank you, Father, Lord of heaven and earth, because you have hidden these things from the wise and the intelligent and have revealed them to infants'" (Luke 10:21).

Following Our Leader's Lead

The passages I have just shared with you are not new to me, but for years I thought that the ministry of power was only for the select few — you know, apostles and saints and all. Certainly I should not be expected to do that sort of thing. But then I came upon Jesus' shocking words, "Very truly, I tell you, the one who believes in me will also do the works that I do and, in fact, will do greater works than these, because I am going to the Father" (John 14:12). I could no longer evade my personal responsibility and involvement.

This, however, was not good news to me. I was concerned about where such notions might lead. I was worried that people might step from the sovereignty of God and attempt things in their own strength. I was anxious about the pride and presumption in all this authoritative talk. Most of all I was afraid people would fall off the deep end . . . afraid I would fall off the deep end.

But quickly I saw that the danger of superficiality is clearly as perilous as the danger of excess, perhaps more so. In my concern over falling off the deep end, I realized that I just might fall off the shallow end. My desire to maintain religious respectability could easily result in a domesticated faith. I knew that I dare not let this happen. I must be willing to step out even if the waters looked deep.

Besides, there are precious people who desperately need help. Some years ago I met a distinguished-looking woman while giving a series of lectures in Santa Barbara, California. I shall call her Gloria. The focus of my lectures was Contemplative Prayer, and the atmosphere of the meetings had been enhanced by the relaxed beauty of stately eucalyptus trees and red-tiled haciendas. Following an afternoon session, Gloria asked for an appointment, and so we stepped into a lovely library room, where we could be uninterrupted. I remember the solid oak bookshelves and beautifully crafted hardwood table in the centre of the room. I also remember the refined dignity with which Gloria carried herself. "Sophisticated," I thought to myself.

But the story she told that day was anything but sophisticated. A deeply spiritual person, Gloria had suffered from six months of intense affliction from the evil one. That is the only way I know to describe it. You see, six months earlier, while on a week-long silent retreat, Gloria, suddenly and unexpectedly, experienced acute stomach pains. "I doubled over in agony," she told me. "Then I felt a presence: a horrible, awful presence. I began weeping profusely. I felt unbelievably heavy on my feet, heavy as though I was carrying a cross. Then I saw a monstrous thing. It was huge, dark, ugly. It spoke with a gravelly voice, like an animal. The impression came to me, 'The devil is trying to eat me up!'"

Bent over with pain, Gloria laboriously made her way to the chapel. She sprinkled herself with holy water and prostrated herself on the floor, saying, "I will worship only God." There on the floor of the chapel she fell asleep.

When Gloria awoke, she felt somewhat better. At the evening liturgy she received Eucharist and then went to bed, hoping that the incident had passed. In the middle of the night, however, she was yanked awake. "My body was jerking so violently," she told me, "that I feared my neck would break. All I could think of was, 'The devil is trying to destroy me!'" She staggered down the hall and pounded on the door of the room occupied by the priest overseeing the retreat. Awakened from a sound sleep and unsure what to do, he called one of the sisters at the retreat house, and together they sat up with Gloria until the darkness subsided a little. "I know they thought I was mentally ill," Gloria confided to me. "What else could they think?

"The episodes and the darkness have continued now for six months." Gloria was sharing with me in a straightforward and utterly lucid manner. "Then, in your lecture on prayer, you warned of spirits that are opposed to the way of God, and I thought maybe you would understand my story. I cannot talk to just anybody. Please, can you help me?"

I had been listening now for perhaps forty minutes, and I knew I was in the presence of someone who was completely rational. I sensed that the afflictions Gloria had been experiencing were from the enemy of her soul. I said firmly and, I hope, compassionately, "Yes, I can help you." (Actually I was not nearly as confident as my words sounded, and I knew that if any help was forthcoming, it certainly would not be from me. But I also knew that this was no time for theological hair-splitting.)

Placing my hands on Gloria's head, I prayed with all the authority and tenderness I could muster. I ordered the darkness — whatever it was — to leave and to go into the strong arms of Jesus. Gloria began weeping . . . a deep, inward weeping accompanied by huge sighs. I invited the peace and the love of God to enter her, filling every aspect of her mind, body and spirit. And the darkness left. The peace came. Together we sat in perfect silence, sensing the flow of grace and mercy.

That was ten years ago, and the darkness has never returned. Reflecting on this event recently, Gloria told me in a telephone conversation that the prayer on that day was "like a sonnet spoken over me". I like her description and would only add that, if so, then it was a sonnet from above.4

Common Sense Counsels

A few simple counsels are needed in these matters. First, I hope you will not assume from this story that every stomach pain is an attack of the devil. More often than not a pain is a pain is a pain! There is nothing more to it than that. We need not go looking for a demon under every bush. Besides, many of our prayer efforts in this realm are not on the dramatic, cosmic scale at all. Instead they focus on much more mundane – though equally important – matters. In the power of God we learn to take authority over everyday issues like our eating habits and our sexual fantasies and our fears and our failures.

Second, we do not have to put on some special voice or jump up and down or do anything bizarre to function in this realm. If the power of God is present, then we do not need any special effects, and if the divine authority is absent, then all the gymnastics in the world will not make up for the deficiency. So, rather than try to be something we are not, we can speak normally and do whatever seems appropriate to the situation.

Third, we have special resources to draw upon. It is common to experience unusual anointing of the Holy Spirit for specific ministry situations. When appropriate we should wait for the power of the Spirit to increase, all the time surrounding ourselves with the light of Christ and covering ourselves with the blood of Christ and sealing ourselves with the cross of Christ. In addition many of the angels of God have been assigned to aid us in our battle. We can ask God for their help.

Fourth, while we deal firmly and decisively with evil, we always remain gentle and compassionate with the individual. People should not be put on display, nor should their situation be exploited in any way. These are precious persons for whom Christ died, and we are to show them the greatest courtesy and respect at all times.

Fifth, Authoritative Prayer is not a substitute for disciplined habits of living. Many times people need not deliverance but discipline. In such cases our task is to help them enter an overall pattern of living that involves the normal disciplines of the spiritual life.[5]

Sixth, in this work we will do well to stay connected with others. This is no hit-and-run kind of ministry. At times God may want a solitary Elijah or John the Baptist, but his more customary pattern is to anchor us in communities where there can be accountability and support. This also allows us to be with people without being the centre of attention – a great blessing in itself.

And seventh, while we always want to be bold in the boldness of God, we must immerse our efforts in the most profound humility of spirit. Frankly, there is much that we do not know and much that we cannot do. Sometimes I wish I could just walk into intensive care units and mental health wards and bring people to wholeness, one after the other. But I cannot do that, and I know of no one who can. "You lack faith," some may tell me. I am sure they are correct. In fact, I am sure I lack many things. I do not, however, lack trying, and I will continue trying, for sometimes – not always, but sometimes – the most wonderful things happen. And when they do, we can only thank and bless the God of heaven.

From Heaven to Earth

Ordinary forms of prayer proceed from earth to heaven. We are asking for forgiveness, or giving thanks, or seeking healing. To use a spatial image, it is prayer upward.

But Authoritative Prayer moves in exactly the opposite direction. We are bringing the resources of heaven to bear upon a particular matter on earth. It is prayer downward, if you will.

William Law declares that prayer is a mighty instrument, "not for getting man's will done in heaven" but "for getting God's will done on earth".[6] Dr Ole Hallesby highlights the same reality when he writes, "Prayer is the conduit through which power from heaven is brought to earth."7 We are, in effect, praying from heaven to earth.

The Apostle Paul tells us that after God raised Jesus from the dead, he "seated him at his right hand in the heavenly places, far above all rule and authority and power and dominion. . . . And he has put all things under his feet" (Eph. 1:20b–22a). His point is a simple one: Jesus, by means of his ascension and heavenly reign, has authority over every spiritual and material power.

Next the Apostle brings you and me into the picture. God, says Paul, has taken those who have been saved by grace through faith "and raised us up with him and seated us with him in the heavenly places in Christ Jesus" (Eph. 2:6). Not only has Jesus been placed in a position of authority above all created things; we have been placed there as well.

This leads logically into Paul's famous description of the spiritual warfare we wage and the spiritual resources we have available to us (Eph. 6:10–20). The flow of his argument runs like this: Christ's heavenly position of authority (Eph. 1) gives us our heavenly position of authority (Eph. 2) which results in the ability to wage the warfare of the Lamb against all principalities and powers (Eph. 6). We exercise Authoritative Prayer from this heavenly position of authority.

Waging the Lamb's War

As a means of advancing the kingdom of God, Authoritative Prayer is focused primarily upon coming against the principalities and powers of this present darkness. Paul writes, "Our struggle is not against enemies of blood and flesh, but against the rulers, against the authorities, against the cosmic powers of this present darkness, against the spiritual forces of evil in the heavenly places" (Eph. 6:12). In saying this Paul means not that the "blood and flesh" are unimportant but that the real battle goes deeper. Behind absentee landlords of ghetto flats are the spiritual forces of greed and avarice. Behind unreasoned and excessive resistance to the Gospel message are demonic forces of disobedience and distraction. Underneath the organized structures of injustice and oppression are principalities of privilege and status. Aiding and abetting the sexual violence and the race hate and the child molestation that are such a part of modern society are diabolical powers of destruction and brutality. Therefore, says Paul, when we face, for instance, people who are deaf to the Gospel or laws that are cruel and unjust or leaders who are oppressive, then we are also dealing with cosmic principalities and powers that are straight from the pit.

In Authoritative Prayer we are engaged in the warfare of the Spirit against the kingdom of darkness. In the Apocalypse, the last book of our Bible, Christ is pictured as both the sacrificial Lamb and the conquering King (Rev. 5 and 19). This great eschatological vision of conquest by suffering is a description of the total mission and struggle of the pilgrim people of God. Ole Hallesby writes, "The secret prayer chamber is a bloody battle-ground. Here violent and decisive battles are fought out."[8]

But remember, we are told that the gates of hell cannot withstand the onslaughts of the Church (Matt. 16:18). The kingdom of darkness goes into full retreat when we take up the full weapons of our warfare. "Therefore take up the whole armour of God," writes Paul, "so that you may be able to withstand on that evil day." And these are weapons of real power: the belt of truth, the breastplate of righteousness, the shoes of peace, the shield of faith, the helmet of salvation, the sword of the Spirit, the life of prayer (Eph. 6:13-18).

Christ, writes James Nayler:

> puts spiritual weapons into [our] hearts and hands ... to make war ... conquering and to conquer, not as the prince of this world ... with whips and prisons, tortures and torments ... but with the word of truth ... returning love for hatred, wrestling with

God against the enmity, with prayers and tears night and day, with fasting, mourning and lamentation, in patience, in faithfulness, in truth, in love unfeigned, in long suffering, and in all the fruits of the spirit, that if by any means [we] may overcome evil with good.9

Exercising our Authority

Spiritual warfare is not something we talk about; it is something we do. How do we do it? We do it by breaking all the destructive vows – both conscious and unconscious – that lie over the lives of people. Many have condemned themselves with inner vows of sickness and failure and death. Seeing these things and knowing that it is not good for people to be in such bondage, we speak the word of authority that breaks the curse. Some have curses lying over them from the generations that have gone before: the curse of alcoholism, the curse of mental illness, and more. Whether the curse is physical, emotional or spiritual, we break it in the name and by the authority of Jesus.

How do we do it? We do it by taking authority over the sicknesses of mind and body and spirit. Sickness is an enemy, and we are to fight against it. We speak balance into phobic and neurotic personalities. We rebuke fevers and choke off the blood supply to cancer cells. We call for wholeness and well-being to come sweeping into the lives of people.

How do we do it? We do it by coming against every "mountain" that hinders our progress in God. We command fears of all kinds to leave and never return. We stand against evil thoughts and suspicions and distortions of every sort. We bind the spirit of anger and jealousy and gossip, and release the spirit of forgiveness and love and faith.

How do we do it? We do it by demon expulsion. Wherever we find evil forces at work, we firmly demand that they leave. We are in charge, not them. In the ministry of power we take authority over whatever is opposed to our life in the kingdom of God.

How do we do it? We do it by coming against all social evil and institutional injustice. We blow the trumpet against institutional structures that guarantee the poverty of the poor. We oppose unjust laws that demean and dehumanize those for whom Christ died. We work for laws of equity and justice. We give to the poor; we feed the hungry; we shelter the homeless. All these things and much more are the work of Authoritative Prayer. It is work that throughout is done in the spirit of deepest prayer and greatest humility, for we are trusting in the power of God, not our cleverness. Richard Sibbes writes, "What cannot prayer do when the people of God have their hearts quickened, and raised to pray? Prayer can open heaven. Prayer can open the womb. Prayer can open the prison, and strike off the fetters."[10]

In the strong name of Jesus Christ I stand against the world, the flesh and the devil. I resist every force that would seek to distract me from my centre in God. I reject the distorted concepts and ideas that make sin plausible and desirable. I oppose every attempt to keep me from knowing full fellowship with God.

By the power of the Holy Spirit I speak directly to the thoughts, emotions and desires of my heart and command you to find your satisfaction in the infinite variety of God's love rather than the bland diet of sin. I call upon the good, the true and the beautiful to rise up within me and the evil to subside. I ask for an increase of righteousness, peace and joy in the Holy Spirit.

By the authority of almighty God I tear down Satan's strongholds in my life, in the lives of those I love, and in the society in which I live. I take into myself the weapons of truth, righteousness, peace, salvation, the word of God and prayer. I command every evil influence to leave; you have no right here and I allow you no point of entry. I ask for an increase of faith, hope and love so that, by the power of God, I can be a light set on a hill, causing truth and justice to flourish.

These things I pray for the sake of him who loved me and gave himself for me.

— Amen.

Radical Prayer

*To clasp the hands in prayer is the beginning of
an uprising against the disorder of the world.*
— Karl Barth

Radical Prayer goes to the root, the heart, the centre. The
word radical itself comes from the Latin *radix*, which
means root. Radical Prayer refuses to let us stay on
the fringes of life's great issues. It dares to believe that
things can be different. Its aim is the total transformation
of persons, institutions and societies. Radical Prayer, you
see, is prophetic.

Oregon Epiphany

In the spring of 1978 Carolynn and I drove to the Oregon
coast for a few days of rest from a demanding winter
schedule. On our first morning there I got up before the sun,
though not before the sun's light. Carolynn was still asleep,
so I quietly slipped out for an early walk on the beach.
Other than the ever present sea gulls, I was quite alone.
The tide was out, and the night mist was just beginning
to flee from the morning's encroachment. Nearby was a
huge monolith well known in the area as Haystack Rock.
Nesting atop the rock were squadrons of tufted puffins —
stocky black birds with reddish bills and white tuft bands
on their heads. With the tide going out, I was able to walk
almost completely round this magnificent rock fortress,
which rises straight out of the sand. I marvelled at its
stubbornness in standing against the unrelenting attack of
ocean waves.

The sun had now broken over the distant mountains. The

sheer splendour made me catch my breath. I exclaimed out loud, "This is beautiful!" Now, I was not in the least trying to be religious in this; I was simply taking in the wonder of light and trees and ocean and mist. There was, however, a response – a clear, unadorned, frank response – "I know, I made it." I blurted out, "Thank you, Lord!" Again, there was a response, "You're welcome."

I stopped dead in my tracks. I do not know about you, but I am not used to "hearing voices".[1] Yet what followed, while unusual, was not strange in the least. It was more like an ordinary dialogue between friends than like the silly science fiction stereotypes we see in the media. The experience lasted for perhaps an hour and a half, though I had no watch with me to tell for sure. I worshipped, laughed, gave thanks and even at one point asked some questions that had often troubled me. To one question in particular I think God chuckled good naturedly at my naïvety.

What happened next is hard to explain. I had come to a cliff overlooking the beach. On top was a forest of hemlock, Sitka spruce and Western cedar. I was admiring one giant Western cedar especially. I knew it took several centuries for this tree to attain its present size. Then, as I took three steps to the right, I saw what had been hidden from my view by the healthy tree – another extremely large but obviously rotting Western cedar. Some sprouts of green went out on two sides, but it would only be a matter of time before the tree died, for its centre was exposed – apparently it had been struck by lightning in some far distant past. Aside from the huge size of the two trees, there was nothing unusual in the scene.

But then, as I examined the decaying tree, the word of the Lord came to me, saying, "This is my Church!" When I heard the words, tears came to my eyes. I had worked in churches all my life, and I knew it was so – the Church, while huge and with some vestiges of life remaining, was decaying. Then, for some reason unknown to me, I turned 180 degrees and looked back at Haystack Rock in the distance. The tide had come in by then and the rock was completely surrounded by water, the waves savagely breaking against it. The divine word continued, "But this is what my Church is going to be!" Great hope rose up within me as I stared at this massive icon of strength and endurance.

Then I was given instruction that I assume was one of the primary reasons for the encounter. It was the guidance to pray for the rising up of a new generation of leaders – prophets of the apostolic mould – leaders who could once again gather the people of God into communities of radical faithfulness.

With this, the experience seemed to draw to a close and so I made my way back to tell Carolynn all the things I had seen and heard. Over the years since this encounter I have sought to pray in the way I was instructed, though not as faithfully as I am sure I should. But also I get inklings that vast numbers of people around the globe have been given similar guidance, so that great waves of prayer for the rising up of prophetic leaders has been ascending to the throne of God throughout the years. Now I believe we are beginning to see prophets emerging – many of them in Third World countries – prophets who are calling people into fresh, bold expressions of faithfulness and obedience.

The Prophetic Messenger

I am aware that some people have theological reasons for believing that the charism of the prophet ended at the apostolic age. For still others the word is no longer useful because of contemporary abuses and stereotypes. I understand these concerns; even so I have chosen to continue to use the word prophet both because this was the way it came to me on that Oregon beach and because there is a rich tradition in the Bible that informs what I am talking about.

What do these prophets look like? They come from every class and category of people. Some are educated; others are illiterate or semi-literate. Some come from organized churches and denominations; others come from outside these structures. Some are women; some are men; some are children.

To the person they love Jesus with their whole heart. They all evidence the call of God upon their lives and the hand of God upon their ministries. It is of no consequence to them who is up front, who gets the attention, or who is remembered in the annals of history. Few of them, in fact, are known to the custodians of the modern media for they lack those elements necessary to be "newsworthy" – money, power and scandal.

For the most part they are insignificant and irrelevant even in the world of religion. It is not that they lack influence; it is that the place of influence is viewed as unimportant. Who cares if a few thousand tribespeople in Zaïre come into obedience to Christ? It is not that they lack impact; it is that the kind of impact is seen as irrelevant. Who notices if anonymous people in Los Angeles begin loving their enemies and sharing their goods with one another? To normal human reckoning they are the little people, but in the kingdom of God they are truly the great ones. They are the spiritual heirs of Deborah and Elijah, of Amos and Jeremiah, of Paul and the daughters of Philip.

Under their leadership and by the power of the Holy Spirit the people of God are once again being gathered. (I am speaking not organizationally but organically.) We are witnessing in our day a whole host of children and women and men who are getting hooked into a different order of reality and power.

These are those who have seen the stone cut without hands smashing the kingdoms of this world and becoming a great mountain that fills the whole earth (Dan. 2). These are those who have seen this living stone – the very stone that the builders rejected – become the head of the corner, and they themselves have become like living stones built into a spiritual house, a holy priesthood (I Pet. 2). These are those who have come into the kingdom of our God and of his Christ.

These are the ones who can envision a new future, a future of righteousness and peace and joy in the Holy Spirit. They are being taken over by a holy power to do the right. They are being brought off bondage to human beings. They cannot be bribed or manipulated or flattered. They love their enemies and pray for those who despise them. In time their very presence and actions will bring down those structures that are sustained by greed and pride and fear. Their simple non-cooperation with the oppression, prejudice and class strife of modern culture will transform the world almost beyond recognition.

I believe that you who read these words are among this company of the committed. The hand of God has been upon you, wooing you, winning you, drawing you to himself.

As important as the prophetic messenger is, the prophetic message is more important. The prophetic message envisions a radical way of living and a radical way of praying. We must now attempt to sketch out the basic outlines of this message.

Spiritual Defiance

The true prophetic message always calls us to a spiritual defiance of the world as it now is. Our prayer, to the extent that it is fully authentic, undermines the status quo. It is a spiritual underground resistance movement. We are subversives in a world of injustice, oppression and violence. Like Amos of old, we demand that "justice roll down like waters, and righteousness like an everflowing stream" (Amos 5:24). We plead the case of the orphan and the widow, or whoever the helpless ones are in our context. In our prayers and in our actions we stand firm against racism, sexism, nationalism, ageism and every other "ism" that separates and splits and divides.

We become the voice of the voiceless, pleading their cause all the way to the throne of heaven. We demand to be heard. We insist that changes be made. "Biblical prayer," writes Walter Wink, "is impertinent, persistent, shameless, indecorous. It is more like haggling in an outdoor bazaar than the polite monologues of the churches."[2] Like Abraham we bargain with God over the fate of the city (Gen. 18). Like Moses we argue with God over the fate of the people (Exod. 32). Like Esther we plead with God over the fate of the nation (Esther 4).

Our spiritual defiance involves attempting to change God's mind when we believe that to do so is consistent with God's unchanging love. "Sometimes," writes Donald Bloesch, "the prayer of faith involves defiance of God bordering on presumption."[3] Martin Luther says that "the might of prayer" is "so great" that "it has overcome both heaven and earth". He could even speak of "conquering God" in the sense that we are seeking to bind God to his own promises.[4]

We speak to God about the bruised and the broken, the helpless and the homeless. We speak to others as well. Our spiritual defiance leads to firm, aggressive action against all injustice and oppression. We are enraged that people are thrown into prison at the whim of an unjust ruler, or that the child down the street is emotionally or physically abused. We are insulted that our culture defines choice in such a way as to pit a woman's body against herself, or that it defines life in such a way as to grind the poor all the more deeply into their poverty. Instead we must turn a deaf ear to media caricatures and prayerfully discern the way of Christ amid the complex issues of our day.

The weapons of our resistance make us appear to be completely irrelevant to a world based on power, efficiency and control. We speak the truth. We pray for our enemies. We refuse to cooperate with injustice. And yet, incredible as it may seem, these weapons are powerful in pulling down strongholds and bringing to birth the righteous and peaceable kingdom of Jesus.

Social Holiness

The true prophetic message always calls us to "social holiness", to use the phrase of John Wesley. By our praying and by our living we sabotage all class and rank and status distinctions.

Jesus was, and is, a social revolutionary. When he healed the sick he did more than cure diseases: he healed the sickness in a society that would cast these people aside. When he pronounced his beatitudes upon the people, he was taking up those classes and categories that society deemed to be unblessed and unblessable. He told these "sat upon, spat upon, ratted on" people that they were precious in the kingdom of God. He blessed the children; he spoke to an outcast woman; he hobnobbed with a wealthy crook (Mark 10:13–16; John 4:1–26; Luke 19:1–10).

We are to do likewise. In our praying and in our living we value all, breaking down every barrier. The class barriers have shifted somewhat in our day. The slender people we value; the fat we don't. The successful people we value; the failures we don't. The powerful people we value; the helpless we don't. The intelligent people we value; the ignorant we don't. And on it goes, *ad nauseam*. But for the children of the kingdom it is not important *who* a person is, only that a person *is*.

Jesus' social revolution went all the way to the corridors of religious power. In the Sermon on the Mount he told the people, in essence, that the entire temple ritual system could dry up and blow away and their blessedness would still remain. Jesus, you see, set people free rather than put them in bondage.

And so do we. By our prayers and by our words we liberate people, not bind them to us. When we pray for others we are leading them to Jesus, their present Teacher, so they have no need of us any more. Any faith that makes the blessedness of people dependent upon anyone or anything other than God himself is, to that extent, a false faith.

Social holiness takes us beyond our comfort zones and our geographic borders. When Jesus defined neighbour with his parable of the good Samaritan, he was flying in the face of the popular view of neighbour, namely that he is someone like us. Under the tutelage of the Spirit Peter too came to the insight that "God shows no partiality, but in every nation anyone who fears him and does what is right is acceptable to him" (Acts 10:34b-35).

A venerable old sage once asked his disciples, "How can we know when the darkness is leaving and the dawn is coming?"

"When we can see a tree in the distance and know that it is an elm and not a juniper," ventured one student. "When we can see an animal and know that it is a fox and not a wolf," chimed in another.

"No," said the old man, "those things will not help us."

Puzzled, the students demanded, "How then can we know?"

The master teacher drew himself up to his full stature and replied quietly, "We know the darkness is leaving and the dawn is coming when we can see another person and know that this is our brother or our sister; for otherwise, no matter what time it is, it is still dark."

Embracing the Whole World

The true prophetic message always calls us to stretch our arms out wide and embrace the whole world. In holy boldness we cover the earth with the grace and the mercy of God. This is a great task, a noble task. God has placed into our hands the destiny of the world, and by means of our prayers we hold back the divine wrath. Helmut Thielicke writes, "The globe itself lives and is upheld as by Atlas' arms through the prayers of those whose love has not grown cold. *The world lives by these uplifted hands, and by nothing else!*"5

So we throw caution to the winds and pray not just for

individuals but also for nations, not just for the renewal of the Church but also for the transformation of the world. We pray for and work for the kingdom to come on earth – on all the earth – as it is in heaven.

Here is how a wonderfully wise woman of prayer taught me to pray for the nations.[6] We are to begin, she said, by focusing on one nation and prayerfully discerning what kind of nation it should be. If it is an aggressor nation, for example, we may sense that it should retreat from its self-aggrandizement and begin "sending out into the world little golden arrows of trade and commerce and financial cooperation."[7] At times we may narrow our prayers to those who make the decisions that can change the course of a nation towards rightness. We bless the broken bits of virtue these leaders already display and ask that they, like the loaves and the fishes, will be multiplied and used for good.

Then, most important, we repent for the sins of the world. In this we will do well to begin with our own country – whichever country that may be. Since no nation is blameless before God, we stand as a representative of our own nation and repent for her sins.

This is no small task, as any who have tried it can testify. We must pass beyond all propaganda jargon and national self-interest and kneel in sorrow and sadness for the arrogance and selfishness and greed that cause national injustice. Having done this, we can also repent on behalf of other nations as well. We open even greater spiritual resources when we are given the grace and forgiving power to repent in the name of our enemies.

In addition we hear the voice of the true Shepherd calling us to go to all peoples with the liberating message of life in Christ. We do so with boldness of faith but also with humility of heart, for we know that Jesus, the true light, has already been shining his truth into the hearts of people (John 1:9). Our task, therefore, is to see where God has been working and into that context proclaim the everlasting Gospel of Jesus Christ. George Fox writes, "Let all nations hear the word by sound or writing. Spare no place, spare not tongue nor pen; but be obedient to the Lord God . . . and be valiant for the Truth upon earth . . . walk cheerfully over the world."[8]

When we do these things, we have come to the place where we love others for God's sake and not our own. We are therefore given a boundless compassion for all peoples.

Christian Community

Our commitment to the entire world must also be made specific, and so the true prophetic message always calls us to Christian community. We do not live in isolation, and we do not pray in isolation. The Christian number is plural, not singular.

The Church scattered must become the Church gathered. We do not yet know exactly what forms these new gatherings will take in our day. Frankly, we are entering a kind of "spiritual centrifuge". A centrifuge is an apparatus that rotates at such tremendous velocity that existing densities break up and new densities emerge.

We are seeing this happen right before our eyes. Old densities, old ways of arranging our religious lives, are breaking up and new arrangements are emerging. It remains for all of us who have been gathered together by Jesus Christ, our ever-living Prophet, to envision the future.

In the days ahead we can expect Christian community to take one of four primary expressions, though there will be infinite variations on each basic form: institutional, communal, personal spiritual mentoring, and small group spiritual formation. These four expressions do not need to be exclusive of one another, and in many places they will all function together. Allow me to describe each of the four briefly.

Many of our institutional structures will survive and even thrive. Some of the prophets, like St Francis so long ago, will hear the call to "build my church" from within existing structures. Their way will not be easy, for the obstacles are many. Jesus' observation about the futility of putting new wine into old wineskins sets the difficulty into bold relief (Matt. 9:17). One of the most crucial issues facing institutional life will be how to find a place for the functioning of the prophetic ministry. Can we give a prophet's honour to those with the prophetic mantle, or must we always kill them?

The task will be monumental and there will be setbacks, but gains will be made as well. God is in the business of breathing new life into dry bones. There is a great Reformation teaching that the Church reformed is always reforming. I believe this is indeed possible, and steady prayer needs to arise for those called into the ministry of reforming the Church and the churches. We want to rejoice in every new burst of life, every creative force of renewal.

Communal life is the most intensive expression of Christian community, and it has existed in all the ages of the Church. Though I am not a member, I am close to a group that is communal, calling themselves the Friends of Jesus Community. These four households have pooled their resources in order to buy a small apartment complex in the inner city to work to heal the wounds of racism. They write: "As Friends of Jesus, our call to intentional community came out of our conviction that we must have a closer fellowship and sharing with each other if we were to resist the wrong emphases of our culture and be faithful to God's call to share our lives with the poor and powerless."9 From first-hand knowledge I can say to you that their witness is indeed remarkable on many levels. Numerous other groups have attempted similar ventures.

Those seeking communal expressions of Christian community must wrestle with major issues: how to maintain proper authority without becoming authoritarian, how to maintain a high level of intentional community life without becoming ingrown, how to make this way of life accessible to families with small children and couples who are highly mobile. Vigorous prayers need to arise for prophetic vision to create new solutions to old problems.

Some, in their ongoing life in the way of Christ, have found it helpful to seek out individuals who could mentor them in the things of the Spirit. Spiritual director is the old term for this; others use the term spiritual friend. Personally, I prefer to speak of a spiritual mentor. Spiritual mentors are people gifted in discernment, wisdom and knowledge. Their task is to help people see the footprints of God in their lives and, now and again, to urge them to move in directions that they might not go otherwise.

This is an expression of Christian community, but it is not intended to stand alone. It necessitates other expressions of group life, especially in corporate worship. The great challenge for those moving in this direction is to find ways to develop enough spiritual mentors in a reasonable period to have a substantial impact on the life of the Church. Otherwise it will become the exclusive interest of the privileged few. We must pray for God to make a way where there is no way.

One model of Christian community that shows tremendous potential for the future is small group spiritual formation. This is an approach that seeks to provide both nurture and accountability. For example, every week I meet a small group of four whose goal is to help each other become better disciples of Jesus. We do this by means of five questions to which we respond at each meeting. The questions are simple enough, but at times they search us to the depths. I list these questions for you: consider how you might respond:

What experiences of prayer and meditation have you had this week?

What temptations did you face this week?

What movements of the Holy Spirit did you experience this week?

What opportunities to serve others have you had this week?

In what ways have you encountered Christ in your study of the Bible this week?[10]

Many issues need to be resolved for those committed to small group spiritual formation: how to develop spiritual mentors while maintaining shared leadership, how to allow for the free proliferation of groups without destructive excesses, how to maintain accountability without legalism. Holy prayers are needed in order to dream new dreams and see new visions.

Whatever the specific shape of our life together, it is of the utmost importance that we pray in community. While prayer is often private and personal, it is never outside the reality of the worshipping, praying fellowship. In fact we cannot sustain a life of prayer outside the community. Either we will give it up as futile, lacking the support and watchful care of others, or we will make it into a thing of our own. Without the discerning life of the Christian community we will quickly turn prayer into a face-saving, self-justifying monologue.

Christian community is a gift of God created by the power of the Spirit and based upon our forgiveness in Jesus Christ. We all live under the gracious shadow of the cross, forgiving and being forgiven.

Dallas Willard writes, "The aim of God in history is the creation of an all-inclusive community of loving persons, with himself included in that community as its prime sustainer and most glorious inhabitant."[11] I believe that God is gathering just such a community in our day. It is a community that combines eschatology with social action, the transcendent Lordship of Jesus with the suffering servant Messiah. It is a community of cross and crown, of conflict and reconciliation, of courageous action and suffering love. It is a community empowered to attack evil in all its forms, overcoming it with good. It is a community of unselfish love, and witness without compromise. It is a community buoyed up by the vision of Christ's everlasting rule, not only imminent on the horizon but already coming to birth in our midst.

The Royal Law

Divine love, *agape*, alone can sustain the community that God calls into being; therefore the true prophetic message always calls us to that dynamic love of God and love of neighbour that are at the heart of the Gospel. We love God by loving our neighbour, and we can love our neighbour only as we love God. The two commandments form a seamless robe.

When we try to love our neighbour without loving God, we begin imposing what Bonhoeffer calls our "wish dreams" on to the relationship, which in the end destroys it. Unaided human love loves others for its own sake, while *agape* loves others for God's sake. Human love reaches out expecting a return, needing a return, demanding a return. *Agape,* in contrast, gives, expecting nothing in return. "This is why," writes Bonhoeffer, "human love becomes personal hatred when it encounters genuine spiritual love, which does not desire but serves."[12] To attempt to love our neighbour without an ongoing love relationship with God will destroy community.

When we try to love God without loving our neighbour, we cut ourselves off from the "pulmonary artery" of God. God's love demands expression; it cannot stand alone. It is how God "breathes", if you will. Just as our blood *must* flow from our heart to our lungs, so God's love *must* flow out to his creation. Therefore, if we love God with all our heart, soul, mind and strength, we will be drawn of necessity to our neighbour. We see the face of God in our neighbour and to neglect our neighbour is to neglect God. If we forget our neighbour in our zeal to love God, we will soon forget God as well. It is only through the royal law of love that our deeds of mercy and compassion become a blessing. Without it, try as we might to do otherwise, our serving will always be tinged with condescending arrogance. St Vincent de Paul says, "It is only because of your love, only your love, that the poor will forgive you the bread you give them."[13]

Prayer makes our love flow freely, both vertically and

horizontally. As we pray, we are drawn into the love of God which irresistibly leads us to our neighbour. When we try to love our neighbour, we discover our utter inability to do so, which irresistibly drives us back to God. And so we enter into that never ending fellowship of love that gives Christian community its life.

Finis

Perhaps you have noticed that we have come full circle. I began this book with the words of St Augustine: "True, whole prayer is nothing but love." And here we are back to love again. Throughout the course of our journey I have tried to describe something of the heart of God which reaches out in utter accepting love and woos us into the intimacy of prayer. We saw some of the ways God's loving friendship draws us *inward* into the transformation we need; changing us, moulding us, forming us. We were invited *upward* into the intimacy we need: adoring God, resting in God, listening to God. We heard the call *outward* into the ministry we need: healing the sick, suffering with the broken, interceding for the world.

Two millennia ago at an early-morning breakfast by the Sea of Tiberias Jesus had only one question for Peter: "Simon son of John, do you love me?" (John 21). Jesus did not ask him about his effectiveness, or his skill, or anything but his love. Three times Jesus asked, "Simon, do you love me?" Peter struggled for an adequate response to that probing query. Finally, he blurted out, "Lord, you know everything; you know that I love you." Assured of his heart, Jesus gave Peter work to do: "Feed my lambs."

The same question is asked of us. The same work is given to us.

———————————◆———————————

A Benediction
May you now, by the power of the Holy Spirit,

*receive the spirit of prayer. May it become, in
the name of Jesus Christ, the most precious
occupation of your life. And may the God of
all peace strengthen you, bless you and give
you joy.*

— Amen.

Notes

Coming Home: An Invitation to Prayer

1 Samuel Taylor Coleridge, "The Rime of the Ancient Mariner," in *The Oxford Anthology of English Literature*, vol. II, ed. Frank Kermode and John Hollander (New York: Oxford University Press, 1975), p. 204.

2 Julian of Norwich, *Enfolded in Love: Daily Readings With Julian of Norwich*, trans. Members of the Julian Shrine (New York: Seabury, 1980), p. 1. In the fourteenth century Julian was a woman's name. This is not the case today and so in the text of this book I have used the name Juliana to more clearly identify her. Other writers have done this as well; e.g. see Kenneth Scott Latourette, *A History of Christianity* (New York: Harper & Brothers, 1953), p. 650.

3 Donald L. Alexander, ed., *Christian Spirituality: Five Views of Sanctification* (Downers Grove, IL: InterVarsity, 1988), p. 182.

4 *Hymns for the Family of God* (Nashville, TN: Paragon Associates, 1976), Hymn 222.

5 Just a brief comment about the stories — personal and otherwise — in this book. Where other people are involved, I have received permission to share their story. Here and there I have changed minor details in order to protect the anonymity of the individual. Regarding myself, I am normally reluctant to share personal prayer experiences openly. In the case of this book, however, as best I can determine, I was instructed to share these things with you by a higher authority.

Chapter 1 Simple Prayer

1. Emilie Griffin, *Clinging: The Experience of Prayer* (San Francisco: Harper & Row, 1984), p. 5.

2 *The Collected Works of St Teresa of Avila*, trans. Kieran

Kavanaugh and Otilio Rodriguez (Washington, DC: ICS
Publications, 1976), p. 94.

3 John Dalrymple, *Simple Prayer* (Wilmington, DE: Michael
Glazier, 1984), p.13.

4 C. S. Lewis, *Letters to Malcolm: Chiefly on Prayer* (New
York: Harcourt, Brace, & World, 1964), p. 22.

5 Madame Guyon, *Experiencing the Depths of Jesus Christ*
(Goleta, CA: Christian Books, 1975), p. 47.

6 Mary Clare Vincent, *The Life of Prayer and the Way to
God* (Still River, MS: St Bede's Publications, 1982), p. 8.

7 Griffin, *Clinging*, p. 10.

8 The value of "uneventful prayer experiences" was
suggested to me by Emilie Griffin and is discussed in
chapter 1 of *Clinging*.

9 Joseph F. Schmidt, *Praying Our Experiences* (Winona,
MN: Saint Mary's Press, 1989), p. 21.

Chapter 2 Prayer of the Forsaken

1 George Arthur Buttrick, *Prayer* (New York: Abingdon-
Cokesbury, 1942), p. 263.

2 *The Journal of George Fox* (Cambridge University Press,
1952), p. 9.

3 Howard Macy, *Rhythms of the Inner Life* (Old Tappan,
NJ: Fleming H. Revell, 1988), p. 95.

4 Lament Psalms: Individual – 3, 5, 6, 7, 17, 22, 25, 26, 27,
28, 35, 39, 41, 42–43, 51, 54, 55, 56, 57, 59, 61, 63, 64, 69,
71, 86, 88, 102, 109, 130, 140, 141, and 143; Communal
– 60, 74, 79, 80, 83, 85, 90, 124, 126, 137, and 144. From
A. A. Anderson, *The Book of Psalms*, vol. 1, *The New
Century Bible Commentary*, ed. Ronald E. Clements and
Matthew Black (Grand Rapids, MI: Eerdmans, 1981),
pp. 38–39.

5 James Walsh, ed., *The Cloud of Unknowing* in *The
Classics of Western Spirituality* (New York: Paulist,
1981), p. 145.

6 Bernard of Clairvaux, *The Love of God*, ed. James M.
Houston (Portland, OR: Multnomah, 1983), p. 107.

Chapter 3 The Prayer of Examen

1 Madame Guyon, *Experiencing God Through Prayer*, ed.
Donna C. Arthur (Springdale, PA: Whitaker, 1984), p. 51.

2 Ibid. pp. 51–52.
3 *The Collected Works of St Teresa of Avila*, p. 94.
4 Ibid.
5 Anthony Bloom, *Beginning to Pray* (New York: Paulist, 1970), p. 49.
6 As quoted in ibid., p. 46.
7 Guyon, *Experiencing the Depths*, p. 53.
8 Ibid. p. 56.
9 Virginia Stem Owens, endorsement for *Life Path: Personal and Spiritual Growth Through Journal Writing* by Luci Shaw (Portland, OR: Multnomah, 1991).
10 Frank C. Laubach, *Learning the Vocabulary of God* (Nashville, TN: Upper Room, 1956), p. 5.
11 Ibid. p. 17.
12 Ibid. pp. 7–8.
13 Ibid. p. 7.

Chapter 4 The Prayer of Tears

1 Gregory of Nyssa, *De compuncione* 1.10, PG 46:829 D as quoted in Irénée Hausherr, *Penthos: The Doctrine of Compunction in the Christian East* (Kalamazoo, MI: Cistercian, 1982), p. 27.
2 Abba Anthony, *Vitae Patrum* 7.38; PL 73:1055C, as quoted in Hausherr, *Penthos*, p. 41.
3 Jonathan Edwards, ed., *The Life and Diary of David Brainard* (Chicago: Moody, n.d.), pp. 34–35.
4 Raïssa Maritain, *Adventures in Grace* (New York: Longmans, Green, 1945), pp. 182–85.
5 M. Basilea Schlink, *Repentance: The Joy-Filled Life* (Minneapolis: Bethany, 1984), pp. 28, 33.
6 *The Letters of Ammonas*, trans. Derwas J. Chitty (Oxford: SLG, 1979), p. 18.
7 Hausherr, *Penthos*, p. 139.
8 Mme Lot-Borodine, *Vie Spirituelle* 48 (1936) 65-110, as quoted in Hausherr, *Penthos*, p. 138.
9 Adrienne von Speyr, *Confession*, tr. Douglas W. Stott (San Francisco: Ignatius, 1985), p. 50.
10 Lewis, *Letters to Malcolm*, p. 98.
11 Phineas Fletcher, untitled poem from *Hail, Gladdening Light: Music of the English Church*, Cambridge Singers dir. John Rutter (UK: Collegium Records, COLCD 113,

1991) Stereo/digital compact disc.

12 Richard J. Foster, *Celebration of Discipline* (San Francisco: Harper & Row, 1988). See Chapter 10, "The Discipline of Confession".

13 St Symeon the New Theologian, *Oratio* 32; PG 120:480 C, as quoted in Hausherr, *Penthos*, p. 172.

14 Thomas à Kempis, *The Imitation of Christ*, tr. William C. Creasy (Macon, GA: Mercer University Press, 1989), p. 23. Although there have been many fine English translations of *The Imitation*, I heartily endorse this fresh translation by William Creasy because he has succeeded in creating a text that elicits an experience similar to that of the original reader.

15 St Theodore the Studite, *Great Catechesis* 27; ed. Papadopoulo-Kerameus (St Petersburg: 1904), p. 191, as quoted in Hausherr, *Penthos*, pp. 131–32.

16 St John Chrysostom, *De paenit.* 7.5, PG 49:334, as quoted in Hausherr, *Penthos*, pp. 127–28.

Chapter 5 The Prayer of Relinquishment

1 Andrew Murray, *With Christ in the School of Prayer* (Springdale, PA: Whitaker House, 1981), p. 211.

2 Catherine Marshall, *Beyond Our Selves* (New York: McGraw-Hill, 1961), p. 94.

3 *The Journal and Major Essays of John Woolman*, Phillips P. Moulton, ed., *A Library of Protestant Thought*, (New York: Oxford University Press, 1971), pp. 185–86.

4 Søren Kierkegaard, *The Journals of Kierkegaard*, ed. Alexander Dru (New York: Harper & Brothers, 1959), p. 245.

5 A. W. Tozer, *The Pursuit of God* (Harrisburg, PA: Christian Publications, n.d.), p. 45.

6 As quoted in *The Lord of the Journey: A Reader in Christian Spirituality*, ed. and comp. Roger Pooley and Philip Seddon, (San Francisco: Collins Liturgical in USA, 1986), p. 292.

Chapter 6 Formation Prayer

1 For a good discussion of *conversatio morum* see Chapter 5 of Esther de Waal, *Seeking God: The Way of St Benedict* (Collegeville, MN: Liturgical, 1984).

2 Jean-Pierre de Caussade, *The Sacrament of the Present Moment* (San Francisco: Harper & Row, 1982), p. 22.

3 Dallas Willard, "Looking Like Jesus", *Christianity Today*, vol. 34, no. 11 (Aug. 20, 1990): pp. 29–31.

4 St Ignatius of Loyola, *The Spiritual Exercises of St Ignatius*, tr. Anthony Mottola (New York: Doubleday, 1964). Several recent workbook-style manuals help to apply the Ignatian retreat idea into contemporary settings. A good example is Sister Helen Cecilia Swift *A Living Room Retreat* (Cincinnati, OH: St Anthony Messenger Press, 1981).

5 Timothy Fry, ed., *The Rule of St Benedict in English* (Collegeville, MN: Liturgical, 1982), pp. 32–38. James Bryan Smith and I have revised this material for the modern reader, found in the *RENOVARÉ Devotional Readings*, vol. 1, no. 12. In the eleventh century Bernard of Clairvaux wrote a kind of expanded commentary on Benedict's twelve steps, called simply *The Twelve Steps of Humility*. He also wrote a follow-up book called *The Twelve Steps of Pride*. The two books are published under one title: *The Twelve Steps of Humility and Pride*, ed. Halcyon C. Backhouse (London: Hodder and Stoughton, 1985). More recently, Albert Edward Day, in his book, *Discipline and Discovery* (Springdale, PA: Whitaker House, 1988), gives fifteen steps into humility.

6 Bloom, *Beginning to Pray*, p. 35.

7 As quoted in Day, *Discipline and Discovery*, p. 82.

8 See Thérèse of Lisieux, *The Story of a Soul*, tr. John Beevers (New York: Image, 1989). There is also a good chapter on Thérèse in Gloria Hutchinson, *Six Ways to Pray from Six Great Saints* (Cincinnati, OH: St Anthony Messenger Press, 1982).

9 As quoted in Hutchinson, *Six Ways to Pray*, p. 87. See also Thérèse's biography, *Story of a Soul*, pp. 126–29.

10 Henri J. M. Nouwen, *Making All Things New* (San Francisco: Harper & Row, 1981), p. 69.

11 As quoted in Vincent, *Life of Prayer*, p. 62.

12 Evelyn Underhill, *Abba* (Wilton, CT: Morehouse-Barlow, 1982), pp. 32–33.

13 Bloom, *Beginning to Pray*, p. 33.

Chapter 7 Covenant Prayer

1 Dietrich Bonhoeffer, *Meditating on the Word*, tr. David McI. Gracie (Cambridge, MA: Cowley, 1986), p. 31.
2 Thomas Kelly, *A Testament of Devotion* (New York: Harper & Row, 1941), p. 53.
3 *Hymns for the Family of God*, Hymn 404.
4 As quoted in *Friends of Jesus Community Newsletter*, vol. 1, no. 5 (Dec. 1990).
5 Tozer, *Pursuit of God*, p. 11.
6 "Contemplation", *Service Book and Hymnal* (Minneapolis: Augsburg; Board of Publication Lutheran Church in America, 1958), Hymn 483.
7 Richard Baxter, *The Saints' Everlasting Rest* (London: Epworth, 1962), pp. 146–52.
8 Dalrymple, *Simple Prayer*, p. 47.
9 Bloom, *Beginning to Pray*, p. 86.
10 Thomas Merton, *The Sign of Jonas* (New York: Harcourt & Brace, 1953), p. 288.
11 Baxter, *Saints' Everlasting Rest*, p. 152.

Chapter 8 The Prayer of Adoration

1 Douglas V. Steere, *Prayer and Worship* (New York: Edward W. Hazen Foundation, distrib. by Association Press, 1938), p. 34.
2 Ole Hallesby, *Prayer*, tr. Clarence J. Carlsen (Minneapolis: Augsburg, 1959), p. 141.
3 *Sitivit sitiri Deus* (God thirsts to be thirsted after). As quoted in Vincent, *Life of Prayer*, p. 25.
4 Lewis, *Letters to Malcolm*, p. 90. I am indebted to Lewis for these four points.
5 Ibid.
6 Ibid.
7 Ibid.
8 Ibid. pp. 89–90.
9 Sue Monk Kidd, *God's Joyful Surprise* (San Francisco: Harper & Row, 1987), p. 200.
10 Annie Dillard, *Pilgrim at Tinker Creek* (New York: Bantam Books/Harper's Magazine Press, 1974), p. 278.
11 See Glenn Clark, *I Will Lift Up Mine Eyes* (New York: Harper & Brothers, 1937), p. 107.

12 Lewis, *Letters to Malcolm*, p. 91.
13 Baxter, *Saints' Everlasting Rest*, pp. 136–37.

Chapter 9 The Prayer of Rest

1 Kelly, *Testament*, p. 124.
2 *Hymns for the Family of God*, Hymn 86.
3 Bloom, *Beginning to Pray*, pp. 92–94.
4 Eugene Peterson, *Contemplative Pastor* (Dallas, TX: Word, 1989), p. 110.
5 Ibid.
6 Ibid. p. 111.
7 P. T. Forsyth, *The Soul of Prayer* (Grand Rapids, MI: Eerdmans, 1916), p. 32.
8 Kelly, *Testament*, p. 45.
9 Lewis, *Letters to Malcolm*, pp. 67–68.
10 Louis Bouyer, *The Spirituality of the New Testament and the Fathers*, vol. 1 of *A History of Christian Spirituality* (New York: Seabury, 1982), p. 313.
11 Henri Nouwen, *The Way of the Heart: Desert Spirituality and Contemporary Ministry*, (New York: Seabury, 1981), p. 70.
12 The group is called "SEE Christ" (Spiritual Enrichment Encounters with Christ). The members take turns planning the activities of the day's retreat. Usually there are several one to two hour periods alone in silence followed by group interaction and prayer. For further ideas on the practice of Solitude, see chapter 7 of Foster, *Celebration of Discipline*.
13 François Fénelon, *Christian Perfection* (Minneapolis: Dimension Books, 1975), pp. 155–56.
14 An interesting footnote to this story occurred about eight years later when I was asked to lead a committee through a nine-month study process which did indeed bring about a beneficial resolution to the situation.
15 Henri J. M. Nouwen, *Lifesigns: Intimacy, Fecundity, and Ecstasy in Christian Perspective* (Garden City, NY: Doubleday, 1986), p. 71.

Chapter 10 Sacramental Prayer

1 *The Book of Common Prayer and Administration of the Sacraments and Other Rites and Ceremonies of the Church, together with The Psalter and Psalms of David:*

According to the use of The Episcopal Church (New York: Seabury, 1979), pp. 320–21.

2 Lewis, *Letters to Malcolm*, p. 16.

3 Ibid. p. 5.

4 Christians differ over such things as the number of sacraments or how God's grace is mediated through the sacraments. For our purposes, however, it is not necessary to distinguish between what is sacrament proper and what is sacramental in a more general sense. I choose the term "means of grace" to discuss this less specific understanding of God's mediated presence. Our concern is to see the ways the life of prayer is enhanced by God's grace coming to us through his created world.

5 As quoted in Dietrich Bonhoeffer, *The Psalms: The Prayer Book of the Bible*, tr. James H. Burtness (Minneapolis: Augsburg, 1974), p. 25.

6 This classification is Dietrich Bonhoeffer's. See ibid. p. 27

7 As quoted in ibid. p. 23.

8 As quoted in Alexander Schmemann, *For the Life of the World: Sacraments and Orthodoxy* (Crestwood, NY: St Vladimir's Seminary Press, 1988), p. 139. St Maximus is not using the word "symbol" (*symbola*) in opposition to "real". That became a distinction in later centuries. When he says "symbol", he means that the Bread and the Wine "embodies" the reality "as its very expression and mode of manifestation".

9 Lewis, *Letters to Malcolm*, p. 104.

10 I am fully aware that both the Quakers and the Salvation Army do not use outward sacraments, stressing instead the spiritual nature of communion with God. (Some branches of Quakerism give freedom of conscience over the use of physical elements.) Even they, however, are sacramental in the sense that they believe God's life often comes to us through his created world.

11 *Dr Martin Luther's Small Catechism with Explanation* (Rock Island, IL: Augustana Book Concern, 1957), p. 56.

12 P. T. Forsyth, *The Church and the Sacraments* (London: Independent, 1947), p. 141.

13 E. M. Bounds, *Power Through Prayer* (Grand Rapids, MI: Zondervan, 1979), p. 27.

14 Ibid. p. 70.

15 Forsyth, *The Church and the Sacraments*, p. 141.
16 See Barry Liesch, *People in the Presence of God* (Grand Rapids, MI: Zondervan, 1988), p. 168.

Chapter 11 Unceasing Prayer

1 In order the quotations are from the following sources: Brother Lawrence, *The Practice of the Presence of God* (Philadelphia: Judson, n.d.), p. 60; *Writings from the Philokalia on Prayer of the Heart*, trans. E. Kadloubovsky and G. E. H. Palmer (London: Faber & Faber, 1975), p. 85; Julian of Norwich, *Showings*, tr. Edmund Colledge and James Walsh (New York: Paulist, 1978), p. 253; *On the Prayer of Jesus: From the Ascetic Essays of Bishop Ignatius Brianchaninov*, tr. Father Lazarus (London: John M. Watkins, 1965), p. 60; Gloria Hutchinson, *Six Ways to Pray*, p. 10; Frank C. Laubach, *Letters by a Modern Mystic* (Syracuse, NY: New Readers Press, 1979), p. 23.
2 William James, *Varieties of Religious Experience* (Bergenfield, NY: New American Library, 1958), p. 24.
3 The word "hesychastic" or "hesychasm" comes from the Greek word *hesychia* which means tranquillity or peace. Hesychasm is a Christian form of living the spiritual life that has its roots in the first hermits who fled to the barren deserts of Egypt and Syria during the fourth century. In the fourteenth century there was a renaissance of hesychasm among the monks at Mount Athos, and since that time it has been associated with Eastern Orthodoxy.
4 *Writings from the Philokalia*, p. 85.
5 See Helen Bacovcin, *The Way of a Pilgrim* (New York: Doubleday/Image, 1979).
6 For a useful discussion of breath prayer see Ron DelBene with Herb Montgomery, *The Breath of Life: Discovering Your Breath Prayer* (Minneapolis: Winston, 1981). I am indebted to these authors for some of the contemporary practical applications of hesychasm.
7 Timothy Ware, ed., *The Art of Prayer: An Orthodox Anthology*, comp. Igumen Chariton of Valamo, tr. E. Kadloubovsky and E. M. Palmer (London: Faber & Faber, 1966), p. 97.
8 Brother Lawrence, *The Practice of the Presence of God* (Old Tappan, NJ: Revell, 1958), p. 9.

9 Ibid. (Doubleday/Image edn, 1977), pp. 65, 57.
10 Kelly, *Testament*, pp. 31, 35.
11 Laubach, *Letters by a Modern Mystic*, pp. 20, 12; Laubach, *Learning the Vocabulary of God*, p. 8.
12 Kelly, *Testament*, p. 124.
13 Lawrence, *The Practice of the Presence of God* (Doubleday edn), p. 67; Laubach, *Learning the Vocabulary of God*, pp. 8–9.
14 Guyon, *Experiencing the Depths*, pp. 125–26.
15 Ibid. pp. 110–11.

Chapter 12 The Prayer of the Heart

1 Jean-Nicholas Grou, *How to Pray*, tr. Joseph Dalby (Greenwood, SC: Attic, 1982), p. 18.
2 Joachim Jeremias, *The Prayers of Jesus* (Philadelphia: SCM, 1967), p. 111.
3 Dalrymple, *Simple Prayer*, p. 38. Some scholars will go as far as to suggest that behind all Jesus' references to God as Father which are in our Greek New Testament are Hebrew and Aramaic Abba language.
4 This song is copyrighted by Carol Lacquement Penick. Information regarding melody and permissions can be obtained by writing to her at 107 Shannon Drive, Greenville, SC 29615, USA.
5 Kenneth Swanson, *Uncommon Prayer*, p. 198. It was Ponticus Evagrius (346–399) who first systematized this order. In the West John Cassian (360–435) took these three stages and transformed them into what we today know as "purgative prayer" (lips), "illuminative prayer" (mind), and "unitative prayer" (heart).
6 Buttrick, *Prayer*, p. 264.
7 Swanson, *Uncommon Prayer*, pp. 211–12.
8 Guyon, *Experiencing the Depths*, p. 122.
9 See Brennan Manning, *The Wisdom of Accepted Tenderness: Going Deeper into the Abba Experience* (Denville, NJ: Dimension Books, 1978).
10 As noted in Vincent, *The Life of Prayer*, p. 81.
11 *The Complete Poems of John Donne*, ed. Walter Hendricks (Chicago: Packard, 1942), pp. 270–71.

Chapter 13 Meditative Prayer

1 Jim has published this story. For his more expanded

NOTES   285

description see *Christianity Today*, vol. 35, no. 8 (July 21, 1991), pp. 29–31.

2 For a full discussion of the various forms of meditation as well as a detailing of the biblical foundation for meditation, see Chapter 2 of *Celebration of Discipline*. Also my booklet, *Meditative Prayer*, (Downers Grove, IL: InterVarsity, 1983) contains additional material.

The Bible does not make anything like careful distinctions between meditation and contemplation. Over the centuries, however, devotional writers have often distinguished the two in the following way: while meditation focuses primarily on a rumination upon Scripture, God, his works, the creation, and other significant devotional writings, contemplation consists in resting in the loving awareness of God and is not usually attached to any particular thought or Scripture passage.

In my own writings, when I have only one opportunity to speak to the issue, I have followed the biblical pattern of using meditation and contemplation interchangeably. In this book, however, I will follow the division between the two that has developed over the centuries of the Church, though I certainly do not want to make too much of the difference.

3 Dietrich Bonhoeffer, *The Way to Freedom* (New York: Harper & Row, 1966), p. 59.

4 Alexander Whyte, *Lord, Teach Us to Pray* (New York: Harper & Brothers, n.d.), p. 251.

5 Ibid. p. 249.

6 As quoted in Lynn J. Radcliffe, *Making Prayer Real* (New York: Abingdon-Cokesbury, 1952), p. 214.

7 St Francis de Sales, *Introduction to the Devout Life*, tr. John K. Ryan (New York: Doubleday, 1955), p. 84.

8 Whyte, *Lord, Teach Us to Pray*, pp. 249–51.

9 Gregory of Nyssa, *The Life of Moses* in *The Classics of Western Spirituality*, tr. Abraham J. Malherbe and Everett Ferguson (New York: Paulist, 1987), p. 137.

10 *The Confessions of St Augustine*, tr. Rex Warner (New York: Mentor/New American Library, 1963), p. 51.

11 Brother Ugolino di Monte Santa Maria, *The Little Flowers of St Francis* (Garden City, NY: Doubleday, 1958), p. 277.

12 Julian of Norwich, *Enfolded in Love*, pp. 6, 1.

13 à Kempis, *The Imitation of Christ*, pp. 41, 32, 68, 69–70.
14 I have teamed up with James Bryan Smith to compile
    writings from fifty-two of the devotional masters from
    Gregory of Nyssa to Dietrich Bonhoeffer. It is under the
    title of *Devotional Classics* and is soon to be published
    by HarperSanFrancisco. This volume provides one reading
    per week for a year. Each section contains an introduction
    to the author, excerpts from his/her writings that are
    abridged and revised for the modern reader, reflection
    questions, a brief Bible study which parallels the reading,
    an annotated bibliography of key writings of the author,
    and finally, a brief reflection essay which makes a bridge
    between the devotional reading and contemporary
    culture. This volume can be ordered from a bookshop
    or by writing *RENOVARÉ*, P.O. Box 879, Wichita, KS
    67201–0879, USA.
15 As quoted in Steere, *Prayer and Worship*, pp. 58–59.
16 à Kempis, *The Imitation of Christ*, p. 7.
17 Thomas Merton, *Spiritual Direction and Meditation*
    (Collegeville, MN: Liturgical, 1960), p. 98.

Chapter 14 Contemplative Prayer

  1 As quoted in Thomas Merton, *Contemplative Prayer*
    (Garden City, NY: Doubleday/Image, 1971), p. 30.
  2 As quoted in ibid. p. 42.
  3 Catherine de Haeck Doherty, *Poustinia: Christian
    Spirituality of the East for Western Man* (Notre Dame, IN:
    Ave Maria, 1983), p. 216.
  4 Lewis, *Letters to Malcolm*, p. 11.
  5 Steere, *Prayer and Worship*, p. 11.
  6 As quoted in Donald G. Bloesch, *The Struggle of Prayer*
    (San Francisco: Harper & Row, 1980), p. 86.
  7 Richard Rolle, "The Fire of Love," in *Varieties of Mystic
    Experience*, ed. Elmer O'Brien (New York: Mentor-Omega,
    1964), p. 133.
  8 Bernard, "Sermon LXXXIII on the Song of Songs", in
    O'Brien, *Varieties of Mystic Experience*, p. 105.
  9 Albert C. Outler, ed., "Journal", in *John Wesley* from
    A Library of Protestant Thought (New York: Oxford
    University Press, 1964), p. 66.
 10 Julian of Norwich, *Showings*, p. 254.
 11 As quoted in Swanson, *Uncommon Prayer*, p. 163.

12 Guyon, *Experiencing the Depths*, p. 125.
13 Dalrymple, *Simple Prayer*, pp. 109–10.
14 Thomas Merton, *The Hidden Ground of Love*, ed. William Shannon (New York: Farrar, Straus and Giroux, 1985), p. 156.
15 Walter Hilton, *The Stairway of Perfection*, tr. M. L. Del Mastro (Garden City, NY: Doubleday/Image, 1979), p. 71.
16 Guyon, *Experiencing the Depths*, p. 127.
17 There is a division among the great devotional writers over the use of the imagination in contemplation. Some view it as a useful aid; others feel it should be reserved for meditation rather than contemplation; still others believe it should never be used. At times the issue has been tied to the Iconoclastic Controversy of the eighth century and following in which many felt that the use of icons was a form of idolatry. William of St Thierry, a twelfth-century Cistercian monk, for example, believed that praying with images was idolatry because God was found only in the purity of relationship in his image stamped in every human being. Many of the Puritan leaders in the seventeenth century had similar convictions.

I have chosen to side with those who see the imagination as a useful aid in Contemplative Prayer. This is not a law, but a practical help. I do not draw a hard line between meditation (where the imagination is much more widely accepted) and contemplation. Also, while contemplation is usually wordless, it does not necessarily need to be imageless. Indeed some of the great contemplatives, such as Juliana of Norwich, received profound visions from God during times of contemplation.
18 As quoted in Foster, *Meditative Prayer*, p. 14.
19 As quoted in ibid. p. 20.
20 As quoted in ibid. pp. 21–22.
21 *Confessions*, pp. 200–1.
22 As quoted in F. Ernest Stoeffler, *The Rise of Evangelical Pietism* (Leiden: Brill, 1965), p. 149
23 Gerhard Tersteegen, *The Quiet Way* (New York: Philosophical Library, 1950), p. 23.

Chapter 15 Praying the Ordinary

1 Merton, *The Sign of Jonas*, p. 238.

2 Bloom, *Beginning to Pray*, p. 59.
3 Grou, *How to Pray*, p. 82.
4 As quoted in Hutchinson, *Six Ways to Pray*, p. 62.
5 *The Rule of St Benedict*, pp. 82–83.
6 See Robert J. Ringer, *Winning Through Intimidation* (Greenwich, CT: Fawcett, 1974).
7 See Edward Hays, *Prayers for the Domestic Church* (Easton, KS: Forest of Peace Books, 1989).
8 See D. Elton Trueblood, *The Common Ventures of Life* (New York: Harper & Row, 1965).
9 These words are taken from a song "Holy Ground" in the music album by John Michael Talbot, *Come Worship the Lord*, vol. 2, (Brentwood, TN: Sparrow, 1990).

Chapter 16 Petitionary Prayer

1 C. W. F. Smith, "Prayer", in *The Interpreter's Dictionary of the Bible*, vol. 3 (Nashville: Abingdon, 1962), p. 858.
2 Forsyth, *The Soul of Prayer*, p. 38.
3 Hans Urs von Balthasar, *Prayer*, tr. Graham Harrison (San Francisco: Ignatius, 1986), p. 251.
4 Forsyth, *The Soul of Prayer*, p. 63.
5 Lewis, *Letters to Malcolm*, p. 58.
6 Forsyth, *The Soul of Prayer*, p. 14.
7 Lewis, *Letters to Malcolm*, p. 28.
8 As quoted in C. S. Lewis, *Letters to an American Lady*, ed. Clyde S. Kilby (London: Hodder & Stoughton, 1969), p. 73.
9 Helmut Thielicke, *Our Heavenly Father: Sermons on the Lord's Prayer* (New York: Harper & Brothers, 1960), p. 110.
10 As quoted in ibid. p. 119.
11 Ibid. p. 133.
12 *Hymns for the Family of God*, Hymn 118.
13 H. H. Farmer, *The World and God* (London: Nisbet, 1935), p. 129.

Chapter 17 Intercessory Prayer

1 Forsyth, *The Soul of Prayer*, p. 53.
2 Ambrose of Milan, *On Isaac or the Soul*, viii, 75 J.P. Migne, *Patrologia Latina* 14, p. 557. For further information see Bloesch, *The Struggle of Prayer*, pp. 35, 48.

3 Bloesch, *The Struggle of Prayer*, pp. 36–37.

4 The discerning reader will have realized by now that I have not included a chapter on the prayer of guidance. Now you know why. For the most part the modern fascination with "how to discover the will of God" betrays a failure to see that as we know God, we know his will. Some unfortunately are looking for techniques rather than intimacy.

5 John Calvin, *Sermons on the Epistle to the Ephesians* (Edinburgh: Banner of Truth Trust, 1975), p. 683.

6 *Presbyterian Times* (March 20, 1990). This is a newspaper published by the National Korean Presbyterian Church. I am indebted to Jung-Oh Suh for the translation of the article, "Myong-Song Presbyterian Church Built by Prayer Alone", pp. 1, 8–9.

7 Buttrick, *Prayer*, p. 263.

8 As quoted in Bloesch, *The Struggle of Prayer*, p. 87.

Chapter 18 Healing Prayer

1 Unlike the other incidents in this book, I am not able to confirm this story in terms of this gentleman's present emotional state. Several years after this event we lost contact with each other, and I have not seen him since. He was, however, perfectly normal for the time I knew him, and he and his wife even came to visit us once after we had moved to another state.

2 Swanson, *Uncommon Prayer*, p. 185.

3 Besides healing, some of the more common uses of the laying on of hands are as follows:

i)   Blessing. Usually this was a tribal blessing. In Genesis 48:14–16 Jacob laid his hands on the heads of Ephraim and Manasseh saying, "the angel who has redeemed me from all harm, bless the boys". When the people brought children to Jesus, it was so he would lay hands on them and bless them (Mark 10:13–16).

ii)   Baptism in the Holy Spirit. According to Acts there are three principal ways by which the baptism in the Holy Spirit was received: through the obedience of faith (Acts 1:4–5, 5:32), through the ministry of the Word (Acts 10:44–46, 11:15), and through the laying on of hands. In Acts 8:5–17 the Samaritan believers received the

Holy Spirit through the laying on of hands by Peter and John. In Acts 9:17 Paul received the Holy Spirit through the laying on of hands by Ananias. In Acts 19:1–6 the disciples at Ephesus received the Holy Spirit through the Apostle Paul's laying on of hands.

iii) Spiritual Gifts. Spiritual gifts are given by the sovereign act of God (1 Kings 3:5–12; 1 Cor. 12:7–11). They are also received through the laying on of hands. Paul laid his hands on the disciples at Ephesus, and they received the gift of prophecy (Acts 19:6). The young leader Timothy was encouraged to continue the effective use of the gift that was given to him by the laying on of hands (1 Tim. 4:14; 2 Tim. 1:6).

iv) Special Ministry. Joshua received a special endowment of wisdom by the laying on of hands by Moses (Deut. 34:9). Hands were laid on the Levites for empowerment to exercise their office (Num. 8:10–26). The Apostles laid hands on the first deacons so they could care for the daily distribution of food with wisdom and equity (Acts 6:6). Hands were laid on Barnabas and Saul to commission them on their mission endeavour (Acts 13:3).

4 It is likely that Paul had in mind here a gifting and commissioning into leadership, somewhat akin to our concept of ordination. If so, the concern would be not to bring people into experiences of leadership before they are ready, that is, where the exercise of power and authority would lead to pride and various other abuses. In cases of Healing Prayer it appears that the laying on of hands was done quite freely.

5 As quoted in Bengt R. Hoffman, *Luther and the Mystics* (Minneapolis: Augsburg, 1976), p. 196.

6 Francis MacNutt, *Healing* (Notre Dame, IN: Ave Maria, 1974), p. 153.

7 St Augustine, *The City of God*, tr. Gerald G. Walsh and Daniel J. Honan (New York: Fathers of the Church, 1954), p. 450. This and many other stories are recorded in some detail by Morton T. Kelsey in his book, *Healing and Christianity: In Ancient Thought and Modern Times* (New York: Harper & Row, 1973).

8 *City of God*, Book XXII.8, p. 445.

Chapter 19 The Prayer of Suffering

1 The phrase "what is lacking in Christ's afflictions" has caused considerable debate. Because of the presence of the definite article in Greek — "*the* afflictions of Christ" — it is possible that this refers to a definite or well-known entity such as the Jewish apocalyptic concept of the birth pangs of the Messiah which will usher in the age to come. If this is the case (and present scholarship leans in this direction) then the idea is as follows: with the death and resurrection of Christ the age to come has been inaugurated. The present evil age continues and so Christians live in the overlap of the two aeons. The woes of the Messiah, the afflictions of Christ have already begun, and when their appointed limit has been reached, the age to come will be consummated, and this present evil age will pass away. All Christians participate in these sufferings and through them enter the kingdom of God (Acts 14:22; 1 Thess. 3:3–7). The Apostle Paul through his sufferings is contributing to the sum total of these eschatological afflictions. Hence, by helping to fill up the predetermined measure of afflictions, Paul is bringing the full consummation of the age to come all the closer.

2 Pope Paul VI, "The Role of Suffering in the Life of the Church", *The Pope Speaks*, vol. 19, no. 2 (June 26, 1974), p. 170.

3 *St Augustine: Sermons on the Liturgical Seasons*, tr. Sister Mary Sarah Muldowney (New York: Fathers of the Church, 1959), p. 86.

4 Kelly, *Testament*, p. 71.

5 Glenn Hinson, "The Contemplative View", in *Christian Spirituality*, p. 179.

6 As quoted in C. S. Lewis, *The Problem of Pain* (New York: Macmillan, 1961), p. vi.

7 Grou, *How to Pray*, p. 83.

8 Dietrich Bonhoeffer, *The Cost of Discipleship*, 2nd edn, tr. R. H. Fuller (New York: Macmillan, 1963), p. 166.

9 From Rob Goldman, "Healing the World by Our Wounds", *The Other Side*, vol. 27, no. 6 (November–December 1991), p. 24.

10 As quoted in Bloesch, *Struggle of Prayer*, p. 132.

11 Ibid. p. 77.

12 Martin Luther, *Lectures on Romans*, ed. and tr. W. Pauch (Philadelphia: Westminster, 1961), p. 349.

13 As quoted in Friedrich Heiler, *Prayer*, tr. and ed. Samuel McComb (New York: Oxford University Press, 1958), p. 279.

14 As quoted in Arthur Wallis, *God's Chosen Fast: A Spiritual and Practical Guide to Fasting* (Fort Washington, PA: Christian Literature Crusade, 1986), p. 67.

15 Søren Kierkegaard, *Edifying Discourses*, vol. 4, tr. David Swenson and Lillian Swenson, (Minneapolis: Augsburg, 1946), p. 113.

16 John Calvin, *Commentaries on the Epistles to the Philippians, Colossians, and Thessalonians*, tr. John Pringle (Grand Rapids, MI: Eerdmans, 1948), p. 164.

17 This story is recorded in Paul Yonggi Cho, *Prayer: Key to Revival* (Dallas, TX: Word, 1984), p. 86.

Chapter 20 Authoritative Prayer

1 Fyodor Dostoevsky, *The Brothers Karamazov*, ed. Ralph E. Matlaw, tr. Constance Garnett (New York: W. W. Norton, 1976). Some of the most relevant passages are in Books Four and Six.

2 *The Journal and Major Essays of John Woolman*, p. 112.

3 C. S. Lewis, *Mere Christianity* (New York: Macmillan, 1943), p. 60.

4 In preparation for writing this story I went over the entire sequence of events with "Gloria" on the telephone. Her words, placed in quotation marks, come from this phone conversation. Some people may find this story troubling because they have always felt that Christians cannot be "demon possessed". They are correct in the sense that demons cannot completely control or "possess" a Christian. Actually the term "demon possessed" is improper and a poor translation of *daimonizomenoi*. We are talking more about demonic influence and affliction than we are demonic ownership and control. To my knowledge there is no passage in the Bible which flatly states that Christians cannot be "demonized", as it has come to be called. This is an argument from silence, of course, but when it is coupled with passages that seem

to suggest demonic influence upon believing peoples, then we can make a fairly strong case for the possibility of the demonization of Christians. Saul, it appears, had the "Spirit of the Lord" upon him and "an evil spirit" which tormented him (1 Sam. 10 and 16). The crippled woman Jesus calls a "daughter of Abraham" was bound by an evil spirit for eighteen years (Luke 13:10–17). The person Paul says should be handed over to Satan for the destruction of the flesh is evidently a Christian, for Paul adds, "so that his spirit may be saved in the day of the Lord" (1 Cor. 5:1–5).

5 I, of course, have written about this extensively in *Celebration of Discipline*. I would also like to call your attention to Dallas Willard's *The Spirit of the Disciplines* (HarperSanFrancisco, 1988) as well as many of the classics of devotion such as William Law's *A Serious Call to a Devout and Holy Life, the Spirit of Love*, ed. Paul G. Stanwood (New York: Paulist, 1978) and Jeremy Taylor's *The Rule and Exercises of Holy Living, and the Rules and Exercises of Holy Dying*, comp. Roger L. Roberts (Wilton, CN: Morehouse-Barlow, 1981).

6 William Law, *The Spirit of Prayer and the Spirit of Love*, ed. Sidney Spencer (Canterbury: Clarke, 1969), p. 120.

7 Hallesby, *Prayer*, p. 117.

8 Ibid. p. 98.

9 *A Collection of Sundry Books, Epistles, and Papers, Written by James Nayler, etc.* (London: no pub., 1716), p. 378.

10 Alexander Grosart, ed., *The Complete Works of Richard Sibbes*, vol. 3 (Edinburgh: Nichol, 1862–64), p. 186.

Chapter 21 Radical Prayer

1 I am using the language of "hearing" but I do not mean something that could be recorded on tape. Most certainly this is an internal "hearing", but it is also an experience distinct from having a nice idea pop into one's head. Personally I have had only three experiences of this kind, this one being the second. In each case they have come at a critical turning point in my life.

2 Walter Wink, "Prayer and the Powers", *Sojourners*, vol. 19, no. 8 (October 1990), p. 13.

3 Bloesch, *Struggle of Prayer*, p. 79.

4 Martin Luther, *Luther's Works*, ed. Jaroslav Pelikan, vol. 6 (St Louis: Concordia, 1961), p. 158. See also Bloesch, *Struggle of Prayer*, pp. ix, 49.

5 Thielicke, *Our Heavenly Father*, p. 109.

6 The person was Agnes Sanford, and she has written about this way of praying in her many books, especially *The Healing Light* (Plainfield, NJ: Logos, 1972), chapter 15, and *Behold Your God* (St Paul, MI: Macalester Park, 1973), chapter 13.

7 Sanford, *The Healing Light*, p. 160.

8 *The Journal of George Fox*, p. 263.

9 Dorothy Craven, "Sharing in Community", *Friends of Jesus Community Newsletter*, vol. 2, no. 6 (December 1991).

10 These questions are part of a larger programme of spiritual formation. For further details write to: *RENOVARÉ, P.O.* Box 879, Wichita, KS 67201–0879, USA.

11 Dallas Willard, "Studies in the Book of Apostolic Acts: Journey into the Spiritual Unknown", (unpublished study guide).

12 Dietrich Bonhoeffer, *Life Together*, tr. John W. Doberstein (San Francisco: Harper & Row, 1954), p. 35.

13 This quotation is from the 1947 French movie, *Monsieur Vincent* (Paris: EDIC/Union General Cinematographique). The scriptwriters, Jean-Bernard Luc and Jean Anouilh, put these words into the mouth of St Vincent, and, although this is undoubtedly poetic licence, the idea is certainly consistent with the life and spirit of St Vincent.

Scripture Index

Subject Index